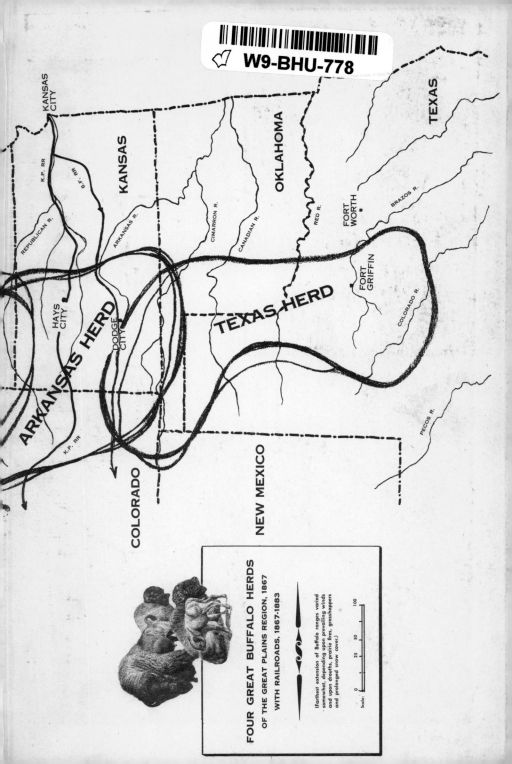

KANSAS CITY

TEXAS

K.P. RR

S.F. RR

KANSAS

OKLAHOMA

REPUBLICAN R.

ARKANSAS R.

CIMARRON R.

CANADIAN R.

RED R.

FORT WORTH

BRAZOS R.

HAYS CITY

DODGE CITY

ARKANSAS HERD

TEXAS HERD

FORT GRIFFIN

COLORADO R.

K.P. RR

COLORADO

NEW MEXICO

PECOS R.

FOUR GREAT BUFFALO HERDS
OF THE GREAT PLAINS REGION, 1867
WITH RAILROADS, 1867-1883

(farthest extension of buffalo ranges varied
somewhat, depending upon prevailing winds
and upon drouths, prairie fires, grasshoppers
and prolonged snow cover.)

Scale: 0   25   50   100

THE
BUFFALO
HUNTERS

THE BUFFALO HUNTERS

THE STORY OF THE HIDE MEN

BY

Mari Sandoz

HASTINGS HOUSE, PUBLISHERS, NEW YORK

•

CONTENTS

vii

The endpapers show a rough map of the approximate ranges of the four great Buffalo Herds, which overlap, due to seasonal migrations.

FOREWORD

THE buffalo, the American bison, once roamed most of what is now our nation. Cortez found this creature "with the hump like a camel and hair like a lion's" at Anahauc, deep in Mexico in 1521; others saw buffaloes at the head of navigation of the Potomac in 1621. They had spread into northern Saskatchewan too, and west to the coastal plains. But the region of the buffalo's best adaptation was probably the Great Plains. Here he roamed the open prairies in the vast dark herds that were uncountable, even apparently inestimable, for the estimations varied by tens of millions.

The Great Plains lie between the Rocky Mountains and the bend of the Missouri out of Dakota and reach like a great awkward thumb from Canada down as far as the Pecos, deep in Texas. This region is half the size of all the United States lying east of the Mississippi. It is cut by a succession of east-flowing streams, like a vast, many-runged ladder that the buffaloes climbed northward in the spring and descended in the fall, moving from water to water.

Other animal life had found what is now the Great Plains very compatible, at least for a time. The reptilian monsters, the dinosaurs, had lived here, the big horned *Brontops,* the early rhinoceroses, giant pigs, early camels, the mastodons and the great wooly mammoth, the long-horned bison and the sabre-toothed tiger. Many were larger than the American buffalo and many lived longer in the region; many were more lovely and some more intelligent—for example, the little eohippus that grew into the horse that was to have such a portentous connection with the buffalo herds in historic times. But whether larger or more intelligent, none grew as numerous as the buffalo; perhaps no animal of any size except the much punier creature, man, ever grew as numerous on the whole earth as the American bison upon the Great Plains, and no animal ever adjusted to his environment more completely.

ix

The buffalo's habit of feeding into the wind led him in casual annual circles, three, four hundred miles across. Usually he moved by easy stages over the nutritious prairies, always in what were, for that particular herd, warmer regions for the winter, cooler in the summer. There were, roughly, four of these great herds. Their migratory circles overlapped and each one wintered on the late growth of the gramas and other, seedier grasses, including the tall varieties that lifted through the snow where another herd had spent a short time in mid-summer, feeding on the seed-rich annuals and the earlier mats of grama.

There was apparently no disease on all the continent that threatened the buffalo in any number. In addition he had the great recuperative powers apparently fostered by the drier temperate regions. He survived many injuries that might seem fatal. Usually only the old died of a broken leg, say, and even a shattered hip socket was known to heal, leaving the buffalo as lusty a runner as any.

There was no sabre-toothed tiger to pull this buffalo down, no cat larger than a mountain lion, ineffective on the treeless plains and against the thick hide and the dense hair. Wolves followed the herds, to fall upon the weak, the injured and the old left unprotected. Coyotes, buzzards, ravens and magpies hung around to clean up the bones. Only the Indian managed to kill any appreciable number of buffaloes and he knew he must have all the help he could get, and prepared the hunts with elaborate ceremonials to bring the buffalo close and to assure a good hunt. The Indians danced the return of the herds as some peoples danced the return of the sun.

The buffalo was almost the sole subsistence of the Plains Indian—his shelter, clothing, food and fuel. The buffalo furnished most of the amusement and entertainment too, and was involved in many of the Indian's tests of courage and character, and a large part of his ethics and his religion. Often after a successful hunt the finest robe, painted and quill-embroidered, was taken to some high hill and left there in a ceremonial offering of thanksgiving to the Great Powers, and to the buffalo for all those of his kind who had died that his brother, the Indian, might live.

The mother figure so usual in the legends of the Plains tribes is generally, in one guise or another, the buffalo woman, the woman with the buffalo wisdom. This is true not only of the nomadic hunting tribes like the Sioux and the Cheyennes but also of such corn-planting hunters as the Pawnees. The author recalls

hearing an old Pawnee of the buffalo days tell his story of the
beginning of the world:

Once, long ago, all things were waiting in a deep place
far underground. There were the great herds of buffaloes and
all the people, and the antelope too, and wolves, deer and
rabbits—everything, even the little bird that sings the *tear-
tear* song. Everything waited as in sleep.

Then the one called Buffalo Woman awoke, stretched her
arms, rose and began to walk. She walked among all the
creatures, past the little *tear-tear* bird, the rabbits and all the
rest and through the people too, and the buffaloes. Everywhere as she passed there was an awakening, and a slow
moving, as when the eyes were making ready for some fine
new thing to be seen. Buffalo Woman walked on in the good
way, past even the farthest buffaloes, the young cows with
their sleeping yellow calves. She went on to a dark round
place that seemed like a hole and she stood there a while,
looking. Then she bowed her head a little, as one does to
pass under the lodge flap, and stepped out. Suddenly the
people could see there was a great shining light all about
her, a shining and brightness that seemed blinding as she
was gone.

And now a young cow arose and followed the woman, and
then another buffalo and another, until a great string of them
was following, each one for a moment in the shining light
of the hole before he was gone, and the light fell upon the
one behind. When the last of the buffaloes was up and moving, the people began to rise, one after another, and fell into
a row too, each one close upon the heels of the moccasins
ahead. All the people, young and old and weak and strong
went so, out through the hole that was on Pahuk, out upon
the shining, warm and grassy place that was the earth, with
a wide river, the Platte, flowing below, and over everything
a blueness, with the *tear-tear* bird flying toward the sun,
the warming sun. The buffaloes were already scattering over
the prairie, feeding, spreading in every direction toward the
circle that is the horizon. The people looked all around and
knew this was their place, the place upon which they would
live forever, they and the buffalo together.

But this buffalo was a very large and tough-hided animal
to be fought and killed with only the stone-headed spear and
arrow and very fleet for unmounted men. So the hunts for meat

and robes were usually managed by a whole village or band, everybody to share in the harvest, for as with the buffalo, none could save food for himself alone while others stood by hungry. In 1492 the present United States held perhaps little over two hundred fifty thousand Indians while the buffalo was estimated all the way from fifty to one hundred twenty-five millions, depending to some extent upon whether the estimator had seen the wide dark herds of the Great Plains.

Nothing the Indian could do changed the drift of these tremendous herds. They moved over the prairie as the stars moved, and truly as the wind, and there seemed only two possible plagues that could break the wealth of their number: Another Ice Age or the return of the great drouth that drove most animal life eastward across the Missouri. But if such a drouth came the buffaloes would perhaps head straight into the warm, dry southwestern winds that brought the drouth, moving deeper into the dying regions, until the dust of the powdery earth would rise over them, perhaps touched to gold by the lowering sun as they hurried on in their hope of water and of grass.

But this is not the way it happened, nor were the buffaloes pushed back by a great encroaching icefield. It was modern man who came, bringing with him his horse, the first creature able to overtake the buffalo, and bringing also the long and powerful extension of his arm that was his fire weapon. Close behind him came the fire road that brought and carried away. But for a long time the buffalo showed little fear; perhaps like the Indian and the white man too, he felt that his very numbers secured him against all diminution.

MS

BOOK I

THE REPUBLICAN HERD

CHAPTER I

THE PORTENTOUS MEN
OF 'SIXTY-SEVEN

ALL the horizon lay bleak and grey with late November, the Indians gone, the scattering of antelope quiet on the empty prairie, the white of their rumps barely showing. An eagle flew high over the breaks, soaring, circling, while on the tableland the snowbirds fluffed themselves out round and fed busily in their little circles. But suddenly they lifted, tossing like dead leaves on the light southeasterly wind. Then they were gone, perhaps to sleep in some sheltered spot, perhaps hurried by the delicate perception of a sound that seemed to germinate in the earth, a faint vibration that grew in the air. The antelope were gone too, now, and the deer from the buckbrush along the bottoms as the sound became a far rumble that rose and spread. A wolf, whitened by approaching winter, stood on a ridge a while, looking back, his tail an erect plume against the clouded sky.

Then the buffaloes appeared on the northwest tableland, singly at first, then in twos and threes coming down the breaks, and in little strings along the narrow trails. More and more of them came, their running a deep rumble in the earth, their dew claws rattling, the ponderous humped shoul-

3

ders thrusting forward, great shaggy heads down, grunting, their noses turned into the wind.

Those in the lead stopped to sniff at the frozen creeks and the fall ponds along the river bottoms, shying from the thin ice and then crowded out upon it, pushed by the dark herd behind until the ice sagged and cracked. In the deeper holes they went clear down, others driven upon them, striving for footing on the struggling mass, perhaps to go under too. And still they kept coming, thicker and thicker, crowding hard upon the leaders. This was the way two thousand buffaloes had been left in the quicksands of the Platte River when the great herd moved north in the spring migration, and why they could be driven over any bank or cliff if the scattered van could be turned, as the Indians sometimes turned them with waving blanket or with fire, to plunge over the Chugwater bluffs up in Wyoming, and in many other less likely places.

But now the main body of the herd was coming, one dark cover over all the upper forkings of the Republican River. They came by the thousands, tens of thousands, perhaps by hundreds of thousands too, for no eye could encompass them all—one great dark moving robe that reached from horizon to horizon; a fine thick robe soft as Indian-tanned that spread over all the breaks, the canyons and the broad sweep of the valleys, fitting close as fur to the chilling earth.

And as they slowed and settled to feed a little, to rest, the wind freshened. A few grey flakes of snow began to fall; then more, and by night the storm had closed down, the storm whose coming had urged the buffaloes to move very fast until they struck long grass bottoms and the protection of bluffs and canyons against the cold wind veering into the northwest. It was a swift November snow, the third of the season, and the temperature dropped far below zero. But the second night the sky cleared and the next morning the sun crept over the sparkling plains, the vast snow-swept prairies unbroken by tree or bush away from the stream lines or the steeper breaks.

The snow was light, not over eight, ten inches on the level, and the buffaloes got up, one after another, until the whole white plain seemed rising under some curious, darkening yeast. Grunting they shook themselves and went to feeding, their wool still caked with white as they searched out the tall joint grasses sticking through the shallow drifts. Their small hoofs cut up the snow on the barer stretches. Their breath wreathed the great heads and shoulders in the cold, and lifted in a pale cloud of frost that hung over all the vast herd, the sign that the eyes of every Indian, Sioux, Cheyenne, Arapaho and even Kiowa, and every white hide hunter sought.

As the sun moved over the breaks of Medicine Creek, a man pushed his way through the flap of a canvas tipi hidden in a canyon. His long black hair was tangled into his beard, his clothing stiff and dirty. He took one long habitual glance towards the picketed horses and then all around the canyon wall for Indian sign.

"Clear day, Jim!" he called back into the smoky tent. "Not a cloud no place—"

Almost at once Jim Hickok came out too, tucking his beaver-tan hair inside his short buffalo coat as he stepped into the early sun. He was cleaner than his skinner, and lighter complexioned, with flowing mustaches and a pale stubbling of beard. He looked around carefully too, and then climbed up the canyon wall to see farther, shading his eyes with a long slender hand.

"There they are!" he said, motioning towards the pale smudging along the horizon to the southwest. "A powerful big herd!"

When the smell of coffee hung in the canyon the hunter was ready, leaving his helper to fetch up the camp with the hide wagon. Rifle in scabbard and his eyes protected from snowblindness with a heavy streak of soot across his bare cheekbones, he started. He wore gun-barrel chaps, the leather saturated with buffalo tallow to keep the snow water out, with a heavy cartridge belt over his buffalo saddle coat. Even in the bulky coat Jim Hickok was plainly a slight man, with well-cut, fur-lined gloves to protect his delicate hands. Instead of the fine faunching black mare he usually rode he was on a light grey today, a little slower if it came to a run from the Indians or a buffalo stampede, but much less conspicuous against the snow.

The hunter proceeded cautiously towards the vanishing frost cloud, keeping to the broken country, to the barer, rougher ground already thawing off enough to help hide the tracks of his horse, and where he could get out of sight very fast, perhaps even stand off a dozen angry bucks, Sioux or Cheyenne. Many Indians, peaceful even a couple of years ago and content to hang around the forts and trading posts between their big hunts, were making trouble all summer and into this fall of 1867. They didn't like the settlers pushing into the buffalo country or the Union Pacific railroad that roared its way up the Platte. Now another string of tracks had come hurrying up the Smoky Hill River of Kansas like a snake chasing a mouse along a wagon rut. With the long overland haul to river shipping, only the well-tanned Indian robes had been worth the freight but now that the railroads had tapped the buffalo ranges, even flint hides, the untanned, wind-dried skins, paid out. Hunters were swarming in to kill buffaloes by the thousands, the ten thousands, generally taking nothing but the hide, leaving all the meat to stink on the prairie wind. Now the hides were priming towards winter, heavy and well-furred, but they were priming for the Indians as well, and the meat fat for their hungry roasting fires. As surely as they wanted robes and fancied juicy hump ribs they would be out after the big Republican herd too, and any man who carried as fine a scalp as Jim Hickok better keep his eyes peeled.

By the time the hunter got sight of the herd it had broken up to feed, the small bunches scattered dark over the snow as far as he could see with his fieldglasses. He swung around to approach against the wind, topping every snowy little rise on his belly. But there was no boom of hunting rifles and the buffaloes remained quiet, undisturbed, certainly not disturbed by Indians, who were contemptuous of the hideman's still or silent hunt. They took their meat and robes with whoop and galloping horses in the thundering chase and the great surrounds.

When the snuffling, grunting buffaloes were just over the ridge, Jim Hickok hobbled his horse in a draw and crept close upon a small bunch of about fifty. He pushed a wall of snow together before him, laid his rifle across the top and, selecting the leader, aimed for the lights, the lungs. The report was loud on the cold wet air, the puff of smoke very blue, but through it he saw the fat young cow give a little jump and run a few steps, bright blood streaming from her nostrils to the snow. Several shaggy heads lifted to look. Two cows up close started a low bellowing in their throats at the smell of the blood and then suddenly they began to move away, one picking up speed, the others looking, deciding to fall in. Soon the whole bunch would be in flight. But the hunter brought down the running cow and then the other one, going in the opposite direction. She was up again and headed straight for Jim, as though her little eyes had located him, or she caught his enemy scent. So he fired another, a faster shot that brought her down in a lurch, forward upon her great head, her body rocking a little as she kicked, and was still.

By now the whole little bunch was excited, rolling their anger in their deep throats, the two old bulls pawing the earth at the stink of death, hooking their horns threateningly this way and that, their long beards waggling. But they too, waited for a leader, and each time one tried to start there was the boom of the gun until the heated barrel had burned away all the snow support. Besides, the hunter would soon have to move to keep the shifting buffaloes from catching his scent and stampeding. He aimed for one of the big bulls, but let him get too far away. He missed, and then the other one too, both fine, dark-robed animals; missed them clean like a greenhorn tenderfoot popping away with a derringer. Maybe Jim had buck fever too, even after all his years with guns, or perhaps the barrel was too hot, and the stinging smoke blinded his eyes.

The hunter examined the sights, adjusted them a little and gave himself time to cool too as he rubbed the barrel with snow. This still hunting with a heavy rifle was very different from the swift jump of pistols in some smoky little frontier saloon, or shooting from a buffalo horse charging along beside a great bull, almost within touching distance. That was sport; this was hides and a stake that Jim Hickok needed, a new stake from hides that were as good as gold up at the hide yards of the new station the Union Pacific railroad had located at Sidney Barracks on its way through western Nebraska a few months ago.

When fourteen buffaloes were down and one crawling away, dragging his hindquarters, the rest apparently had enough of the thundering noise, the infuriating smell of blood and the curious actions of the bleeding. They were quitting the hunter, bunching their ponderous shoulders close together as for protection but walking in their swinging pace, ready to break into a trot, a gallop. Stiff from inaction and cold, Jim got up and ran around the side, barely taking the time to glance over the white prairie for Indians, who could be coming up on him in line with the buffaloes from any side, almost. He kept to the cross wind and dropped down to shoot from a bank as the buffaloes passed. His buck fever had passed and he got eight more, scattered out in a ragged, fleeing line, the two big bulls among them, great and black on the snow as the others all drew away, leaving them bleak and alone. He ran after the rest a ways and the little bunches they were tolling along, hoping to head them with his scent. Then he noticed a tight little herd in a box canyon quietly sunning and chewing their cuds out of the cold northwest wind. Only one, a young spike bull, was stand- ing, his wet nostrils out, testing the air uneasily.

This bunch Jim managed better, dropping the first two that started to break for lower ground with a bullet apiece. They went down in the narrow neck of the canyon, almost closing it as they kicked and died. The others tried to climb the steep sides or stopped to snort and bellow at the fresh blood, their little eyes rolling. The hunter picked them off one by one until suddenly he realized he was out of ammunition—his belt and his pockets empty, and only the two cartridges in his hand left. Not only was he out of am- munition but he was at least three miles from his horse. It was a chilling realization that a man so long on the plains would be foolish enough to shoot himself out of trigger feed, that the man who was bragged up in *Harper's Maga- zine* last February as the fastest man with the draw would let himself be caught afoot and alone in the Indian country with an empty gun.

Coke, the skinner, was nowhere in sight and there were no shells to waste signaling him now. Surely Jim Hickok, the one called Wild Bill, should have his famous white- handled pistols along, but they were too valuable to lose crawling on his belly through the snow. Besides, they were better for show than for defense and entirely too light, too short-ranged against a wounded buffalo, or to hold off attacking Indians.

Yet the hunting this first day had gone very well. Forty-two buffaloes were down in the little canyon here, sixty-five altogether, and the sun still high as a man's shoul- der. But Jim was stiff and wet and cold. He crawled into a clump of brushy weeds up at the canyon's rim and looked all around with his fieldglasses. There was what looked like a dissolving thread of smoke far off north, perhaps from the rising column of an Indian signal, but nothing more came, and otherwise there seemed only earth and sky and grazing buffaloes all around. By the time he got back to his horse, Coke was busy skinning at the first kill and had a sirup bucket of hot coffee waiting in a heated firepit beside the wagon. Although the hunter was ravenous, he refilled his cartridge belt before he did anything else. He did it silently, without speaking a word to his helper, as often happened for days between them.

The two men were not finished skinning when darkness came but they could not risk working by the coal oil lantern that would surely toll any murdering redskins within miles. A good, experienced man, Coke had worked fast. He skinned out the heads of the two big bulls with the hides, to sell for rugs or wall robes, but the others he ringed at the neck close up behind the curled horns. He slit the skin down the grass-fat belly from throat to the root of the tail and down the inside of each leg to the knee. Then he staked the head securely by driving a wagon rod through the nose into the freezing earth, took a hitch of rope around a thick wad of the hide from the back of the neck and fastened it to the doubletrees. With a sharp whipcrack Jim started the horses up and ripped the skin off, leaving the tallowed carcass bare. Most of the kill was still warm and only one hide was torn, but those left over night would have to be taken off with the curved skinning knife, painfully, inch by inch. It would be tedious but that too, was part of the business and Coke whistled a little through his teeth as they took a heavy wagon load of the hides to camp, the rest left for tomorrow.

So the two men worked come-day and Sunday, Coke shooting some too, when the buffaloes were moving out very fast, until there were only patches of snow left along the slopes, like the spotted flanks of a pinto pony. Some days

Jim shot as high as fifty or sixty but seldom more than they could skin out, and as the buffaloes grew rested and more alert, particularly on windy, moving days, it sometimes dropped down to twenty. The weather remained cold and the hides pegged down on the prairie dried so slowly they had to be left behind as the herd began to drift southward. Another month free from molestation and Jim Hickok would have his stake, be ready to return to Ft. Hays and the famous customers gathered in the back room of Drum's saloon, men like General Phil Sheridan, General Custer and his brother Tom, and always at least a dozen prominent easterners come to look at the long hairs, the gunmen and Indian fighters.

But Jim Hickok waited a little too long. He had found several nervous, scattered little bunches of buffaloes, nervous from Indian chases, he knew, and so he moved the camp east, nearer to the settlements, where the herd was thinning fast but the hunting seemed safer. They still had not actually seen an Indian.

Then one afternoon as the two men pegged down a new haul of hides, hammering hard to drive the wooden pickets into the bare, frozen ground, they were suddenly surrounded by at least twenty-five mounted Sioux Indians, so suddenly not even Hickok could jump for his gun. Another party whooped down between the hunters and the rougher breaks to cut off escape that way, although there were already a dozen warriors between them and their horses, and the tent with the buffalo guns too. It was two men against at least fifty angry-faced warriors, a few with their guns up, many with arrows set to the string. In the open the longer range of the buffalo rifles would have given the two hunters the advantage until the cartridges ran out. Now they had only their Colts in the holsters laid out of the way while they pegged down the dirty hides, and the Indian weapons were drawn upon them to stop any motion toward the guns.

Coke knew a little sign talk and at Jim's low urging, he tried to bargain with the Sioux, but he got only a snarling

"All!" from the man who seemed to be the leader, and the flat-fingered circling motion of the hand that indicated they were going to take everything. "Kill our buffaloes!" the man roared out, with a final accusation: "You!"

While the Indians looked steadily down their weapons the others picked up the pistol belts and went through the tent, bringing out the buffalo guns, throwing out the small kegs of powder and the bar lead and the cases of cartridges dug from the cache hole under the bed robes, sweeping everything into their yawning hide sacks to sling across their horses. Coke was shaking inside his bloody skinner's pants and Jim Hickok had to stand with his hands empty of all except the useless pegging hatchet and watch this happen, his face pale and furious under the dirt and powder smudges of the day's hunt. The Indians pushed the wagon up close to the tent. One of them stooped to it with flint and steel to burn what they could not carry away. All Jim's property was going to the bloody redskins, and his guns too, and probably both of their lives. Wild Bill Hickok, the Prince of Pistoleers, had let a bunch of dirty, skulking Indians come up on him easy as a still hunter up on the stupid buffaloes.

As the Indian fanned the sparks to a smolder in his tinder of grass, the impatient young warriors pushed up closer with their guns, arguing among themselves, others crowding in with arrows and war clubs ready. But there was a far whooping, and another Indian came down over a little rise, whipping his yellow pinto at every jump, roaring out in his harsh Sioux, "Stop! Do not harm the white men; we are not the ones to make war first!"

Slowly the warriors nudged their horses apart to make way for the newcomer with the one feather of a chief in his hair. They did it reluctantly, sullenly, some curling their lips in snarling threats. But they did move back, and the chief slipped from his horse, kicked the rising smoke of the fire to pieces, and held his hand out to Jim in the white man way. "Me Whistler," he said, making the thumbing sign towards himself as he spoke the traders' word for his name.

Angrily, arrogantly, although the chief had surely saved his life for the moment, Jim Hickok shook his long hair loose from his collar, tossing it to curl over his shoulders. "Me, I'm Wild Bill Hickok," he said. "I remember seeing you around Morrow's ranch up near the Platte—"

Hou! it was so, the chief agreed, nodding his understanding, his teeth white in the dark face. Firmly he motioned the rifles and all the rest of the goods brought back, the powder and the horses too. Then he and the two white men went inside the tent to squat beside the little emigrant stove while Coke stuffed it full of dry buffalo chips. Over a smoke they visited a little, with Coke's smattering of sign talk to help. When a big bucket of coffee boiled up it was passed around outside for the warriors, with plenty of sugar for the tin cup. There were big handfuls of raisins too, the men cracked the seeds with satisfaction, but their eyes still turned to the pile of powder, lead, cartridges and other goods that Whistler had made them give up.

In the tent the old chief reminded the hunters that he had always been known as a peace man, but all this last summer troops had chased the Indians back and forth through their buffalo country. Nobody had been caught but it was hard to make meat and robes while running. Then too, the hide men were killing the Indian's buffaloes, his cattle, taking the skins while the Indians were not allowed to sell the robes they made at all. It was an angering injustice. In addition all the soldiers marching around and the hunters shooting stirred up the buffaloes too much for the arrow, the only way the Indians could hunt now that they were not permitted to trade robes for guns and powder or to buy ammunition. Besides, it kept their men busy protecting the women and children from the whites, who had plenty of guns.

Jim Hickok said he had shot at no one here, but that

he would not stop hunting. "The buffaloes belong to the man what gets 'em," he insisted, and Whistler had to admit that the Sioux had never denied any one the right to make meat. It was the waste of the herds for only the hides that grieved him and angered the warriors to fighting.

When old Whistler left, his blanket was heavy with tobacco and powder and lead. His warriors rode in single file behind him, their blankets held close about them in the golden evening light of winter, the younger men lagging a little, as though still minded to sweep back upon the guns and all the ammunition there beside the old tent.

Finally the Sioux seemed gone and then Jim Hickok let loose the fury that almost always found a swift and natural outlet in the lightning draw. By the time he quieted, Coke had gathered up much of their scattered belongings out of the dusk. He piled everything into the side-boarded wagon, spread the tent over the top and hooked up the team in the darkness. Quietly, without striking even a match, they moved out over the prairie, the wheels creaking on the frozen ground. Jim rode ahead on his black mare. She stopped cautiously every now and then, turning this way or that from some gully or washout, or to listen, snorting, clearing her keen nose. But there seemed no scent of danger and no sound except the howl of the wolves and the high thin voices of the coyotes answering them. They were made restless by the coming change of weather but otherwise too lazy for much howling, with all the meat left by the hunters, several thousand fat carcasses, the entrails easy to drag out with no hide to gnaw away.

Several times Jim had to turn his horse from the grunt and snore of sleeping buffaloes. Once he was so close in the darkness that the man-smell penetrated their stolid resting and they sprang up awkwardly, joints cracking in the darkness, and were gone in a thunder of hoofs on the frozen ground, fortunately missing Coke and his wagon, although their noses led them straight in his direction. They passed very close in the dark shaking of the solid earth, the man so stiff from fright he could scarcely climb off the wagon when they were gone.

After awhile the two men stopped to gnaw on some frozen jerky, not daring to build more than an Indian fire, a handful of broken buffalo chips glowing red for a few minutes under a dry hide, to boil up a tin can of coffee. Then they crawled into their sleeping robes, the pickets of the horses within hand reach. But although Coke was soon snoring, Jim could not forget the danger, particularly the indignities, of the day. He was the man who, it was said, got the nickname of Wild Bill from the wild account he gave of the McCanles killing at his murder trial six years ago, the man who had probably killed at least a half dozen others besides the Virginian, Dave McCanles and those with him at the Rock Creek station of the Overland Stage in Nebraska back in 'Sixty-one. To such stories Jim Hickok said nothing, one way or the other. He had done many kinds of hired-handing, from living in a company dugout as horseherder for the Rock Creek station to house gambler in some of the best saloons in Kansas, including Hays and the other boom towns as the Kansas Pacific moved westward up through the Smoky Hill Trail country on its way to Denver and the gold mines. Last winter he chased horse thieves and then drove illegal timber cutters from the public lands for the government. It was claimed by some that he spent most of that time up in Nebraska trapping beaver, and there was a story that he got into a two-gun saloon fight up there and dropped four cowboys before he got a bullet in the arm. Although three of the men were supposed to be dead, later accounts said the only casualty was the truth, that Bill wasn't carrying two guns, that he wasn't even in the saloon. But now, after many months of sporadic scouting for the army, interspersed with short hide hunts and standing off the hostile summer Indians, this man who stirred such storytelling had let himself be surrounded by a little bunch of wintertime, agency Sioux, to be rescued by one of the most despised characters of the frontier—a peace chief.

The truth was that the fastidious Wild Bill hated the hide business, this crawling over the prairie, perhaps through snow or mud and fresh buffalo droppings. A man was always bloody and soiled, always full of vermin and buffalo mange, conspicuous anywhere with his continual scratching. Yet Bill liked the test of holding a small bunch of buffaloes together in the still hunt as he picked them off, the clumsy animals confused, frightened, stupidly waiting to be shot. But he hated most of all the blood and stink of the great awkward hides, heavy as lead and limsy as rags while green, and then board-stiff when dry enough for the hauling wagons. What he needed was a big outfit with a cook, a lot of skinners and haulers, a big comfortable wall tent with his monogrammed bay rum bottles and a good stove for hot water to shave and to soothe the cold from his hands. Then, with enough armed help around so no devilish redskins could creep up on a man, he would only need to shoot down the buffaloes.

Perhaps he hated the isolation, the lack of admiration most of all, that and the cold which crept into his bones and kept his long thin fingers stiff as frozen tallow. He was made for finer things, as his mother assured him long ago, before he got into trouble back home in Illinois. But now he was thirty and had tried out several kinds of work, followed several wild geese since the fight with another canal driver in which both fell into the water. The other man didn't seem to be coming up and Jim Hickok struck out for the west, thinking he had killed a man. Since then he had moved on repeatedly over gun fights, and had actually stood trial for the killing of McCanles and the two men with him at Rock Creek. But those times were behind Wild Bill Hickok now. He usually had the law on his side these days, was the law, but it didn't pay enough, and although he had filed on two homesteads, one in Kansas and then one in Nebraska, somehow he never had much to his name except debts. He hadn't been running in luck the last year with the pasteboards, particularly not while scouting for the new regiment, the Seventh Cavalry. There were a lot of Hard Cases and card-sharpers among them and just enough Bible packers to lend a little respectability and a sense of recklessness.

Scouting wages didn't go far either, and there was the new weskit Wild Bill was having made. It would be of fine corded silk the color of a pale sand dune in the sun, embroidered in sprays of prairie roses like the one, great as a man's palm, that was pressed between the pages of the *Harper's Magazine* he always carried in his gripsack, pressed full blown beside the picture of Wild Bill Hickok, the Prince of Pistoleers. With the new weskit there would be a black broadcloth cape lined in plaid silk and boots with embroidered patent leather tops, the heels two inches high, with a little more build-up inside, for Wild Bill liked to fancy himself much nearer six feet than he was, particularly now that eastern visitors expected him to be tall as they believed everyone was in the west, even men like Sheridan, Custer and Kit Carson, no bigger than the family runt.

But the tailor would be waiting for his money at Kansas City, the garments to be shipped out to Bill at Hays only if he could raise the cash ahead of time, in addition to what he already had on tick there.

"Coke," the hunter whispered, nudging his partner. "We'll make one more try—"

The skinner moved sleepily under his robe. "You forgettin' all them Sioux bucks? Next time they mightn't be no old coffee-cooler like Whistler come tearin' up to stop 'em," he muttered.

Wild Bill and Coke stayed another month, although both Sioux and Cheyenne parties kept coming through now, so the camp could never be left alone, but had to be moved along from kill to kill. Yet they were never attacked. Perhaps old Whistler's rescue gave them general protection; perhaps it was because they were always on the alert now and camped in places where many Indians would die in an attack. Indians were always spooky about getting their men killed.

In this extra month Bill got twelve hundred more hides, good, prime, thick-furred robes that brought twice the price of their early take. Bill hired a trader's freight outfit to haul in his accumulated caches. Then the first clear day after he sold the lot, the receipts augmented by a few hands of poker with the troopers of Sidney Barracks, Bill rode southward over the two hundred fifty miles of winter prairie to Hays, Hays City now the end of the track with the first train in just ahead of the snows, and already three big dance halls opened and twenty-one saloons.

Jim had his tailor bill paid and more than three thousand dollars in gold and yellowbacks in his money belt. With the swagger of its weight and importance, he headed straight for the bath house at Hays. Later he came out in the new rose-embroidered weskit, with frock coat and checked trousers, the flowing cape, and the handsome boots so well fitted to the slender feet with insteps high as a lady's. Now he was the Wild Bill of the card tables. With his hand carelessly at his holster he went down the middle of the dusty street. He kept away from the shielding alleys and was cautious as he passed the late wagons and the hitchracks with shivering horses hunched together in the squares of windowlight. There was a wild shot or two as some galloping troopers hit town, but otherwise everything seemed quiet. Drum's saloon, too, would be duller now that little Phil Sheridan was stationed at Ft. Leavenworth, leaving his regular place in the back room empty, and that General Custer, suspended for a year, was shorn of the swank that went with the command of the Seventh Cavalry. But the brawling Tom Custer would be around, and the troopers flush from the paymaster's arrival at the post today. They and the hundreds of buffalo hunters driven in by a general blizzard off west last week ought to make good pickings.

Before Wild Bill reached the light that spilled from

the windows of Tom Drum's, he stooped to flick away the dust on his boots with his handkerchief. Then he threw back the two sides of the cape to show the red silk tartan lining, settled his shining curls about his shoulders and walked easily through the saloon door, into the noise and light.

At twenty-five Lonesome Charley Reynolds still carried an innate neatness although by 1867 he had spent seven years on the frontier, much of that time in trapper dugouts. As often before, he was hunting alone this fall, his hide wagon hidden in a tight little canyon. He knew this Republican region that cut across the Kansas-Nebraska border better than any other man of white blood except Buffalo Bill Comstock, and perhaps it was the Indian in Bill that gave him his superior knowledge.

As always Lonesome Charley rode very cautiously out of his canyon; most cautious about the Indians. He knew many of those around on these hunting grounds by name, both Sioux and Cheyennes, and some were once his friends, before he had to shoot one and wound some others. Besides, there was a rising anger among the Indians over so many killed by the troops, and the Cheyenne village destroyed last spring. They had saved their lives that time but little more, and went angrily to the Medicine Lodge treaty conference in south Kansas. They complained a great deal there, particularly against the new railroads and the buffalo hunters.

"Why do they kill and not eat?" an old chief had demanded at the conference, to a great agreeing roar of *"Hou! Hou!"*

But they had received no reply and since then men much longer in the Indian country than Charley Reynolds were found dead, face down along the trails and around the buffalo camps. He would keep out of sight.

On the trans-Missouri frontier the badge of a man was his hair: the braid and scalp lock of the Indian; the careless, tangled growth of the trapper, mountain man and buffalo hunter; the drake tails of the freighter and settler; the careful, tumbling locks of the frontier dandy. But Charley Reynolds kept his hair short under his beaver cap, and as neatly combed as any city man. His flowing mustache was neat too, his clean-shaven cheeks darkened across the bones with grease and gunpowder against the blinding sun on snow. At the edge of the canyon Charley got off his old zebra dun mustang and crawled to the rim, a handful of the snow on his cap as an extra precaution. "By God," he said, speaking as to a companion, a keen-eared one who could catch Charley's soft speech. "By God, a man oughta get into some business where he don't have to bust every rise on his belly like a snake."

Yes, and watch his tracks like the jackrabbit who doubles back and sits with his round, unblinking eyes out for an enemy on his trail, open even in his sleep, because, being a rabbit, he had neither tooth nor claw for his defense.

But Charley Reynolds knew no business except frontiering—scouting, trapping, hunting, and fighting Indians when necessary. As he looked slowly around the skyline, he knew it would always be so, for once more his heart began to pound under his ear-flaps. Off on the horizon was a frost cloud, a pale flat line like white smoke against the purplish west of a winter morning—a great herd, and very compact judging by the breath haze. The hunter wiped the frozen drip from his nose with the corner of the bandana around his buffalo collar and climbed clumsily back into the saddle. At the first opportunity he reined into the tracks of a herd of wild mustangs, following their direction as far as he could. He rode slumped forward in the saddle, squinting all around the white plain for smoke or the flash of a mirror signal.

When Charley Reynolds first returned from three years in the Civil War, he had hired out to a trader. They were attacked by Indians near the Smoky Hill River, the trader killed and his outfit looted. Charley got away to a wolfer's empty dugout and stood off the Indians until dark, killing one and wounding at least two more. He escaped in the night, but the redskins remembered. Last year when he came back to the headwaters of the Republican to make hides they gave him no rest. His camp was burned, a bullet was put through his coat, and once he had to kill his wounded horse in a buffalo wallow for breastworks, firing from behind it, careful this time to hit no one seriously, holding the warriors off until a hail storm came roaring like a stampeding herd of buffaloes over the valley. The Indians hurried away to shelter and Charley didn't wait for their return. Realizing that sooner or later they would get the drop on him, he went to work up at Morrow's roadranch on the Platte. It was a hangout for Indians but as one of Jack Morrow's hired hands he was immune. Charley Reynolds was a quiet, soft-spoken, accommodating man, and, as usual, got along very well, even with the Sioux loafing around there. But finally he had a little trouble with a drunken, trigger-happy officer from Ft. Mc-Pherson. Charley's bullet cost the man an arm and since then the soldiers too were laying for the lonesome hunter.

"You always looked to me like a man that tends to his own business," Big Jack Morrow told his hired hand. "But with the army after you, you better quit the country till the dust settles." So Charley had ridden southward and wintered with his brother in Kansas. When he started back to the buffalo country last spring he said they would not see him again until he had money enough to live in comfort. Although this might take years, a life-time, he started with no more truck than for a few weeks' hunt. "Travel light if you're goin' far," a white-haired old beaver trapper once told him, and Charley Reynolds intended to go very far indeed.

Now he had hides cached in half a dozen places, and many loads to his credit at the trail and railroad stations. He could have made more money by taking the tongues out too, but the smoking they required would surely have drawn the bucks riding down on his camp. He took chances enough with his little buffalo chip fire, the smoke of it a pungent whiff to a sharp Indian nose. Even his pale grease light, a strip of rag stuck on a wire over a tin cup of skunk oil and lighted into a fingernail of flame, was dangerous. Still, with luck he would get at least two thousand hides, perhaps twenty-five hundred this season, half of them good winter robes worth around two-fifty each—a very fair haul for one man alone.

Without luck—well, without luck little Charley Reynolds would not need the hides or the money. But the Indians who got him would know they had been in a fight.

Beginning in 1825, when all the trans-Missouri region was Indian and buffalo country, twenty-eight eastern tribes were forced to give up their homes and move, without permission from the resident Indians, into the present state of Kansas, there to have land and buffaloes forever. But already the white man was pushing in from the east. He marked out trails too, one to Santa Fe, the Overland up the Platte, and later the road of the 'Forty-niners through the Concho River region of Texas, all through the Indian lands. The trailers shot the buffaloes, destroyed the grass and drove away the herds that had sometimes held them up for hours, even days, with their passing. The emigrants brought new diseases too, particularly the cholera that killed so many Indians. The growing resentments and pressures brought a series of treaties thrust upon the Indians, first just to sell their rights to the trails and to establish intertribal peace on the Plains. Often the treaty payment goods did not come but the trails were not given back. With travelers always in sight, the buffalo grew much wilder, the tensions and angers greater. Frightened and foolish emigrants shot at friendly Indians and brought retaliation—and more and more troops to pursue the redskins into their treaty-right grounds. Some were caught, usually only the easy-minded friendlies, their women and children killed. This made more angry warriors, brought more depredations.

In 1854 the eastern tribes had had to move from their so-called permanent homes in Kansas, give them up to settlers. By then the desire for the Indian's land had changed him from the Noble Red Man that princes and lords came to study, into a blood-thirsty savage standing in the path of progress. The most insignificant incidents were magnified and mismanaged into bloodshed. The killing of a crippled Mormon cow brought a young West Pointer into a peaceful Sioux camp with a cannon and too much whisky aboard. He shot the head chief down and was wiped out himself, starting what turned out to be twenty-three years of intermittent war with these Indians. There were retaliations, more breaking of treaty agreements, more falling upon friendly camps.

The Indians of the north Plains only attacked those who pushed into their region but south the Comanches and Kiowas had long raided the Mexican and Texas settlements, taking captives. In 1864 Col. Kit Carson had a serious engagement with these tribes at the old Adobe Walls in the Texas Panhandle. Outnumbered, even with his cannon, he got less than a draw.

By then the new trail up the Smoky Hill River to the Colorado gold mines, more emigrants shooting at friendlies, and the buffalo hunters on the Indian ranges had brought on the Indian War of 1864, which closed the Smoky Hill and the Overland Trails to all but strong forces of troops. Settlers and emigrants were killed, and the year ended with the massacre of the Cheyennes, men, women and children, at Sand Creek, Colorado, where their agent had told them was a safe place for those who wanted to be peaceful. This was followed by the vengeance march, January 1865, of Sioux and Cheyennes up to the Powder River region in Wyoming, the Indians pillaging and burning the road ranches on the way and driving the troops into their little posts. The next summer a wide three-pronged military expedition invaded the Powder and Yellowstone country with orders to take no male prisoners over twelve years. The orders were superfluous; the troops retreated, mostly afoot and starving, without one real engagement.

The national temper was not improved, and in 1866 three forts were planted illegally on the new Bozeman Trail through the Powder River region. The Indians held them under perpetual siege and in December they decoyed Captain Fetterman's eighty-one men to their deaths. And then in the spring the hated Union Pacific railroad came roaring up the Platte and the Kansas Pacific, anxious to get some of the great government subsidy of cash and land too, started up the Smoky Hill. The railroads offered cheaper transportation than the bull trains and made the dried, the flint hides, pay out. In the meantime the Indians were forbidden to trade robes for guns and ammunition.

With hundreds of buffalo hunters like Wild Bill Hickok and Charley Reynolds getting ready to shoot their way into the herds, the wilder Indians waited only until their ponies were strong with spring. To stop their raids, Hancock and Custer took the field in April 1867 ostensibly to meet with the Indians in a peace council, but they had fourteen hundred men, including artillery and with pontoons, evidently to ford Kansas rivers far beyond the peace grounds. Old-timers at Ft. Larned had laughed to see the expedition go out. "Looks like Hancock'd know them western rivers is mostly sandbars from when he was down fightin' old Santy Ana," one of them said.

"Oh, them pontoons'll come in handy in the cactus, an' 'll shure kill a lot a Indians laughin'."

But the Cheyennes hadn't laughed as the force drew up near their big camp gathered on Pawnee Fork of the Arkansas River for the peace council. They had been peaceful, still wanted to be, but they had seen their women and children shot down in piles on the winter snow of Sand Creek less than three years before. When the great army approached, this time with cannons, they fled, leaving the empty village and all their goods behind for Hancock's burning. Custer, a novice at Indian fighting, had tossed his long hair back, set his hat close and started out to round up the Cheyennes like a herd of longhorns. He rode out with dash and flying guidon, but he met what any experienced Indian fighter would have anticipated—a great trail that melted before his eyes. All summer only small detachments managed to engage the Indians, generally a handful of warriors trying to sweep away the cavalry horses. A few Indians were killed and some troopers, but far more soldiers died of cholera that summer than both white men and red together from gun and bow.

The Indians of north Kansas, angered by Hancock's attack on the Cheyenne camp, had harried the hunters all summer, while their southern relatives and allies were at the Medicine Lodge treaty conference that was planned to get the redskins out of the way of the third western railroad, this one to come up along the Arkansas River, over much of the Santa Fe Trail. There was still little raiding down there, and that little against the trails and settlements because few hunters made the thin summer hides so far from the railroad. But along the Kansas Pacific survey west from Hays to the Colorado line, and northward as far as the Platte, hide hunting was big money, and protecting this growing enterprise proved a severe initiation for the Seventh Cavalry. The regiment was less than a year old, conspicuously raw, the leadership inexperienced and floundering despite the cooperation of troops from older units and the scouting of experienced frontiersmen like Buffalo Bill Comstock. Wild Bill Hickok, who knew the region fairly well from his hunting although he understood little about Indians, had also scouted for the troops part of the summer. But not for Custer. Apparently one long-haired dandy was enough in his column.

Custer had managed to get through the Indian country to the Platte by early July without an engagement, but by then his command was rebellious, with wholesale desertion as soon as the danger of the scalp knife hovering about

their flanks was past. Custer, perhaps led into exaggeration,
reported that around forty of his troops vanished in one
night. The next day, while the column made a halt near the
Platte with the railroad just across the river, seven mounted
men and five afoot struck boldly for it, right before the commander's eyes. Furious at this open insubordination and derision, Custer had the men pursued, commanding in the
shrill, high voice of his anger that none was to be brought
in alive. Those with horses got away. The five afoot were
shot down, two falling like 'possums, the other three actually
wounded, one to die ten days later. After that the desertions
dwindled, perhaps because the column had started back south
and once more marched through Indian country with angry
warriors buzzing all around both flanks, but without the arms
and ammunition for an attack. Many of the over-marched
troopers recalled the story that in the Civil War, two years
ago, a whole division had rebelled against the young general,
and that ninety men were arrested for mutiny from one regiment. There was no denying Custer was relentless with his
men, but Hardbacksides took his punishment along with
them.

At Ft. Wallace, out ahead on the Kansas Pacific survey,
near the Colorado line, there were many letters to greet
Custer. Abruptly and without permission he left his command, riding to his wife at Ft. Hays, and followed her to Ft.
Riley. He gave fear of cholera as the reason, although there
was no report of the disease at Hays but a lot of it with him
in the field, his own troops sick and dying.

There had been laughter and talk about Custer and
his women among the hunters scouting for the general, and
around the buffalo camps that they passed—women they
claimed were in Custer's field wagons, and about the Indian
maidens often around his quarters. Gossip traveled fast and
maybe it got back to Hays and the Mrs., the scouts told each
other. Some of the couriers said that Elizabeth Custer had all
their goods packed, "Like she was flying with the geese."

The department commander was not satisfied with the reasons that Custer gave for his hurried trip to Ft. Hays. He was placed under arrest, charged with deserting his post and with ordering that none of the deserters up at the Platte be brought in alive. Tried, Custer was suspended from his rank and command for a year. Grant, then Secretary of War, approved the sentence the same day, something that Custer was not the man to forget. This promptness made it impossible for General Sheridan, the new department head, to help his dashing commander of the Seventh.

So the Hancock campaign of 1867 ended in humiliation. Custer had not contacted the Indians in even one engagement and the rest did little more, although the expedition cost millions of dollars and stirred up the Indians so that many soldiers, railroad workers, hunters and defenseless settlers were killed, but almost no Indians. To those who said that Custer was sacrificed for Hancock's failure there was the reply that Hancock could not be blamed for the general's earlier troubles back at West Point and in the Civil War. Last year, when Custer was out campaigning with President Johnson for a favorable Congress, some newspapers reminded their readers that in the war he had ordered lashes meted out to his officers without trial and with no charges ever preferred against them.

But no one could deny that under Major Elliott the morale of the Seventh was falling even lower. Ordered out to pursue some depredating Indians, he prepared the six companies as for a grand review, everything slicked up and polished, flags and guidon flying, strings of wagons and ambulances trailing along behind. The hide men watched his column pass their camps, spit into the dust and looked more carefully to their own Indian precautions. Such parading through the buffalo country would really keep the redskins at a boil.

Once more an occasional settler was found with his back full of arrows, and more hunters and freighters were

shot, or disappeared. There was talk too, of graft and fraud
in the army freighting, involving officers. A Denver newspaper reported a rumor that Butterfield hired the Kiowas
to hold up his wagon train so he could get damages. But next
year was presidential election, a new administration coming.

As the Cheyennes worked northward from the village
that Hancock had burned back in April they had killed a
few troopers guarding the railroad graders and took a few
captives as their southern allies did, raising a wave of terror
that swept the eastern fringe of the buffalo country and drove
the settlers from their homes. In one vicinity the homesteaders organized a company of militia and threw up a sod
blockhouse for refuge. By then most of the angry Cheyennes
had reached the Platte. They ditched a Union Pacific freight
at Plum Creek and killed several of the crew. One man was
scalped alive; he recovered but learned to keep his hat on.
The warriors had plundered the cars and filled their hide
sacks. Some young bucks rode over the prairie letting bolts
of bright calico unroll in the wind behind their running
horses, whooping and laughing.

A couple of newspapers thought that the wrecking and
killing was done by white men in paint and moccasins, so
unskilled, their scalping so inexpert. But the Indians never
denied the attack, although those who came to the little peace
council at North Platte in September claimed they were not
in it. To the questions about white captives taken in Kansas,
the few Cheyenne chiefs present said they were with other
bands—some of the Southern Cheyennes who raided with the
Kiowas and Comanches. There was much talk to the Indians.
They must make peace, settle on agencies where there would
be regular issues of food and goods or else troops would come
marching against them. The friendly Sioux chief Spotted
Tail smiled a little. It seemed he had seen troops marching
all summer through the buffalo country that was the Indians'
by treaty right.

Through the big talk of both sides it was plain the whites wanted to crowd the Indians to a few agencies no bigger than hide corrals, out of the way of the railroads, the settlers, cattlemen, miners, and the hide hunters. The chiefs talked about these same people—the railroaders, settlers, and hide men—but they wanted all such whites driven from the buffalo ranges where the Indians intended to remain. They were particularly angry over the hunters in their rich Republican country, the men who killed off their herds, their cattle, as the chiefs called them, for the hide, while the Indians were not permitted to sell any robes at all. They didn't speak of the contraband traffic—the railroads renting freight cars to the illicit traders, recording only the weight hauled. That was not getting their rights, and it was not enough. Besides the illegal traders could cheat the Indians. They had to sell at the price offered or let the well-tanned robes mold and rot.

The government councilors scolded the chiefs as the white men did their children and told them that the hide men and the trade in robes were not proper subjects for this conference, which was for peace. Then they gave out the pres-ents, including some powder and ball for the wilded buffaloes. Afterward the peace commission moved on to Ft. Laramie and the Indians went out to their fall hunts.

When Charley Reynolds saw the hunting villages come, the guns of their hunters booming in the chase, he began to haul his hides up to the great dark ricks at Sidney. But this hunter sat in at no game, shook no dice and drank no whisky even when others wanted to set up. Lonesome Charley was building him a stake.

Most of the meat shot by the buffalo hunters of 1867 was left to rot on the prairie to fatten the wolves, the buzzards and the long-tailed magpies. The juices soaked the earth and would darken the surrounding grass into lushness for many years. The bleaching bones were so thick that large reaches of the Republican country would look white as from eternal frost. But there were some who hunted only for the meat. One party operated very systematically, the one hired by Bill Cody to fill his contract with the Kansas Pacific railroad, heading west past Ft. Hays towards Colorado and the gold in the mines of the mountains. From early spring the railroad had twelve hundred men in the construction gangs. Cody's contract called for twelve buffaloes a day, eviscerated and ready for the meat wagons, and paid him five hundred dollars a month, it was said, to supply them. In addition he also furnished meat for the troop encampments guarding the route.

Cody had killed buffaloes for the railroad the summer before and this year he knew how it should be done. He hired Tennis, an experienced plainsman who had hunted the Republican and Smoky Hill region for several years. There were five more men, including young Sutley from Pennsylvania, with two years of normal school training. Each man furnished his own blankets, grub enough for two months, and his arms, as well as two horses, one for packing. Old-timers like Tennis would not be hampered by wagons. "Indians ain't never slowed down by wheels, an' if you ain't got no army to stand 'em off you better keep to legs—horses' or yours," he said as he gnawed off a chew of tobacco.

They outfitted at Hays and headed west with their pack horses, camping on streams with enough timber for wood but not enough to shield the approach of Indians or to draw their encampments. They didn't use Cody's fine showy method of shooting buffaloes from a running horse as he did for visiting celebrities and sportsmen. That called for years of practice and would require a large relay of fast horses, day in and out—enough to tempt the best Sioux and Cheyenne raiders. Tennis taught even the green men how to ride close in to a herd, hobble the horses and creep up against the wind, usually without stampeding the buffaloes until they had several fat young cows down. Summer hides brought little and helped keep the meat clean so the buffaloes were not skinned but they were bled like beeves and gutted of all but the heart and liver, ready for the haulers who followed close.

The cooking and other camp work was rotated, always with two men together to protect the supplies and ammunition. Hunting close enough to the railroad grade to get the meat in fresh brought many encounters with the Indians, who harried the hated track gangs. The Indians all knew Tennis and many stopped by with their bitter chronic complaints. All this hunting with rifles made the game too wild for the bow, and they were not permitted to buy or trade for guns and ammunition. They said this while they had their cup of coffee or a little tobacco for the pipe, and then sneaked around trying to run off the horses, to steal the ammunition, or put an arrow or a bullet into any unwary back. Out in bright daylight, Tennis and his men were little concerned about the Indians, so long as the raiding parties were small enough to be held off by the longer range of their buffalo rifles. Then finally, one early dawn, there was a gunshot in a little clump of brush down at the creek. Indians whipping away as Tennis led the others in shooting from the blankets. They found a dead man down there, one of their own outfit, his rifle still beside him. There was no telling why he went so far from camp so quietly, and at the most dangerous time of day, unless he had heard a disturbance among the hobbled horses. The hunters dug a grave, piling the sod and all on a robe. One of them sheepishly produced a little Bible and after the Twenty-third Psalm was read they carefully replaced the sod and threw the left-over earth into the river.

Cody himself had hunted very little the summer of 1867. He owned the outfit, purchased the provisions and ammunition, directed the freighters and occasionally picked a camp. Mostly he looked after the business from Drum's saloon at Hays. He had a special table there, conspicuously placed to set off his fringed buckskin, the fine belly-tan hat and his flowing yellow hair for the easterners: speculators,

railroad promoters, hide buyers, and the sportsmen seeking
new experiences and new trophies, as well as the gamblers,
gunmen, roadagents and the ladies of Drum's.

The railroad moving steadily westward attracted
many townsite promoters and Cody decided there were
quicker ways to riches than supplying the track crews with
meat, guiding an occasional eastern hunting party or sitting
in at a little poker. He would start a town too, one to be
called Rome, up along the tracks. For this he went alone,
without his audience of admirers and drinkers of his whisky.
He was overtaken by a party of Indians and chased about
twenty miles. When his horse was almost played out he ran
into a wagon from Ft. Hays carrying a dozen soldiers in full
arms. A good peppering of bullets sent the Indians flying.
The next time Cody rode out alone he wounded a buffalo
bull, up so close that the animal gored his horse and then
took after Bill, sent him kicking up dust with his fancy high-
heeled boots. But once more he was rescued.

"That's our Bill, our Buffalo Bill!" Tennis laughed
when he heard the story. "Tolls the Indians and the buffalo
right up handy for the troops—"

But winter came. The graders turned up the frozen
earth in slabs like grey rock and the railroad work shut down.

When the Indians came to the Republican herd for
their fall hunts of 'Sixty-seven, no hide man stayed anywhere
near the large camps, not unless it was some greenhorn who
soon disappeared, perhaps not to be found until the eagles
and the wolves were done and what was left bleached for the
bone pickers. But as the cold settled down the Indians scattered into smaller winter villages set in protected bends
where the wood was plentiful, with young cottonwood bark
for the ponies to gnaw while the snow laid on. There was
little raiding in cold weather and so the company of militia
organized by the Kansas settlers back in August was dis-
banded, but the sod blockhouse was preserved as a refuge.

The Indians hunted and trapped a little and planned ways to get guns and ammunition for the buffaloes, wild from the long pursuit, and to drive out the hunters, and the troops that were sure to come riding again with the spring. In the meantime the women tanned many robes and made bead-work they hoped to trade for goods, and eventually for guns also.

In midwinter the Republican herd broke into small bunches and slowly drifted south of the river before they began their gradual swing around northward along in late January. The boom of the forty-four rifle carried loud on the cold air, and even the pistol and the buckshot-loaded shot-gun. The hides piled up as the hunters shot their way southward, and their top-heavy hide wagons crept along the intricate netting of ruts to the trails and the railroads during the short midwinter thaws.

The summer of 1867 the Great Plains had still been mostly the treaty grounds of the buffalo Indians. The four great herds, usually named for their wintering, their good-robe region, grazed the vast prairie in overlapping annual circles. The Republican herd, mostly summering between the Black Hills and the Big Horns and northward toward the Yellowstone was the main herd of the great Sioux nation, their chief commissary. The southern half of this migratory circle was on the range of the southern Sioux and allied tribes, the north in the region of the Sioux of Red Cloud, Crazy Horse and Sitting Bull, the Northern Cheyennes and Arapahoes, and the Crows. In addition there were always fringe tribes who came in to make meat along the annual migration paths of all the four herds.

The Arkansas herd went north to the Republican region and into Nebraska through July, in January it was back at the Arkansas and below, apparently safe, for by the new Medicine Lodge treaty, the hide men were never to cross south of this stream again. The herd reached down as far as the Cimarron, deep in Kiowa, Comanche and Southern

Cheyenne hunting grounds. These tribal buffalo ranges ran
far southwestward into the Texas herd, which wintered toward the Concho and the Pecos and in the spring skirted the
Staked Plains north through the Panhandle to the Arkansas,
from east of Ft. Dodge up the river into Colorado. The
fourth, the Northern or Yellowstone herd, retreated to the
protecting breaks of the Yellowstone and its southern tributaries for January, and then spread to summer across the
upper Missouri and the Milk into Canada.

These migratory movements were often modified by
extremes of temperature and by drouth, grasshoppers and un-
usual wind direction. Yet they always approximated the great
circular patterns of the cyclonic winds of the Great Plains, as
these winds were mimicked by the swift and comic little
whirlwinds that ran vagrant over the hot summer prairie.
But the herds were vast dark shadows upon the plains even
when there was not one cloud to stand against the sky.

Some put the total buffaloes in 1867 at fifty million,
probably much too high, although it was said that General
Crook, long in the Indian country, favored this number. Most
old-timers believed there were certainly twenty, thirty million buffaloes left, fifteen million, at the very least, summering from the Platte River south to the Concho of Texas.
Sometimes it seemed they did grow out of the ground in the
south country as the Plains tribes believed. Each spring the
Indians watched their herds return northward, their hair
sprouting shining and new, as though they had really come
fresh from the earth, with many thousands of the yellow
calves playing among them.

Yet one old-timer, the Cheyenne peace chief Yellow
Wolf, had predicted, back in 1846, that the buffaloes would
soon all be gone. He tried to hire Colonel Bent's herder to
teach the Cheyennes to grow the white man's cattle so the
Indians need not die when the buffalo had vanished. Perhaps it was the natural pessimism of a small people squeezed
between larger tribes and the encroaching white men. Any-

way, Yellow Wolf's prediction had received only laughter, and now he was dead, killed in the Sand Creek fight three years ago. Long before then several Cheyenne chiefs had asked a government council for one thousand white women as wives for the tribe. They wanted their children to live in the new way that must be learned when the great herds were gone. The eastern councilors had been shocked. They did not realize that to the Cheyennes the children belong to the mother's people, and that these chiefs were offering to let their tribe disappear from the earth so their children's children might live.

Yet fifty million buffaloes, or even twenty million, seemed an inexhaustible number to those who did not know that the estimates of the early herds had varied from the fifty, sixty millions of the first explorers who saw the great midlands to the hundred twenty-five million of those who saw the High Plains also. The conservative estimate was around a total seventy-five million then, seventy million on the prairies and the plains with another five million in the forests. There had also been a mountain buffalo up to about 1840. Yet even in this year of 1867 naturalists called the American bison the world's most numerous ruminant. To this the hunters agreed when luck was with them. "Thick as them damn buffalo gnats—" they bragged.

Now a third railroad was coming up the Arkansas, aimed like a spear through the heart of that great buffalo range. The Indians saw its menace and called it the iron snake, another fire-spitting snake of iron that slept under the snow as the one on the Platte had done, and now the one along the Smoky Hill River. But it would glide out of winter hibernation as the rattlesnake comes from the frost-cloven rocks in the spring, gaunted and hungry.

General Hancock, whose summer campaign against the Indians failed so miserably, had been transferred and General Sheridan now commanded the department. Around Drum's saloon it was promised loudly that Sheridan would make the Indians pay for the humiliation to the suspended Custer. The few times Little Phil rattled his spurs passing through the bar to the back room he seemed somehow a taller man, and very purposeful.

CHAPTER II

LORD OF THE PLAINS

FROM about November twentieth to late December the buffaloes were at their finest; sleek and fat, the pelage thick and glossy-dark; the calves, all except the latest ones, smooth and brown. It was at this time of the year that the sight of the great herds moved visitors from the far world, sportsmen like Prince Maximilian and Sir Gore, and naturalists like Hornaday, to call the American bison the most magnificent of all ruminants. True, the south Indian bison or gaur and the aurochs, the European bison, both surpassed him in height if not in actual bulk. The bull of the American bison usually weighed around two thousand pounds and up, the cows about twelve hundred. With much longer and more luxuriant hair on the head, neck and forequarters, the buffalo was vastly more imposing even singly. In the vast, dark herds of the plains, he was fabulous and unbelievable.

Towards spring, however, the buffaloes faded swiftly, their bleaching hair giving them a rusty, seedy appearance. They began to shed early, sometimes by the last week of February in the Republican herd, and took over half a year to it, dead, matted hair clinging to them in ragged and dirty tufts. To rid themselves of this loosening hair and the vermin in it,

37

they scratched on everything—rocks, banks, trees, telegraph poles and buildings. The only unprotected habitation that the frontiersman could maintain for long was the dugout set into a bank or sidehill too steep for footing. They upset any wagon left on the prairie and rubbed down the flag poles at the army posts. To prevent over-eager defenders of the colors from cluttering up the area with stinking carcasses, orders were still issued at posts like Ft. McPherson, Nebraska, against shooting buffaloes on the parade ground.

On the hump and shoulders the new hair pushed the old off as it came in, dark and often well-matured as early as May, the heads a glossy black. The rest of the body, however, was often still nude as a badly scalded hog into mid-June. Raw, scabby and tender, the buffalo was driven wild by the flies and by the buffalo gnats that were like whirling clouds of fine clinging dust around his nose and eyes and in the sores of his bare skin. Often flight was the only remedy and a thundering run out into the wind of the tablelands left the gnats behind. But the sun burned the buffalo too, and so he retreated to the first mudhole and rolled in it like a great pig, coating his tender hide all over. The mud gathered in thick lumps on the long hair of his forequarters and his head and beard, making an appallingly hideous creature of him. Yet the Indians pursued the mud-caked buffalo as hotly as ever, although they had no illusions about the meat of spring. But hunger sharpens the tooth and the winter parfleches welcome the leanest jerky. Then too, the Indians always preferred freshly killed meat for the cooking fires, and pointed to the unloveliness of the habitual carrion eater, the buzzard, compared to the grace and beauty of animals that fed on flesh or blood that was still warm with animal heat—the eagle, the mink, the ermine and the mountain lion.

By summer the herds were full of romping calves, mostly born from April through June. They followed their mothers many months, perhaps over a year. They were reddish-yellow until August, then the hair fell in patches and by October they were brown, fat and adventuresome.

During the calving season the cows gathered off to themselves, leaving the bulls scattered, or drawn into small herds that were dangerous for the unwary hunter. Often without a cow to take the lead, to draw them away from danger, they stood their ground in sullen stubbornness, and did not try to save themselves at all. Even in the regular herds the bulls were less wary, easier to approach, and meat hunters could creep past them to get at the more desirable but wilier cows. At any pursuit or even the smell of man, the buffalo, unconscious of his strength, fled, and would only fight at bay. Now and then in a hot chase he might turn, swift as light, and overthrow horse and rider, and so was dangerous within the close range of the fuke, as the old hunters called the sawed-off double-barrel shotgun loaded with ball, or with the bow and arrow or spear that the Indian generally had to use. One of the warrior sons of Dull Knife, the Cheyenne chief, was gored to death by an arrow-shot buffalo in a surround. Yet the hunting could be dangerous even with guns, as Bill Cody discovered the time a wounded bull gored his horse and chased him afoot. It got him the name of Buffalo Bill from the laughing soldiers who rescued him.

The flamboyant Cody, with an eye for the publicity, adopted the story as one more exploit, and elaborated it into a duel to the death between the infuriated monarch of the plains and Buffalo Bill Cody armed only with a knife. It had an element of probability. Experienced skinners and butchers sometimes had narrow escapes from buffaloes apparently dead. Up north towards the Yellowstone a hunter was killed by a bull whose tongue he had actually cut out in the belief that the buffalo was dead.

A cow with a new-born calf could be more dangerous than any bull. Usually she left the herd and returned a few hours later with a lanky, new-dropped yellow calf that would

follow at her side until driven away by his successor. For the
first week or so the cow was "on the prod" as the hunters
called it, but they often caught calves a few weeks old, after
the mothers had been shot or driven off. Given a finger to
suck a while the calf followed a man as closely as it had the
mother, doggedly, silently, with only a pig-like grunt for
hunger or thirst. At five months the wild calf could outrun a
relay of three fresh horses and not be overtaken until worn
out by a chase of twelve, fifteen miles, perhaps to die quietly
in the pen or on a rope that night. A buffalo hunter named
Charley Jones discarded the rifle for the rope and built up a
little herd of buffaloes for the ranch he established at Garden
City, Kansas.

The running season, as the westerners called it, was
from July well into September, when the calves were two to
four months old. At its beginning the ease-loving, even sloth-
ful nature of the buffaloes disappeared. Instead of the small
scattered herds of calving time, they now gathered in great
excitement. The bulls chased cows half of the time and
fought each other the rest. The encounters, bull against bull,
were long, threatening and dusty. Heads lowered almost to
the ground, their narrow flanks heaving, their beards jerking, they roared until the earth shook, their bloodshot little
eyeballs rolling as they pawed up dirt and threw it high over
their backs. With thousands of bulls in the herd the roaring
was discernible at one to three miles, even five if the wind
was right and a change of weather in the air.

The actual fight, however, was usually short and harmless. The great heads finally met in a dull thud, insulated,
deadened by the thick mats of hair. There was a frantic strug-
gle, a pushing this way and that, the sharp hoofs straining for
footing, the power of the great shoulders apparently sure to
crush the skulls like the browned puffballs of the prairie. Suddenly one or the other, with a sudden twist, slipped his head
sideways to turn a sharp curved horn into flesh. But the hair
and hide lay thick over the shoulders and the massive neck.

Perhaps the heads met again and again, usually until one or the other of the bulls turned and fled into the milling herd, to take up another stand, with more roaring and pawing of earth. Once in a while a hoof slipped, the adversary's horn cut in under a rib or into a flank, blood ran and the fury grew, until one lay gored and trampled or dragged himself away, every young spike bull, and even an occasional cow now taking a safe hook of a horn at this sudden outcast.

After the breeding season the buffaloes settled down again, separating into small bunches of from twenty to a hundred. Quietly they spread out until the herd covered many square miles, moving as the wind drew them. With their small weak eyes practically lost in the matting of curly hair, they depended almost entirely upon their noses to warn them of danger and so fed into the wind. In this way they sometimes wandered from good range into badlands, or out upon arid waste expanses. When thirsty the whole group set out for the water hole on common impulse. The leader, usually a four-year-cow, started down the nearest draw, the rest as if by signal immediately fell in line with perhaps no more feeding beyond grabbing a mouthful of grass on the move. The trail of a herd in search of water was usually as fine a piece of engineering as any railway surveyor could produce and was governed by the same principles. The buffaloes followed the level of the valley, swerved around high points, crossed and recrossed stream beds in order to avoid a grade. The Indian followed these trails for food and ease of travois travel, and later the white man's roads and railroads. Although the buffaloes used the trails season after season, they were not over twelve inches wide, just enough to let the small hoofs pass with ease. When a trail became deeper than perhaps six inches, whether by wear or washout, it was no longer comfortable and another was started alongside until on slopes there might be fifty trails running close as corduroy.

There was often great crowding and fighting at the water holes and perhaps trampling and death in mires and bogs. Stinking Creek, draining a wide dry region of the upper Republican, was named for the rotting buffaloes caught in its bogs. But once watered the herd settled down to rest with almost every nose pointing into the wind, the young calves playful among their ruminating elders, their tails raised high as scorpions over their backs as they ran, jumped and butted; they rolled in the dust. After a while the herd rose to feed again, gradually strolling off perhaps at right angles to the course from which it came as the wind shifted with the latening day.

Grown buffaloes liked to roll in dry dust, looking, from far off, a little like a flock of black hens dusting themselves. This was not just during the shedding time but in the fall and winter too, the bulls more than the cows. Stretching out full length a bull rubbed his head hard on the ground, using a small curved horn like a sled runner. Then he rolled over his great hump as easily as a horse and scratched his other side, raising a haze of dust all around him. Old bulls usually had over half an inch of the thickness worn off the outside curve of the horns. In wet spots one would get down on a knee, plunge a horn into the wet earth, then the whole head, thrusting the mud up on both sides as he plowed his body into the hole and rolled. Soon another drove him out and then another came, until the little water hole was a deep wallow, empty of the last bit of mud that might cling to wool.

The migratory habits of the buffalo were regular so far as the wind permitted, and usually on a rather grand scale. Sometimes the great herds made their southward move before winter in easy stages, slowly; other times in a headlong rush over long distances, perhaps in a thundering, earth-shaking lope. They might come like a great dark army, four to ten animals abreast, the ragged column reaching clear back into the horizon; or perhaps in a dense mass, the leaders in danger of being trampled into quicksand, bogs or mire, or driven out on treacherous ice. Often thousands were lost in the frozen Missouri, to float up later and lodge against islands and sandbars, the stink driving Indian villages and later white man camps away. There is a legend of a great herd whose leader, a sacred white buffalo cow, was shot. Without direction the herd drifted out upon the fall ice of Lake De-Smet in Wyoming and crashed through, every one lost. The water turned grey so no man would drink it, and for many, many years afterward only white birds settled on the water there—gulls, white geese, and the great white swans that made their nesting homes around DeSmet clear up into the time of Crazy Horse, the 1870's.

The tremendous electric storms of the High Plains destroyed buffaloes too; sometimes one bolt of lightning killed a dozen or two close together. Sometimes while they were gathering into the great running herds, they were overtaken by the tornadoes that swept the southern plains. The buffaloes were very sensitive to the slightest weather disturbance and before a twister they became extremely restless, milling, grunting, pawing the earth, running a little this way and that, tails up high. Then suddenly, perhaps, all broke into a gallop simultaneously, as though some vast unborn wind swept them across the prairie. The instinct that made them rely on their keenest sense, their noses, keeping them into the wind, usually carried the buffaloes away from the gathering storm centers, but the Sioux tell of seeing a long funnel cloud dip down into a stampeding herd somewhere near the bend of the Arkansas River. Then the clouds broke and the rain and roaring wind shut out everything as the Indians, a little war party with two women along, flattened themselves into a washout, holding their horses down with their arms over the necks. But they were soon driven out by the boiling flood that tore through the washout and then were almost drowned out on the open prairie, so dense was the rain.

The next morning the Indians rode over to see where the herd had been. There was no sign of it now as they approached, not a buffalo left in sight, but a broad strip of the prairie was torn and washed bare. The great spreading cottonwood on the creek bottom where so many yellow orioles had nested was gone, nothing left but a stump thick as two whisky barrels, the rest twisted off, torn and scattered up the breaks, bits of it washed in with the piles of trash in the gullies. Finally the Indians saw the buffaloes, many hundreds of them, in a great long rick, as though lifted and sown along for a quarter of a mile, several deep, sometimes four, five on top of each other, broken and twisted, some stripped of their hair, some with the eyes hanging down their faces, drawn out of their skulls. Mixed in with the buffaloes were big loose clumps of hair, weeds, grass, and splintered wood, with a few other animals, antelope and coyotes too, perhaps. The Indians saw the iron of some wagon wheels, twisted and bent, but they saw no horses or men, although some could have been in the big piles or under the sand and mud washed up against the buffaloes by the rain. On a rise off to the side two big prairie wolves skulked like coyotes, looking, their tails between their legs as in fear of some terrifying thing.

"Nobody touched the buffaloes or anything among them, not until the white men came with the wagons for the bones," an old Sioux who was there recalled years later.

Even in blizzards buffaloes faced the wind instead of turning tail and drifting helplessly as cattle did, the longhorns that were trailed up from Texas. With the smell of a storm in the air the buffaloes usually sought a canyon or ravine and settled down to chew their cuds and wait it out, scarcely moving except to trample the rising snow drifts, and perhaps not even that. Sometimes small herds were almost buried and occasionally actually smothered, lost until a thaw came and the buzzards began to circle over them. After a storm the herds scattered out upon the flats and creek bottoms or along wind-bared slopes, wherever grass showed above the snow. A buffalo could fast for days, even weeks. An old Kiowa chief complained at the peace council the summer of 1867 that it seemed very foolish to kill off the buffaloes who looked out for themselves during the winter to make room for the white man's cows that must be sheltered and fed.

The real winter enemy of the buffaloes was crusted snow. Their small sharp hoofs broke through the drifts that held up both the wolf and man. A lone Indian on snowshoes could run up boldly to spear the greatest bull floundering in the drifts, and wolves could tear him down. Old bulls were often in bad shape after a hard winter and yet their percentage kept increasing. By 1867 there were approximately nine or ten bulls to every cow. Even the white man preferred the cow for meat and the Indian always selected the fat young ones to eat and for robes, whether for himself or for market. Cow skins were easier for the women to tan, lighter and more pliable and not so unwieldy for bed robes and lodge skins. Old bulls were killed for shields. The thick skin of the neck and hump was stretched green over a pit of coals to shrink and harden in the slow heat, harden enough to turn an arrow or a spear, perhaps even a rifle bullet if at some distance or at a glancing angle.

The path of the migrating herds was not as fixed, not as direct as, for instance, the deer and the elk climbing to higher altitudes with the softness of springtime. The gentling days turned the buffalo from his southward movement in the first mild spell of late winter. Gradually he began to work northward and often westward, higher up on the slope of the plains too, as the heated air moved in from the west, until the summer nights began to chill and the portentous winds to blow into the coming storms that usually drew him south. But sometimes the nose of the buffalo betrayed him. One of the Sioux who fled to Canada with Sitting Bull told the author the story of a great herd lost because unseasonably soft northern winds had drawn them far into the frozen lands of upper Canada one fall, into the face of the arctic winter. The entire herd starved and froze there, leaving their bones to bleach through the short summers until the whole region was white as with the snows in which the buffaloes had died.

How many were lost? "Ahh-h, it was long ago, and the dead ones were very many," the old Indian replied. "Enough to feed all the women and children a long, long time. Perhaps this many—" touching his two finger-spread hands at the thumbs, moving them from the right shoulder left and downward for the sign of a hundred. Then, instead of counting the number of hundred on the backs of the fingers he made the sign again, one hundred hundred, and then once more. One hundred times one hundred hundred—a million.

But certainly there were not that many?

The old man scraped the bowl of his stone pipe. "Very, very many," he said softly, as to himself.

Although several species of the American bison seem to have disappeared during prehistoric times, the modern buffalo was very vigorous, with few ailments. However a murrain, a *rinderpest* that spread westward from the settlements and the trails in the middle 1820's left many of the great gathering places of the animals dark and stinking. A broad region in southeast Nebraska reaching up to the salt flats where Lincoln now stands was apparently cleaned of all hoofed animals so completely that in 1825 a war party of Sioux returning afoot from a foray against the Missouri tribes almost starved crossing it. Finally they found a dying old bull, his mouth and tongue so horribly swollen and rotting that he could scarcely breathe. But the Indians were so weak and hungry they killed him. Only one man, who was too revolted by the sight to eat of the meat, survived, and in the wintercounts of the Sioux, 1825 is still called the year When the Six Died from Eating the Whistling Buffalo. In 1858 a disease called the bloody murrain killed many cloven-hoofed animals—work oxen, antelope, deer and buffaloes—along the western trails. The stretch of the Overland Trail between Ft. Laramie and Bridger was one long offense to the nostrils. This scourge accounted in a measure, some thought, for the rapid disappearance of the buffalo from the Laramie Plains of Wyoming and along the Platte, although the summer of 1860 so many buffaloes were slaughtered along the trails past Grand Island, Nebraska, that the stench was fearful, and by 1862 the river bottoms to the forks of the Platte were white as fall snow in their bleaching bones.

Yet the real enemy of the buffalo was the incredible extension of the striking arm that the white man carried with him—his powder-stenched shooting stick that reached far beyond any hand-thrown rock, or the spear and the arrow. Before his arrival the buffalo's greatest enemies were the extremes of nature, quicksand, and the lightning-set fires that might be carried by the wind upon the advancing herds. When they finally turned from the fear of smoke, they were perhaps too close and soon overtaken in exhaustion, cornered against some canyon wall or driven over a bluff or cliff, to leave their bones bleaching in broken piles below. In those days the fires ran on until blocked by stream, lake or barren ground, until quenched by rain or the wind swept the flames back to feed upon their own ashes. Sometimes the Indians used fire to hold an escaping herd, ringing the terrified buffaloes for the kill. It was dangerous work in the shifting winds of the plains, and used less since the arrival of the horse, by nature even more afraid of fire than the buffaloes, although he could be trained to it. Since then the Indians fired the early spring prairie to hurry the grass for their winter-weakened ponies, and often the buffaloes were caught in these.

Perhaps the most formidable fire of the buffalo ranges was the one set by General Mitchell in 1865. In January after the Sand Creek massacre of the Cheyennes the fall before, the Indians avenged themselves on a swath a hundred miles wide from Kansas to the Powder River country, burning road-ranches and trail stations, and driving the scattered troops into their posts. Soon afterward a smoke appeared on the morning horizon, growing white and opalescent against the pale winter sky. At first a few green hunters took it for the frost cloud of a buffalo herd, but it kept climbing and stood all around the north and west like the rising wall of a blizzard. It didn't move in with the characteristic speed or send out flying tatters of fog to be followed by a thin sifting of grey flakes and the sharp, wind-driven snow that no living creature except the buffalo could face. Instead the clouds boiled up into the clear January sky like thunderheads. In reply to some uneasy telegraphing, the more remote army posts were told that the fires were started on orders from Mitchell, set at close intervals all along the line of the Platte and the South Fork, from Kearney in middle Nebraska to the foothills of the Rockies near Denver—better than four hundred and thirty miles. The fires had been started in the quiet of early morning so they could spread into a solid front before the wind grew and drove them down upon the Indians and the fleeing animals too. The experienced hunters knew what this was, cursed the perpetrators, and tried to stack their hides that were still spread out to dry on the prairie, hoping that only the outside ones would be destroyed.

All kinds of animals, from rabbit to buffalo, fled before that solid wall of fire. The buffaloes, their eyes too weak and hair-blinded to see the rolling smoke, usually did not catch the whiff of it until quite near. Then, with their ropy tails suddenly up, they turned and stampeded, sweeping in dark thundering waves over the plains, here and there one going down from age, a hoof in a prairie dog hole, or from the burden of a heavy calf, the strong stumbling over them. All those who could, got up to run again, on and on, driven as no hunter could ever drive them, piling up in the canyons, and soon on the level prairie too.

Three days the fire swept southward, the heat exploding the dry seed tops of bluestem and bunchgrass, running up the rises with the speed and roar of an express train. In short-grass country the fire was stopped by the ice of such streams as the Smoky Hill or the Solomon and smoldered there in the bedding places of the buffaloes and in brush and marshes.

Elsewhere it leapt the streams with the wind and ran on, some fireheads going clear to the Arkansas, to spread slowly along the banks, coming together. Yet even here some accommodating wind-blown tumbleweeds carried their sparks and embers across the wide stretch of ice and, reseeded in the well-grassed bottoms beyond, the fire grew again, running itself out deep in the wastelands of the Texas Panhandle.

Millions of creatures were destroyed, all the game dead or driven from an area half again as large as all of New England. But not one Indian was killed. Some had to backfire to save themselves, their camps and their herds, and then ate of the burned game as they hurried their snorting, hungry ponies over the blackened region that lifted itself in great sooty clouds on the wind. The skin hunters, mostly close to the trails in those days, apparently all escaped except three tenderfeet who were found dead in a draw not half a mile from water, their new buffalo guns beside them, only the steel left, burnt, the fine temper of the metal gone. Along the east many settlers were cleaned out, their lives perhaps saved by their dugouts while the cows and pigs and chickens roasted, and sometimes their horses too.

Although the great fire of 1865 was intended against the raiding Indians, it was set along the south bank of the Plattes when the raiders were already well across the river and headed north. Only the peaceful bands were troubled at all, bands led by men like Whistler, the Sioux, who later saved Wild Bill Hickok's life. But they all had to go to the Powder River country for meat, where their young warriors heard the exciting plans of the wilder Indians, plans to drive the white man back towards the Missouri and out of the buffalo country forever. Of course a few whites who had trading houses would be allowed to remain because even the hostiles liked their coffee now, with the white man's sweet lumps in the bottom of the cup. They liked his powder too and the lead that brought down the buffalo who was growing so wild.

The Indians of south Kansas went into Texas, deep

into the country of the Kiowas and Comanches whose warriors rivaled the wildest Sioux. But now it was 1868 and there
were more white men everywhere, and more guns booming
around the herds.

The commerce in prairie hides had been growing a
long time. It was said that many of the British troops in the
Crimea marched on buffalo soles and rode saddles of buffalo
leather that came from the Red River breeds of Canada,
most of it hauled from the Montana plains in their squeaking carts. Many Indian robes went southward. A partner in
the American Fur Company estimated that as early as 1850
at least one hundred thousand robes came in to St. Louis every year; by 1857 an annual average of seventy-five thousand
robes was gathered by the upper Missouri river posts alone.
The Indians killed probably around three and a half million
buffaloes a year during the 1850-1860 period for their needs
and the robes they traded. This included, in addition to the
Plains tribes whose entire subsistence was from the buffalo,
the seasonal hunts of reservation Indians along the eastern
fringe of the buffalo country, and the mountain tribes who
came down for meat, robes and lodgeskins.

The High Plains had an early center of Indian trade
at the present Horse Creek near the eastern Wyoming line.
Here, long before Columbus, ornaments and strange prod-
ucts from as far as Mexico could be traded for white fox
skins, say, or an occasional bit of carved walrus ivory, and
seashells exchanged for quilled pouches or red pipestone.
Here the Sioux got their first wonderful big-dogs that a man
could ride—their first horses, for some fine quilled robes.
The horse of the white man was followed by iron for arrow
and spear points and finally by guns and markets and a thriving business in robes. When the government tried to stop
this trade to keep guns and ammunition from the Indians, to
starve them to the agencies, the villages became wealthy
in robes and very poor in arms and in coffee, sugar and

good flannel cloth. All those destroyed in the years from 1864 through the Plains wars were packed with extra robes and beadwork—fortunes gone up in stinking smoke.

Yet to make enough meat to feed the larger villages of the Republican with the bow called for careful management now. When the ceremonials to bring the buffalo close had been made in old Whistler's Sioux camp, scouts were sent out until some returned with news of a good herd near. Then the lodges were struck and everybody moved together, those managing the hunt riding ahead to keep the over-eager from slipping away and spoiling the surround, while some scouts watched to warn the white hide hunters away with a few flying shots, if necessary.

On the way some of the best hunters with the fastest horses were selected to kill meat for the old and the poor, led by Whistler's nephew, a very serious young warrior. The village camped back from the hunting ground, on a small tributary of the Republican, with good water and wood. In the meantime just over the hill from the buffaloes the hunters stripped to breechcloth and moccasins, bows and quivers ready. They separated into two parties and rode out both ways from behind the feeding herd, moving quietly and keeping down wind as long as possible. When all were ready, in a great arc around the herd, the head men from each side whipped around in front of the buffaloes, whooping. The grazing animals stopped, and, tails up, began to run, but there was man smell everywhere now, many men charging around the herd as the sun goes, with their whooping and the flying horses, the driving arrows.

A few buffaloes that tried to break free went down, others began to circle a little, then more, beginning to mill as in a great flood as the dedicated hunters pushed in past the bulls to the fat cows, some of the others close behind. Arrows sank in behind the running shoulders, perhaps to the feathers or deeper, clear through if they struck no rib, the hunters shouting their "Yihoo!" of triumph as each animal went down. The running buffaloes and horses were like the roar of a great hail over the hard earth, with here and there a horse having to leap a down buffalo, or go down too, the rider dodging for the open prairie. The old bulls were allowed to get away, one now, then another, but the cows and the young stock were kept running in the tightening circle. Once a curved horn dipped down and a horse was lifted up, his belly split to sudden red, the tumbling entrails grey and alive as he fell back, the rider down and dodging too, the cry of alarm that went up lost in the wild thunder of the hunt. He got away but another man had to be picked up and carried away, a great hoof gash in his side, the blood flowing where the flesh hung down like a red rag, the medicine man running up.

Now the circle of the surround was closer, and slower too, the horses tiring, even the buffaloes. Here and there one seemed to be escaping almost under the bows, perhaps pursued and brought down before the rest could try to follow. One with a dozen arrows got clear out but he fell to the crack of a watching gun, the first shot fired. There were half a dozen more bullets and then the last buffalo was struggling to his feet and falling, until struck down by a Sioux war club. Around four hundred buffaloes were scattered over a quarter mile plot, some close as an arrow's length apart, a thick haze of dust over them all. The hunters slipped from their horses now and let them go, to be caught by the waiting boys, while each one sought out his arrows. The women, who had drawn nearer and nearer, were already running in, making the trilling cries of a good hunt, the sun glinting on their long butcher knives as they came, the men who did not hunt running too, to help.

The knives flashed in the late sun and the skins rolled back, with the stench of fresh blood and gut-shot buffaloes. Then the fine pale tallow and red meat lay clean on the skins, the visceral part too, the heads, the great bones for the marrow. Small boys ran excited among the butchers, shouting, bragging, grasping at chunks of raw liver held out here and

there by some good woman, while smaller children, some
on their mother's backs, chewed solemnly at strips of sinew
and gut.

It was sunset when the long line of pack horses came
into the new camp under the hovering layers of blue camp
smoke. They were heavy with meat between the folded
skins, the marrow bones tied on top like thick, pink-touched
bleached wood for the roasting fires. The men unloaded the
meat on spreads of clean marsh grass near the drying racks
the old people built during the afternoon. Hump ribs and
other choice parts were put to roast for the feast, special bits
carried with formal step to the council lodge and laid down
as the men sang their thanks to the meat gatherers. Even the
hunter who got hurt was able to sit up and would soon be
riding in another surround.

As night settled the roasting fires all over the camp
sputtered and flared under the meat, and the fine smell called
in all but the horse herders and the scouts far out, to watch,
for Whistler's camp was not to be surprised by enemies, red
or white.

After the feast the weary ones leaned back to the piled
bed robes, full and happy, perhaps nursing a warm pipe a
little while, or dozing. But the drums called all the rest to
dance and sing, with a special song for those who managed
the hunt very well. It was no longer common to get so many
buffaloes almost entirely with arrows, and in the short time
that the sun moved from the head to the shoulder. Now one
from those with no hunters in the lodge came forward to sing
a song of gratitude that their drying racks had so much fine
fat meat, for although it was fitting that the needy ones always receive a little more than the others, it was also fitting
that thanks be given.

There was one more thing to be done, and for this the
finest skin was selected, a soft, curly one that had a blueness
on the sides, a blueness shiny as on a raven's throat. This
one Robe Woman tanned very soft and worked in her best

bead designs, and then it was taken to a rise where the sun came to sit very early in the morning and the winds of all the great directions blew. There it was left as a thank-offering to their brother the buffalo because so many of his kind had died that the Indian might live. By then the parfleches of Whistler's village were fat from several more good hunts and the lodges warm with many new robes, the beds soft.

After the Civil War, Bates of St. Louis, in the northern trade, and Durfee of Leavenworth, Kansas, together collected around two hundred thousand robes annually, two-fifty thousand in good years. The thin summer skins, mostly from white hunters and tanned for leather, were cheap, from eight fifty to sixteen fifty a bale of ten. The prime, well-furred winter robes, particularly when Indian-tanned, brought much more. As early as 1835 Pierre Chouteau of St. Louis and Robert Crooks of the American Fur Company agreed on forty-eight dollars per pack of twelve skins—eleven seasonable robes and one summer hide.

The Civil War demand for robes and leather had brought many white hunters west, a good proportion of them draft evaders and bounty jumpers, happy to get beyond Abe Lincoln's reach. Hundreds of long bull trains loaded with robes and flint hides came in from the Platte Valley and many moved past Atchison, Kansas, to the levee for steamboats to St. Louis and Cincinnati. By 1864 over a hundred white hunters were killing buffaloes for the hide and tallow on the Saline Fork in Kansas, with similar camps scattered along the other trails, including both Wild Bill Hickok and Charley Reynolds, among them for a while. They helped stir up the Indian War of 1864, which had cut like a bloody knife across the Overland and the Smoky Hill Trails.

But in the Medicine Lodge Treaty signed the summer of 1867, the Southern Cheyennes, the Kiowas and Comanches surrendered all their lands north of Indian Territory, retaining their right to hunt there as long as the buffalo lasted, the troops to keep all hide men out of the Kansas region south of the Arkansas. The payment was to be rations and annuities and a start as farmers: horses, cows and pigs, wagons and plows, and schools and homes for everybody. But the fall and winter passed and the impatient spring too, without sign of the promised goods. It was very difficult for the Indians to understand that the Senate had not ratified the treaty. Their lands were gone, weren't they? Then bring out the goods.

In the meantime the guns of the hunters kept up their roaring, the buffalo grew wilder and the hungry Indians more sullen and threatening as their ponies strengthened with the new grass. "Our chiefs have been fooled by the white man again!" the wild young warriors taunted, and rode against the hide camps, the K. P. railroad builders and the settlers pushing westward. The treaty chiefs had lost so much face they could not stop the raiding, and when the whites pointed out that the Sioux and the Northern Cheyennes made no attacks on the settlements, the chiefs replied that the northern Indians still had their buffalo country from the Platte to the Yellowstone, with no screaming fire road cutting through their ranges, and no guns booming along the creeks and rivers.

But not all the hunters of last fall were back. One who wasn't making hides was Wild Bill Hickok. Before Hays City had seen more than two or three weeks of his fancy cape and vest he had climbed into the saddle to carry messages over the winter prairie to Ft. McPherson on the Platte. He was glad to go. General Custer still had nothing to do but hunt with his hounds. President Johnson, under whom the Seventh Cavalry was created for the general, was in danger of impeachment, and there was talk of running Grant for president —Grant who had fallen over his feet approving Custer's suspension so promptly.

This did not improve the temper of the Custer fanciers in the regiment and after Wild Bill got into a little trouble with them at Hays he hung away from there much of the time, scouting for other troops. As the Indians started raiding again, soldiers took the field, Major Elliott in command of the Seventh Cavalry. But many in Kansas thought that he rode very slowly. Encumbered by a wagon train like a loose section of a joint snake, the marches were held down to fourteen, fifteen miles a day. That was no speed to catch the Sioux and the Cheyennes. The troops found no Indians, not even with Comstock scouting, old Bill Comstock who knew every tra- vois trail and camping ground, and was the best buffalo hunter of the region, the man known as Buffalo Bill before Cody was old enough to lift a gun to his shoulder. But not even Comstock could hurry Major Elliott and the Seventh, and so the Indians went unpunished.

As the Republican winter herd spread north with the summer, toward the White and the Powder River country, the Arkansas herd came into the Republican region. Wild Bill Hickok saw the other hunters making money and de- cided to do a little summer hunting too. On very bright hot days he preferred to stay in camp. The sun bothered his eyes some, but not as much as the glaring new coal oil lamps at Drum's in Hays City, with shimmering circles like pale rain- bows, like winter sundogs, all around the flame.

There was trouble in south Kansas too this spring of 1868 now that the Indians knew another railroad, the Santa Fe, was coming up the Arkansas River. The new grade drew thousands of hopeful laborers from the unemployed in the east. The soup kitchens of the cities were only for the select few certified as the worthy poor by the police chief. Jobless men came to hunt buffaloes too, mostly tenderfeet, with per- haps no more than an old pistol and a jackknife. In a few weeks or even days many turned to outlawry, sometimes as Indians, with moccasins and awkward feathers.

Although the iron tracks crept steadily up the Arkan- sas, in the north the Kansas Pacific ran out of funds at Sheri- dan station, west of Hays City, and laid off most of the twelve hundred laborers indefinitely. These men had seen train loads of flint hides go out last year and heard of the money Wild Bill, Charley Reynolds and dozens of others made. Soon a few of them were found face down on the prairie, their backs full of arrows. There were rumors too, that the hide market was glutted, the bottom dropping out, and so after standing off a raiding party or two, many experienced hunters dropped their wagon tongues at Ft. Wallace, or Hays or Sidney. Some of them sat around the saloons, getting into fights and shooting up the street while they waited for something to come along, or the troops to do something beyond guarding the trails and K. P. tracks.

By August there was raiding along the Saline settlements of Kansas again. The settlers protested to Washington and then sensibly built a few more sod forts and reactivated last year's private militias. Major George Forsyth, aide to General Sheridan and green to Indian fighting, decided on a little informal redskin hunt, maybe show up Major Elliott some said, although another man still around the country, one George Armstrong Custer, hadn't done any better leading the Seventh. With Lt. Fred Beecher and an army surgeon as the core, Forsyth raised a company of fifty civilians: scouts, angry buffalo hunters and post hangers-on. Sheridan's permissive order let him provide the men with Spencer seven-shot repeaters and Colt revolvers, put them on the government payroll and promised them all the plunder—horses, arms and anything else they could capture.

The first few hours the roster lengthened fast, but in the end Forsyth was still short a few men. The undertaking had its lawless aspects—a force of civilians going to attack all Indians on their legal hunting grounds because a few young men of one tribe or another committed depredations. Old-timers knew that success would only bring new raids against helpless civilians, particularly settlers, but more probably Forsyth's scouts would have to be rescued as with most civilian expeditions.

The major was eager to get started and out beyond the telegraph before the vigilantism of the expedition could be grasped in Washington. Few Indian fighters joined up, standing away, instead, from the big talk in the saloons, even at Drum's, where army plans were usually as welcome as a gold piece in the palm or whisky in a blizzard. Many troopers from last summer's campaigns were openly hostile, and some of the officers warned the tenderfoot Forsyth he should have a force of at least two hundred civilians. The Indians were well armed, the best horsemen in the world, and they knew their country.

But such talk was treason to the professed Indian fighters. "Any man-jack of us is worth twenty a them sneakin' redskins," a broad-coupled man they called Whalen protested. "An' probably two Regulars throwed in."

"Two Regulars, hell!" a bluecoat roared and kneed Whalen to the sawdust.

So there was a little shooting. The bartender ducked the bullets and came up with his hands on a neckyoke that he swung both ways, suggesting that they reserve their gunplay for the Indians. Besides, Lieutenant Beecher, although lamed in the Civil War, was an experienced Plains soldier too and Sharp Grover, their head scout, was an old hand in the country.

They finally filled the roster with a quiet little Jew who had been, among other things, a frontier peddler and post handy man, but had little sitting acquaintance with a horse. Almost at once there was another volunteer, an outlaw but a fast man with a gun and not afraid of blood as the little Schlesinger would certainly be. But Schles couldn't be talked out of going now.

"Well, they got a little a everything, salt, pepper and gravel in the grease," one of the old scouts said as he watched Forsyth lead his little party out into the heat of late summer. They were a motley outfit and rode a ragged and awkward column, nobody wanting to eat the dirt.

"Yeh, Beecher there, the nephew of the Bible slingin' Hank Beecher, he's seen Indians before, and them hide men. But the deserters and the outlaws what's been rustlin' Indian ponies—I don't stake much on 'em. Mebby seven, eight real fighters in the whole outfit. I don't look to see 'em come ridin' back with much fight left," a buffalo hunter agreed, and settled himself for more waiting around.

Forsyth and his scouts passed small detachments of troops guarding the railroad and a scattering of buffalo camps. Everywhere the sunburnt men looked after the dusty column and pushed their sweaty hats back, maybe laughing a little. The hunters heard that the Seventh Cavalry was near an Indian village, and laughed at that too. But there could be a fight, with Wild Bill scouting for them, now that Custer was away from the regiment. Bill was filling in for Comstock, killed by Sharp Grover who was riding with Forsyth. Sharp had done the shooting in a Cheyenne camp only a week or ten days ago and he should be able to find the Indians again, although the buffalo hunters along recalled uneasily that he was part Indian and often in their camps, particularly the Sioux.

"That there bastard'll sure lead us into ambush," one of the windy talkers complained when he saw that Grover was getting to ride up with Forsyth and Beecher. But there were half a dozen fast men with a gun ready to shoot Sharp down at the first sign of treachery. Besides, young John Stillwell was out ahead and no one doubted him. Buffalo Bill Comstock would have been better but he wouldn't have gone along on such a wild dog-day chase, not any more than Wild Bill Hickok when Forsyth sent him word, or Bill Cody.

And it was dog-day weather for early September. Remnants of the grasshopper scourge rose in dusty sluggish clouds before the horses where the grass wasn't eaten into the ground, even the browned prairie sunflowers gnawed to the woody stalks. But when the scouts approached the upper Republican streams they suddenly found themselves stirrup deep in the late growth of bottom grass that was ripening towards fall, with the gold of black-eyed susans through it, and the circling flight of blackbirds gathering to go south. Everywhere the brush patches hung dark with chokecherries and the sweet redness of wild plum. Game was thick, driven from the grasshopper-eaten tablelands, with the buffaloes in small scattered bunches now that the running season was over and the southward movements of the fall had not begun.

But here there were no hunters. Beecher knew why when Jack Stillwell picked up a wild travois trail at the Republican. The trail thinned out but it seemed to head towards the shallow Arickaree fork. Forsyth followed, and camped near a sandy island about two hundred feet long and forty wide at the broadest, with one tall cottonwood rising from its scrub willows and the tangle of long bottom grass. Neither Grover nor Stillwell discovered the two big Indian camps down the river about twelve miles, the pony herds unconcealed for anybody who might scout in that direction, the smoke of the evening fires a pale line on the horizon. Forsyth would have ridden away up stream if the Indians had been as unobserving, but at dawn, September seventeenth, they came over the ridge into the bare little valley, whooping, their horses on a dead run upon the scouts, who were almost packed for the march.

"Indians!" everybody shouted, now that they were in plain sight and already sweeping upon some of the loose horses, running seven off immediately.

Forsyth hurried his men from the bare river bottoms to the brushy little island with its one cottonwood. While some worked to quiet the horses the rest threw their packs down for breastworks and young Stillwell and two others went to guard the unprotected lower end of the island. It was so bare that they slipped over to the south bank of the river and hid in a patch of marsh grass.

By then the Indians, painted and stripped for attack, were upon the scouts in a whooping war charge, the crack

of their guns sharp as they came, the horses on the island
jumping and plunging, the men among them ducking for
the ground. As the Indians hit the shallow sandy stream in
the blowing powder smoke, they split and swung both ways
around the island. All except one bold Indian. He rode
straight upon the island, his painted war horse crashing the
tangle of brush and old driftwood caught in it, into the face
of the guns, the well-aimed guns of the buffalo hunters. His
horse leapt the prone men, throwing sand over them, and
then was gone, sending the shallow water into high fans of
spray as he went through the stream. It seemed he was bullet-proof, both he and his horse bullet-proof as steel.

For a moment several of the men stared after him,
certain he would whirl and return. The others had brought
down some Indian horses and one warrior, but Forsyth's thigh
was shattered and Lieutenant Beecher had two bullets and
was dying—the two military men of the disorganized party.
There were several more casualties before the rest could
throw up circular breastworks from the loose soil, keeping
down as they dug, the air thick with bullets and arrows
that cut the brush and grass and even the cottonwood leaves,
and hit among the horses with the dull thud of lead and
iron on flesh.

In the second charge a warrior rode out of the dust
and smoke over the island again. By now one of the mouthy
Indian fighters was throwing sand like a scared badger and
bawling like a settler's bucket calf all the while, unwilling to
pick up his gun or even touch it at Forsyth's command. But
in the dust and smoke the Indians had not noticed the three
men in the tall grass of the river bank, and several were hit
from there. In a pause, while the smoke lifted a little over
the valley, they could see horsemen and travois carrying off
the injured Indians and the dead, while a crying of sorrow
came from somewhere on the wind, women keening for the
dead.

The next charge was afoot, the wily redskins creep-

ing over the rough ground and from weed to weed. Some
ran zig-zag through the shallow water under the smoke and
dropped into the grass of the island within a few yards of the
scouts, digging their own hurried breastworks in the loose
sand. Their guns hit among the men now, and particularly
among the wild and faunching horses. Some went down,
others broke away, until only a few were left, the men all
forced to keep down and so unable to hold off the creeping
Indians. Plainly those on the island had to be driven out. It
cost additional hits among the defenders but it was done.

By now the little knot of white men was in a desperate
situation. With four, five hundred Indians already fighting,
more were coming up all the time, until a solid row, including
many women, watched along the little ridge where the
stream cut in towards it, and still more came, until the ridge
top was dark as with a forest of trees.

On the island there was cursing, praying, and another
attempt to get the big man out of his burrow for the next
charge and to straighten out two others who were shaking
like rabbits. By now Lieutenant Beecher was dead and laid
aside, and they were left with only the wounded Forsyth
to direct them, Sheridan's green aide, with no experienced advice, but dozens of contradictory suggestions, and their
horses all down. He ordered the dead horses dragged into
place around the breastworks of the circular little hole where
the white men lay pushed so close together. Only one among
them still seemed optimistic. Schlesinger, little Schles,
crawled busily around, distributing ammunition, tearing
bandages for the doctor, helping with tourniquets, hurrying
to his gun when another attack threatened. The men had
dug as deep as they could without striking wet sand, trying
to prepare for the next charge, the greatest, and perhaps
the last one, for the Indians were preparing it with great care
and ceremony.

Waiting, the men took hard stock. They were afoot,
with very little hope of standing off the Indians until help

came. Nobody knew where Forsyth's scouts had gone and there was no chance of getting a courier out, a courier afoot in a region buzzing with angry warriors. Yet, although Forsyth's shattered thigh was bleeding badly and very painful even through the morphia, he was working to tighten his command over these civilians. But many were injured now, and the water was getting scarce in the canteens, although it flowed openly on both sides of the island, no longer clear and flashing as it twisted over the yellow sand but red-streaked and soiled by the gut-shot Indian horses, the current digging little channels around their carcasses.

On the island there was only waiting now, with the groans of the wounded, and anger and uncontrolled fear among others, an uncontrolled fear that might have brought a panic as with buffaloes if there had been anywhere to run. There was none of the trained cohesion to which Forsyth was accustomed, but grumbling, disobedience and open derision. One of the outlaws spoke of Fetterman, who had let his eighty-one men be surrounded and wiped out by the Indians up in Wyoming less than two years ago.

"Another goddamn cocky West Pointer!"

Even the hide hunters who could look so confidently down their gun barrels for the shot into the lights, the lungs, of a buffalo, and the frontiersmen who had evaded marauding bands of Indians for years were desperate now that all flight was cut off. Some of the war veterans, those with actual battlefield experience, were a little cooler but coolest of all was the little Jew, the damn fool little Jew Schlesinger.

"Don't you know they'll scalp you!" one of the hunters roared in fury at the cheerfulness still plain in the dirty, smoke-grimed face.

"Ah, yes," Schlesinger agreed. "But it's a poor thing they will get compared to the luxurious locks on some of the frontiersmen here among us—" He managed to laugh a little as he said it, but his nervous hands shook, and his peaked face was gaunt and drawn, for now the surgeon had also been

hit. It seemed that one little man called Schles had better
kept his nose out of other people's business this time.
"—Always I hated the quiet life," he said soberly, and for a
moment even big Whalen forgot his terror in the unconscious humor.

As the charge was prepared Sharp Grover watched
the slope with Beecher's fieldglasses. The leader seemed to
be Roman Nose, considered the bravest of the Cheyenne
warriors, Sharp told Forsyth. He was a seasoned man, long
past a warrior's usual age, but when they wanted him to be a
council chief he said a man who had spent so many years on
the warpath was not gentle or fatherly enough for the council. Roman Nose would be hard to whip, Sharp thought.
The Indians believed him bullet-proof, and the warriors
would follow him to hell.

Once more Whalen and the other two began to cry,
burrowing deeper, while Forsyth cursed that they weren't soldiers, to be placed under arrest. Despite his shattered swollen
leg, he sat up staunchly through this first Indian fight, so
new to it he even had to be told that the Indians who were
whipping their ponies, running them back and forth on the
far slope, were getting them their second wind ready for the
charge.

Finally when it seemed the men on the island could
not bear another moment of waiting, the Indians came, starting slowly, with the loud cries of the women carrying on the
fitful wind. The smoke had cleared considerably and the
scouts could see the approach of the formal array, the painted
Indians, feathers blowing from the spears and shields, half a
dozen men in long, flowing warbonnets. Then suddenly they
whipped their painted horses, Roman Nose the spearhead
of the whooping charge, with the bullets of the hunters hitting all around him in the rolling dust, in the thundering
that shook the earth, until it seemed he truly could not be
hit, or even those around him as they charged in great
waves through the hail of lead. Even when feathers were cut

from heads, and horses began to go down, Roman Nose still
came on, heading the spear of warriors, their bullets throwing sand over the besieged islanders, cutting grass and brush
and flesh. Even now the cowards among the white men
could not be aroused to fight. There was cold anger in Forsyth's commands. He would have had them shot right there
if they were in uniform.

Yet every man was needed, and so the guns kept
booming in the little valley, some of the excited white men
blowing their ammunition as though an arsenal were at their
backs, and still Roman Nose came on in the stinging smoke,
closer and closer upon them. It was true; he could not be
hit. A kind of flat panic hit the men on the island, even Forsyth silent, the shooting almost stilled as Roman Nose led
the charge, barely two hundred feet away. Then suddenly at
the water's edge he went down, shot from the side by Stillwell
and the others hidden in the slough grass. The Indian fell
and lay still, and the charge broke upon his fall as upon a
rock. The running horses split and, turning to both sides,
were away. And as they were lost in the dust and smoke little
Schles carried the good news around the wounded, whispering as though made voiceless by the roar of the attack.

After a while Roman Nose began to crawl a little, stirring the long grass, and some warriors dashed in to carry
him away, the women making their cries as he was brought
towards them, the cries that were for a strong man dying,
Grover and Stillwell knew.

Young Jack knocked over one more Indian as the warriors worked to get the others who had fallen. Otherwise the
Indians kept out of range now, watching from the slope, some
smoking or seeming to eat. About sundown there was a great
keening on the ridge and Grover said that Roman Nose had
probably died. As always the Indians withdrew before dark,
and Forsyth was told that they would not return tonight.
They believed that night fighting was bad luck, perhaps because the dew stretched the bowstring, for it was said that the

arrow does not travel in darkness, the time of rest. But at dawn—

Yes, at dawn; Forsyth knew that. His left leg was broken too, now; he had twenty-three casualties, and his surgeon dying, shot through the head. The men broiled horsemeat and afterward two messengers slipped out, hoping to get through the Indian line somehow to bring relief, at least let the world know how the men on the Arickaree fork died. There was no sound, no shot and when it was hoped they had got through the pickets, they were suddenly back at the island. The second pair sent out included Stillwell and they did not return. There was more fighting the next day, mostly firing at long distance, and the third day the same. A second pair of messengers had started for help and nothing was heard of them either. The horsemeat stank now, even roasted to a crisp, and it began to rain, a fine gauzy curtain across the prairie, giving the yellowed grass an orange transparency, chilling the men, the wounded. Through this only an occasional Indian was visible, humped together on his horse, a hide drawn clear over him.

"They hate rain as much as hens do," Schlesinger laughed. "See how mad they sit in it."

The next morning there wasn't an Indian in sight anywhere, but no rescuers either. Gradually the men dared to get off the stinking island a little ways, carrying the fevered and helpless Forsyth in a blanket between them, his broken legs swollen and festering. They didn't go far from the protection of the island brush, silent, mostly, or wondering about the men sent out. They ate the rotten meat as long as they could and shot a stray coyote who was drawn to the dead Indian horses out on the bottoms. At least his stink was fresh.

Nine days after Forsyth camped there, the cry of "Indians!" went up once more as dark figures came out along the sky. Hopelessly, automatically, Forsyth tried to prepare for another attack from his blanket. But there seemed to be a vehicle behind the riders, a prairie wagon, an ambulance.

Now even the little Jew cried some, his first tears, and made a joke of it, as a small man must in the presence of big bruisers. Soon there were several hundred troops at Beecher Island, as the battleground was now called, and Forsyth's little expedition was rescued.

By now the Indians were far away and no one had much heart for trailing them now. The Cheyennes had withdrawn because they lost one of their great men. Later they said that his bullet-proofing medicine was broken by the accidental eating of meat that had been touched by an iron fork and there had been no time to make the purifying ritual. Forsyth, with his legs swollen thick as kegs with infection, too, would make no call for volunteers for another such venture. Nor would the buffalo hunters, not for a while when few dared to hunt, with the Indians so arrogant in their success. Let the Regulars fight the Indian wars. There was talk around Hays that the Regulars were getting ready to do just that. The Cheyennes would be made to pay for the wounds to the body and the pride of Sheridan's courageous but foolhardy aide.

The fall of 'Sixty-eight spread golden over the High Plains and as the morning frost whitened the lower bottoms of the rivers, the buffaloes, sleek and fat, began to move southward and a few of the hunters came to follow. Ducks clouded the shrunken ponds and rivers, and geese pointed their V's southward. Sandhill cranes passed through, their flocks long strings that rose out of the horizon, in their curious winding, looping way.

But there was no place for the settlers to go, those whose gardens and the crops were cleaned out by the grasshoppers. The Indians, angered over the encroaching hide hunters and the troops that rode against them most of the time the last four years, had swept away much settler stock, and much of the rest was doomed to the same hunger as their owners. By mid-October requests appeared in the newspapers

for clothing and food for the upper Saline country of Kansas
and elsewhere. But the grasshopper invasion didn't discourage the new railroad laid out up the Arkansas. Ground
was broken late in October and the next spring the tracks
would push into the new buffalo ranges.

The army did not wait for spring. It was gathering
near Ft. Dodge on the Arkansas for a powerful strike at the
Indians. General Sheridan set up camp on a hill north of
the post. Custer's Seventh Cavalry was south of the river, the
morale as low as ever, lower than during the period of desertions the summer of 1867. General Sully, an old Indian
fighter, had organized and outfitted the big expedition
against the Indians. He knew how to whip a force together
for a swift winter campaign when snow was on the ground,
the Indian ponies weak, and their trails more difficult to hide.
But he was not an extermination man, or of Sheridan's admiring clique. Besides it was said he drank too much and so,
when his command was ready, he was not permitted to lead
it. Instead Custer, with his suspension expired, was given
command. Now there was optimism around Hays and Ft.
Dodge. Angry and smarting over his humiliation, his year
of inaction, the general was hot to fall upon the Indians, and
with his troopers as restive there would be hell to pay.

From down at Ft. Cobb, in Indian Territory, General
Hazen reported that the Indians belonging to his agency
there were peaceful. Some of the treaty goods promised by
the Medicine Lodge Treaty a year ago had finally come, and
now the hearts of the Indians seemed good.

"They'll be a damn sight better after we strike
them!" Custer had bragged in Drum's saloon at Hays, with
his loud-mouthed brother Tom beside him that last evening
before he went down to take over command from Elliott.
Perhaps he remembered too, that it was General Hazen who
had to arrest him once, long ago, back at West Point, for
surely Custer was not the man to forget. He had the red-
bearded old frontiersman, California Joe, as chief of scouts.

To the tenderfeet who inquired, it was said that both Cody and Wild Bill Hickok had other business. Perhaps it was just as well. Three such long-haired show-offs as Custer and the two Bills could never work together. Who would do the admiring, the applauding?

Besides, scouts got only seventy-five dollars a month. Hide hunting, particularly the winter robes of the lord of the plains, as the visiting celebrities called the buffalo—that was something else.

CHAPTER III

A REVENGE—AND NEW MARKETS

THE fall of 1868 brought the first tangible evidence that the buffalo could no longer be expected to feed all the roving Indians of the plains. Under the treaties of 1867 beef herds were distributed to some of them. They didn't like the meat. Hadn't they let a herd of cattle go clear through their Powder River country to the gold fields of Idaho in the midst of the Bozeman Trail war, when they weren't letting anybody else pass? They hadn't considered the white man's spotted cows worth the killing. The meat stank and was tough and lean. Yet now some of the Sioux, particularly the agency hangers-on up north, were getting hungry enough to eat this beef.

Although it had been announced that the treaties of 1867 would quiet the Indians, many, particularly those who usually hunted south of the Arkansas River, were more troublesome than ever. With them was Black Kettle, the chief who had refused to join the hostile march northward after the slaughter of the Cheyennes at Sand Creek in 1864, and took his small band south of the Arkansas instead. He had tried to keep his warriors peaceful, and in 1866 he made an eloquent speech at Ft. Harker, asking that the government permit no railroads into the Indian country. The fire road up the Platte was driving the buffaloes away and bringing starvation to the Indian. But the Union Pacific was not stopped, nor the Kansas Pacific headed up the Smoky Hill country, and now in 1868 another railroad was coming along the Arkansas right through the heart of these buffalo ranges too. Although the Medicine Lodge Treaty had promised to keep hunters out of all the region south of that river, the hide men pushed in there now. The complaining Indians were told that there were not enough soldiers to guard the two hundred and fifty miles of river against them, as the treaty had promised. So Black Kettle asked about the great cloud of white tents gathering around Ft. Dodge, and the Seventh Cavalry camped south of the Arkansas, doing nothing at all. If they were not there to keep the hunters out of the buffalo ranges, why had they come?

There was no reply, and none was needed. The Cheyenne chief, who had seen troops come shooting into his peaceful camp at Sand Creek, moved away south for safety. He and many others took their people deep into Indian Territory, toward the rough country of the Texas Panhandle, keeping rather close to Ft. Cobb and their friend General Hazen, their military Indian agent. But some of the young men stayed behind to fight the hide men. The Indians knew that General Sully had chased the Sioux around in the upper Missouri country several years ago. Now he was here, in command of the big camp at Ft. Dodge. So during breakfast one fall morning there was rapid firing close in, perhaps right in camp. The soldiers ran out, a great tangle of bluecoats headed this way and that for their guns as fifty or sixty painted warriors rode breakneck right through them and the rows of tents and got out and away in spite of at least five hundred shots sent after them. Taunting and whooping, the Indians were gone in a cloud of dust, to surround a supply train coming to the post. They set fire to the wagons and swept away forty-four mules without much opposition. Gen-

eral Sully sent a small detachment out after the Indians, but
even when, upon second thought, he reinforced the pursuing
party to forty, they captured no Indians.

Apparently this looked like a good opportunity to
President Johnson. With Grant certain to be elected president in November, clearly anything to be done for Custer had
better be done soon. The old Indian fighter, General Sully,
who had whipped his force together, naturally expected to
lead it out against the Indians. Instead he was pushed aside
and the command given to the younger, the battle-hungry
Custer, who had not managed to get one real engagement for
his new regiment or for himself with the Indians. It was a little awkward that the day after Custer was restored to his
command the Indians made some flying charges on his camp
too. There was a great deal of return fire, but not an Indian
was hit or pursued at all. Nevertheless, Custer led Sully's
troops southward with great dash and determination. After
a year's suspension from command he was back, and this
time at the head of a whole expedition, with band and everything, striking for the Indians gathered around General
Hazen, the man who once as officer of the day had to place a
cadet named George Custer under arrest. At Camp Supply,
in Indian Territory, Custer made his final preparations
for a swift blow against the Indians, preferably the Cheyennes. They were the impudent red devils who had caused
most of the trouble for both Hancock and Custer that bad
year of 'Sixty-seven and made Forsyth and with him Phil
Sheridan, the joke of the buffalo hunters. Hazen's frequent
reports gave Custer the approximate camp sites of the Cheyennes. Among his scouts were a lot of Osage Indians, long-
time enemies of the Cheyennes, Ben Clark, one of the ablest
men of the region, married to a Cheyenne, and several buffalo
hunters, including the picturesque red-haired California Joe
with his mule and his bottle. Joe was glad to get a crack at
the Indian pony herds that were half-promised to the scouts,
and to smell out the new buffalo country certain to be opened

to the hide men soon, and to spot some good camping places on sweet water. Cross-eyed Joe was one of the tattered, raggle-bearded, scratching old hide men, usually with a lone camp in the Republican region somewhere, a first class buffalo hunter whose money went for poker and rotgut. He was also one of the best shots on the frontier and he knew the country and the Indians from Mexico north across Milk River. Led by such men and followed by a good wagon train of ammunition and supplies, Custer struck south for the Cheyennes reported somewhere on the Washita, deep in Indian Territory, near the Texas Panhandle.

In the meantime Black Kettle had led a delegation of Cheyenne and Arapaho chiefs to Hazen. The Kettle said they were uneasy about an army coming against them from the north. He and his people had moved down here, far from their own country because they wanted peace. They had never fought the white man of Texas or anywhere south of the Arkansas. Up north the whites killed both their buffaloes and their people and it was hard to control his young men on ground made bloody by so many of their relatives. Now when he and a few Southern Cheyennes along had made a little more meat they would move in closer to Ft. Cobb, away from the troops who seemed to be coming into what was the territory of the Indians. General Hazen replied that he was here as their agent, the peace man for the Indians, but unfortunately he had no control over the soldiers from the north. Still, the Washita seemed a good safe place for peaceful men.

The storm through which Black Kettle and the rest rode home from Hazen shielded the approach of Custer, renamed Hardbacksides by the expedition before they were out three days. In his hurried drive to strike the Indians, to erase the failure of all the summer of 1867, and his own humiliation, he demanded the superhuman from his officers and men. The tough-skinned buffalo hunters and old freighters with the column cursed him as they were driven on in the fall blizzard, but even so the hunters kept their eyes out for buffalo herds to harvest when the Indians were killed off, or at least whipped to some little reservations and certainly not left to roam over all the Indian Territory and the outside buffalo ranges that they claimed through the foolish government treaties.

At the Canadian River Custer left his supply train behind and led his troops, including the mounted band, an ambulance and a string of seven ammunition wagons, southward. Some of the hunters with the big train were glad enough to be left behind, but several went with the ammunition. Even the old cob-pipe men had to chew their tobacco now because all light was forbidden, and all talk and loud commands. Next the ammunition was left behind, the reserve rations and even the overcoats, although there was snow all around. So Hardbacksides rode ahead with his Indian scouts through the snow-white night. Then the Osages detected smoke, and at daylight Custer had his forces distributed and was looking down upon the Cheyenne camp spread along the brushy Washita—the general's and the regiment's first occupied Indian village. It was only fifty, sixty lodges, much, much smaller than the one on the Pawnee Fork last year with Hancock. But that camp was an empty husk. This one was full of Indians. This day must bring glory.

Suddenly a lone Indian out early detected the troops and so Custer charged upon the sleeping Black Kettle village as Chivington's troops had charged upon these Indians at Sand Creek almost exactly four years ago. The trumpet echoed along the river. The mounted band played a bit of Garry Owen on the frozen instruments. Then once more it was bluecoated troops riding down half-naked Indians fleeing among the lodges before the chief could raise his white flag. At the side of Custer rode Hamilton, stirrup to stirrup, until Hamilton fell, shot in the back, some said later by a trooper bullet intended for Custer. Not an Indian had yet fired a shot.

While the scouts took the pony herds, the troops drove

the half-dressed women and children running over the river bank into the ice-bordered stream. The men, vastly outnumbered and outarmed, tried to make a stand to give their families time to escape to the larger Indian camps, out of sight down the river. Black Kettle himself fell in the fire and smoke at the river's edge, half in the ice-rimmed water, his wife beside him.

As the snow reddened and bodies lay strewn about, the white woman and two children, captives of the Southern Cheyennes in camp were killed by the Indians, killed by those who had just seen their relatives ridden down, their heads cut off by Custer's Osage scouts.

It was while pursuing the fleeing that Major Elliott and eighteen men were cut off. Ben Clark had warned Custer that there were many more Indians, Cheyennes, Kiowas, Comanches and Arapahoes just around a bend of the river, bigger camps. Now suddenly Custer was uncertain; only the daring dash of the commander of his ammunition wagons had saved him from the disaster of empty guns earlier in the fight. Elliott had been sent to disperse the Indians coming up from the other villages and to overtake the refugees, and he wasn't returning although the firing in that direction had stopped.

California Joe with the scouts had gathered up the Indian horses, eight hundred seventy-five altogether. But Custer had most of them shot, to spill their dark blood upon the snow too, some of the most beautiful horses of all the Plains tribes. It took well over an hour and the Indians watched it from a rise, well reinforced from the camps below, but they couldn't attack, not with the captured Cheyenne women and children sure to be hit. The buffalo hunters along regretted the loss of the herds too, particularly the fine buffalo horses, worth a lot of money. California Joe had planned to drive them down to Texas to sell.

By now it was afternoon. Custer's men were without rations and needing the overcoats left behind if there wasn'r to be serious frost-bite. Besides, the wagon train left behind might be attacked by the fleeing Indians backtrailing the command. So Custer ordered a swift return to Camp Supply, over the protests that no attempt was made to rescue Elliott and his men, dead or alive. Custer and his Seventh had their victory and now he was impatient to reap the glory.

He started north across the snow with fifty-three captives, all women and children, including no male over ten years old. Mostly afoot, they had to keep up with the mounted command and few of them had any protection except their blankets from the freezing nights—all except the young girls chosen by the officers for their tents. The young daughter of the dead chief, Little Rock, was selected by Custer, and married to him by Indian custom, as he related in *My Life on the Plains* later, and praised her grace and beauty.

Custer made a triumphal return to the post, bringing in the first victory for his regiment. His hair hung long over his shoulders, the polished instruments of the mounted band glistened as they played, and the Osage scouts were painted for war. The other scouts and the troops rode in smartly too, bringing their plodding string of captive widows and orphans, many wounded, their moccasins worn off their feet by the ice and snow. There was celebrating until very late, and the Osages danced the scalps they took until morning. As the celebration grew, Custer's figure for the Cheyenne warriors killed had also grown until he made it one hundred three men, and got the women down to sixteen, the children to a few—one hundred and three blood-thirsty Cheyenne warriors, certainly worth a doughty cavalryman's charge.

The buffalo hunters and the old plainsmen nudged each other and laughed sourly. Hardbacksides was sure spreading himself, killing one hundred and three warriors from fifty lodges, with not over three hundred Cheyennes altogether, Ben Clark and others married to Indians said. Besides, in this tribe so frequently attacked, the men were getting almost as scarce as cows in the buffalo herds—the guns always searching them out. Clark, who had ridden into the camp at Custer's side, estimated that between twelve and fifteen men were killed, not as many as the troopers left behind with Elliott.

This was not a triumphant time for the friends of Elliott, who recalled that the major was still in command of the regiment only a little over a month ago and remembered too, how bitter Custer was all the year of his suspension from his regiment. Now he was once more the only man alive who had commanded the Seventh.

When John Poysell, a contractor along at the fight, told the story of the Washita to his Cheyenne wife she tried to kill herself with a knife and then with wolf poison, strychnine. The post doctor saved her to keen for her dead relatives.

John Wynkoop read the news of the Washita fight with sourness. He had been agent for the Cheyennes in 1864, and told Black Kettle and the rest that Sand Creek was a safe place for peaceful Indians to go. Now once more the Kettle had listened to a white man. Wynkoop, the agent on Pawnee Fork, wrote the Commissioner of Indian Affairs that Black Kettle had been camped peacefully there near his agency all the time last summer when, it was charged, the chief was depredating. Now Black Kettle had been killed, and Agent Wynkoop could no longer countenance such repeated betrayal. Angrily he resigned his position.

Most of the border, however, sighed with relief. The blood-thirsty redskins had been punished, taught a lesson by the gallant Custer and his Seventh. At last settlers, railroad builders, cattlemen and buffalo hunters could go about their business in safety.

Or at least they soon would be safe now that Sheridan and Custer were going right out to pursue the Cheyennes who had escaped, and their wild allies too, the Comanches and Kiowas. It was true that the three military successes over the troublesome Indians of the buffalo country had been over peace men—Little Thunder, the Sioux, on the Blue Water near the Platte in 1855, and Black Kettle at Sand Creek, and then again at the Washita. The hostiles of both tribes were wily enough not to be easily caught, as the buffalo hunters knew. But Custer might succeed.

With a total force of around two thousand men and three hundred wagons moving four abreast, Sheridan and Custer started back to the Washita in December 1868. More hide hunters joined up as scouts and with the wagon train, mainly to locate good buffalo ranges and to see the Indians whipped to a final standstill. From the Washita, Custer hunted the winter camps of the Cheyennes with the daughter of Little Rock as guide. Early in the fall General Penrose had been sent from Ft. Lyon in Colorado to strike the Indians west of Custer's line of attack, to cut off their flight to the wilds of the Panhandle and the Staked Plains. Penrose had Wild Bill Hickok along and others who knew both the Indians and the region better—men like Bent, Boggs, and Ottaby. Even so his command was soon starving. Without forage the horses played out and had to be shot to prevent their falling into the hands of the harrying Indians. Afoot, the troopers waded the same snow as Custer's captive Cheyenne women and children did. In addition Penrose's men were hungry, even with the buffalo-hunting Wild Bill along. Yet the breed Bent and the mountain men Ottaby and Boggs could do no better, perhaps because they were all penned in by the Indians. The only happy news to reach Penrose was that some Mexican buffalo hunters were near enough to sell him a little meat. This should have been a blow to the pride of Wild Bill. To Captain Armes of the command it seemed a foreboding come true. He had helped chase Indians all over upper Kansas the summer of 1867. When orders came for the expedition, he disposed of his property and sent the money home, never expecting to return from this winter push into the Indian's own wild region. Perhaps if the Indians had been as angry as they were eight years later, in 1876, Armes might have proved a prophet. But all they took from Penrose was sixty of his desperately needed mules, putting more men afoot and, in their frightened hurry, making more horses play out. Finally the general and the scouts went out and got four buffaloes, but by then the hard bread was almost gone. Penrose sent Captain Armes back to Lyon for rations, with Bent, Boggs and Ottaby as guides to insure their getting through. They had trouble making Lyon, and by then nobody knew where Penrose was although he must be in dire straits. Toward mid-December Ottaby and two scouts were sent to find General Carr, in the field with the Fifth Cavalry, with orders to rescue Penrose's lost column, hungry, mostly afoot, with the Indians active on his flanks.

But Carr's circumstances proved no less unhappy than Penrose's, except that Carr was perhaps not so completely lost. Sent back by Sheridan because of insufficient forage, he decided to stop to rest his stock north of the Texas Panhandle. His surgeon reported scurvy among the men and their desperate need for fresh meat although they had Bill Cody along, already publicized as the world's best buffalo hunter. To be sure, he had killed most of his meat from Drum's saloon at Hays.

It was February of 1869 before Carr and Penrose finally came in, their forces, including Cody and Hickok, worn out and gaunted, most of their horses gone. The Indians, it seemed, were in prime condition.

It was to be expected that the two generals and their men would take a sour view of Custer's favored treatment in equipment and supplies, and the whole idea of his celebrated Washita campaign. They were backed up in their criticism of his generalship by the buffalo hunters and frontiersmen who were with him and his Seventh. They said Custer sent Elliott in where he had been told the Indians were swarming, and that he himself was saved from the same fate

only by the angry insistence of his scouts, particularly Ben
Clark, who talked very fast to convince the general that
there really were very large Indian villages only a little distance down the river. Once convinced, Custer had hurried
away without even sending a scout to look for Elliott, and
there were those who said he had found this very convenient.

But now the Long Hair was out with his admiring
superior, Little Phil Sheridan, and no one could deny that
Custer was pushing the Indians hard. The Cheyenne girl,
who knew all their campsites, finally led him to their refuge
in the Panhandle. He had a conference there with Medicine
Arrow, the keeper of the sacred tribal arrows of the Cheyennes, and professed only the most peaceful intentions toward the Indians if they would follow him to Ft. Cobb, give
up the white captives he heard were somewhere among them,
and settle down peacefully on their agency. So a pipe was
smoked under the bundle of sacred arrows, and afterward
the keeper scraped out the ashes and dropped some on the
boots of Custer, in the ritual of the pipe. Anyone who lied in
it, who spoke here with a crooked tongue, would die.

A little while later Custer tried to trap the headmen
of the Cheyennes, throw them into irons, but all he got was
four unimportant emissaries, to be dragged away to Ft. Hays.
The Cheyennes kept their word and came in, for Custer
had the guns.

They tried to settle down on the agency, but once
more the promised rations did not come. Finally their relatives captured at the Washita were returned from Ft. Hays.
They told that Custer's wife came there before they left.
They had seen her ride out with her long-haired general,
past the corral where the prisoners were kept. The Cheyenne girl who was married to Custer in the Indian ritual was
in the corral too then, back among the rest, and large with
the son she bore him in the late summer of 1869.

Before then some of the Cheyennes fleeing to the Powder River from the harassment in the south were struck by troops at Summit Springs, with Major North and two companies of his Pawnee scouts along and some buffalo hunters too, as scouts and guides. Once more a Cheyenne camp was destroyed, and the chief, Tall Bull killed. A captive white woman brought up from the south was rescued. Bill Cody came with the expedition but he had a wagon of trade goods to look after and the bad luck to be with a part of the force that was fifteen miles away at the time of the fight. Almost at once he made up for this with a fine story of killing Tall Bull in single-handed combat. Frank North, who had shot the chief himself, laughed when he heard the tall tale, but the hide men along, some who had known Buffalo Bill Comstock when he rode the mail into early Denver in 1859, and around Morrow's ranch over in Nebraska, growled a little at Cody's big yarns and his assumption of the name, Buffalo Bill. Still, old Windy Bill was generous with the whisky in his wagon, particularly when he had been to the barrel himself.

Much depended upon the Kansas Pacific reaching Denver before the branch of the Union Pacific coming down from Cheyenne, but the K. P. was stalled for lack of funds at Sheridan station in northwest Kansas. The promoters looked around for something to catch the public eye, to bring in new financing and to help sell the land given them from the public domain by the government as a subsidy. They gathered up a force of lariat men, mostly Mexicans, who had been roping buffaloes for years. They caught some full grown ones, including two fine big bulls, and dragged them into a box car. With great banner signs along both sides of the car to advertise the railroad and the region it tapped for hunting and for settlement, the buffaloes were started eastward and switched to sidings in one town after another. Crowds of curious sightseers came to look at the great wild monsters of the plains and to hear the barker shout out all the other western

wonders. In Chicago there was a band and a parade of
horsebackers dressed like hunters and cowboys, led by one of
the men who actually roped the buffaloes.

Ever since the first train of the Union Pacific pushed
west from Omaha in 1865 the conductors gladly told ex-
cursionists where buffaloes would probably be found. So
hunters had gone out to North Platte, then to Sidney and
later to the Cheyenne country. But most of the buffaloes that
either wintered or summered along the Overland Trail had
been killed long before the railroad came, and now there
were only the spring and fall crossings, and those shrinking
each year.

There were always buffaloes somewhere along the
K. P. The fall of 1868 a train traveled one hundred twenty
miles between Ellsworth and Sheridan through a continuous, browsing herd, packed so thick that the engineer had
to stop several times, mostly because the buffaloes would
scarcely get off the tracks for the whistle and the belching
smoke. Last spring, between Harker and Hays, a train was
delayed eight hours while an immense herd passed, this
time in one steady, unending stream.

The problem was not buffaloes but accommodations
for the hunters and travelers near the hunting grounds. Several stations west of Ellsworth offered some shelter. Russell
had what passed for a hotel, one large common room with
rows of bunks. But usually there was nothing better than
buffalo robes on the ground of a dugout. The so-called hotel
stations often had a few horses for hire, to be hauled on the
train and unloaded wherever the game was sighted. Eastern
and foreign sportsmen preferred the chase to the still hunt
of the hide men. Usually the buffaloes stood staring at a
horseman until he was within three hundred yards and then
began to move slowly away. When he was within two hundred fifty yards they generally broke into a gallop. This was
the sportsman's moment. A good horse for the chase knew he
was to be in the herd before they had gone two hundred

yards. Buffaloes could run only about two-thirds as fast as a good hunting horse but they had fine bottom and endurance, with extraordinary vitality. If they were not overtaken within five hundred or six hundred yards, the chase was usually abandoned as too long. The danger was not from the buffaloes but from falling horses, with badger dens everywhere, and the great expanses of prairie dog towns, as full of holes as a nutmeg grater.

Although sportsmen were always impressed by the lengthening ricks of hides as they traveled west toward the upper Republican country, they were contemptuous of the stinking hide men and their still hunts. They preferred a fine run with a good horse, a natty breechloading carbine that carried twelve cartridges slung behind the shoulder and perhaps two pistols at the side, giving the hunter twenty-four shots. Sometimes the rest of the party had to hit the dirt when a tenderfoot's wild firing started, and the hospital at Ft. Hays always had what they called buffalo cripples—gunshot men and men with arms, legs and collarbones broken or ribs crushed in falls while running game over badger holes and through dog towns. "Could happen to anybody—" the surgeon always comforted his patients. It could and it did, even to an occasional Indian.

Perhaps the finest publicity for the adventuresome hunter was the great volume of writing and talk that came out of the foolish but brave and desperate fight on the Arickaree. Lieutenant Beecher had been the nephew of Henry Ward Beecher and Harriet Beecher Stowe, whose *Uncle Tom's Cabin* had been presented in every eastern hamlet by wagon troupes as well as at most western stations and army posts. The K. P. took advantage of all this, and newspapers and handbills advertised a GRAND RAILWAY EXCURSION and BUFFALO HUNT on the PLAINS, scheduled from St. Louis, Cincinnati, Chicago and cities farther east—all routed to Phil Sheridan station, which was very near the heroic Beecher battleground but well protected against real danger from hostile Indians. The arrival was always on Tuesday, with the return the following Friday. Stops were promised at all the principal stations coming and going, each set of advertisements featuring the number of buffaloes killed on the preceding hunt.

The price was right too, roundtrip ticket from Lawrence to Sheridan, ten dollars. In the year and a half that Phil Sheridan station was the end of the tracks, it grew into a hell-roarer. The hotel still remained one long bunk room, but there were several saloons and dance halls with their Phil's Girls, as they were called, and plenty of gamblers, horse thieves and murderers. To add to the sense of adventure it was made clear that the trains ran west from Ellsworth to Sheridan only during daylight hours, with squads of soldiers at all the refueling woodpiles and the watertanks to guard against marauding redskins. Beyond Hays the conductor buckled on a pistol and kept his rifle handy for both Indians and roadagents all the way to Sheridan, four hundred five miles west of the Missouri line. It was only a huddle of poor sod shacks and dugouts on the bleak empty plain. Drying buffalo hides were pegged out for miles around, brought here for protection from the hide thieves and Indians who slashed them, also from the wolves who foolishly tore at them now and then, playfully, for there was enough meat rotting on the prairie to feed all the wolves from Sheridan to Siberia. But no matter how poor and drab this end-of-the-line station was, the run to it was into the evening sun of October, and no artist could paint a finer sky.

If the visiting sportsmen were lucky they saw one of the publicized races between the train and the buffaloes. A herd, if close, somehow usually decided at the last minute that it must cross ahead of this roaring, smoking monster, and might actually get on the tracks just ahead of the screaming engine that came pounding upon them. If the engineer couldn't beat the lead cows, he had to whistle "down brakes" or be derailed. Sometimes the train was stopped only a few rods from the panting, thundering herd that swept over the tracks and down off the grade—a dark streaming of animals moving in their cloud of dust while the passengers ran out to pop carbines and pistols at them, particularly at the old bulls lumbering along behind.

Large private hunts could be arranged for people of sufficient importance or money. Several with important guests came out to hunt under the guidance of the Wild Bill Hickok of the romantic magazine and newspaper stories. Towards May, 1869, there was a telegram from Senator Wilson of Massachusetts asking Hickok to guide a large party of gentlemen and ladies in the west. But he was out of the country. He had been carrying dispatches from Ft. Lyon in Colorado to Wallace when a letter from his sister caught up with him. Their mother was very ill. So Jim Hickok, now suddenly Jim again, went home to Illinois for the first time in thirteen years, the first time since the day the man he struck into the canal didn't seem to be coming up.

Wild Bill stayed around home a while as his mother improved but he soon got restless. A few weeks of adulation from the young boys of the community and the shy admiration of the girls and the women, more open around the Ladies Entrance of the saloons, was fine. But there were also denunciations of James Butler Hickok as a red-handed murderer from the pulpits, and rising gossip about his private life. Besides he was even more a stranger in his family than the day he left. He took a trip to Chicago and came home with his head bandaged from a saloon brawl. There was a letter waiting from Senator Wilson. Bill wanted to go back west to hunt for hides, for another stake, but he was broke again, broke as a tromped-on cottonmouth, and the senator's offer meant ready cash. Bill asked five hundred dollars for his services. The senator agreed immediately and sent a list of the places the party would like to observe, and the activities to pursue. In mid-June they left Hays in a grand column of horsebackers and wagon train, the departure delayed by the ladies into the early heat of a hundred-degree day, the men in tight pants, broadcloth coats and top hats, the women in bustled riding costumes and mists of perfume and veiling.

"Some a them Comanches'd shure itch fer the scalp knife if they was to run into that layout," old Apache Bill told the other loafers squatting along the shady side of a hide shed. They nodded their shaggy heads and looked after the senator's outfit as it crawled out upon the hot plain, with the horizon shimmering in heat dances.

But Wild Bill carried out his bargain. His hair was long and curled over his shoulders, the metal of his pistols shone. The party visited the canyons of the Arkansas and swung around to a spot up on the Republican where the Cheyennes had, it seemed, perpetrated a most horrible massacre some years back. It chilled the ladies to delicious horror. "Oh, Mr. Wild Bill!" they exclaimed together, although he was not the one who told the story. For story-telling he had hired a loafer from around Hays at twenty-five dollars a month, found and mounted, besides a guarantee of some good drinkin' liquor every day.

They were out five weeks, with tents, valets, maids and supply train. They returned to Hays sunburnt and gnat-eaten. The night before they left the senator gave a big dinner for Wild Bill, with sea oysters shipped in. He made a frock-coated speech and presented Bill with a brace of ivory-handled pistols, white-handled pistols that Hickok said he would carry with him always. Senator Wilson had turned out quite a gay boy, considering that he came from the land of the Abolitionists. When he heard someone ask newcomers at Drum's "What name you travelin' under?" he laughed heartily, for it was commonly known that Wilson was his travelin' name too, and that far back he was called Colbraith, or so the troops from his home town said.

Out here everybody seemed to have several names. Both Wild Bill and his brother Lorenzo had called themselves Bill Barnes when it suited them, or Billy Barnes, back when they were around Ft. Riley. There were some who said that the John or Curly McCall around town was a brother too, and he did resemble them in a caricatural sort of way. In Wild Bill the long hair was glossy and fell in loose and elegant ringlets, in Jack it was dark, dull and close-curled. The thin beard of Bill was elegant too, like his long womanish hands, his small feet. In Jack McCall the thin wrists were too weak for the work he probably must do to make a living, the thin beard not elegant but adolescent. No flowing mustache could cover up his broken nose as it did the long protruding upper lip of Jim Hickok that got him the name of Duck Bill up in Nebraska (spelled Duch Bill in the warrant for his arrest after the McCanles killing) and Dutch Bill too, perhaps the latter more frequently after he grew the covering mustache. Besides, instead of the proud aloofness of Bill, Jack McCall carried a scowl on his face, his eyes without the steely menace, so no one took his drawing a gun seriously enough to make it worth pulling the trigger.

Before there was much talk about this resemblance, Curly McCall had moved on, perhaps because, as some said, the hot-headed Hickok brothers would take no more from each other than from strangers. Lorenzo joined some buffalo hunters up the Smoky Hill over near California Joe. Wild Bill became marshal at Hays. Within a little over a month Bill felt called on to do a bit of killing—a man called Strawhan, and another Mulvey or some such name, it was said. But it was good for business; running blood makes the whisky flow. Unfortunately another, a more serious trouble was building up like a west Kansas thunderhead for Marshal Hickok—trouble with the troopers of the Seventh, who thought they owned the country, the hunters said angrily.

The colonization agents of the three western railroads all urged travel and western hunts along with settlement, and the newspaper accounts spread fine stories of the sport of shooting the monarch of the plains, and of the small fortunes the hide men were making in just a few weeks. The romantic stories of Badmen and of life worth less than a plugged nickle also fired many imaginations and aroused the concern of a few. It seemed that humanitarians were protesting the slaughter of the Cheyenne women and children at the Washita, the second time in four years, and a few bewailed the vanishing buffalo, both as food for the Indian and as a noble creature from the hand of God. It was four years since hide hunting was outlawed in Idaho, and bills had been broached in other states and nationally too. Nothing had come of these and many besides those who counted their profits in dollars trusted that nothing would come of them. When Sir W. F. Butler in 1867 regretted that his party had shot more than thirty bulls in a hunt at Ft. McPherson below the forks of the Platte, Col. R. I. Dodge told him, "Kill every buffalo you can. Every buffalo dead is an Indian gone."

By now another factor was entering the hide business, the trader with his organized hunting outfits. J. Wright Mooar, an adventuresome young New Yorker had come west with a contract to cut timber along the Smoky Hill River for the government. Around Ft. Hays he ran into White, the meat hunter for the post, and saw that the hides were left with the other refuse of butchering. Mooar was a trader at heart. He shipped twenty-one of the first class hides to his brother in New York. They wouldn't sell, although two-thirds of the hides that Bates and Dufree purchased went to their New York connections. Finally the Mooar hides were given away to a Pennsylvania tannery. But before there was a report on these, John Mooar had seen part of the great Republican herd come in before the winter's first big storm. He sat on his horse in amazement, and that night he wrote his brother an excited letter. Around the post he talked of this phenomenon, so unexpected, even though he had seen the small scattered herds for months. This was more astonishing than the sudden milling crowds around a tenement fire, or the mobs in New York's draft riots during the war, when a thousand were killed in one day.

Then good news came from the Pennsylvania tannery and an order to the Mooar brothers and White for two thousand dry or flint hides at three fifty a piece. By then John had helped a couple of buffalo men, Charlie Rath and Charlie Myers, get five hundred hides together for an English firm, a sample order through Lobenstein, the long established fur trader of Leavenworth.

Swiftly now other tanners became interested. An English firm contracted for ten thousand hides on the first order. Agents came to Hays City and to other shipping points. They found a huge shed at Cheyenne, Wyoming, one hundred and seventy-five by sixty feet and thirty feet high, crammed with buffalo hides, and great ricks at Sidney, at Wichita and elsewhere, with some of the traders long established in the business. It seemed that fine buggy tops, sledge bodies, book bindings, furniture and wall coverings—all the things that needed a strong, elastic leather, had been made from buffalo skin for years.

Now the hide business had a full head of steam and running wild, like a prairie engine hitting a sudden down grade.

Although the end of the K. P. had moved westward, and much of the true frontier with it, General Sheridan made his headquarters at Ft. Hays the winter of 1869-70, one mile west of Hays City. There were around two thousand troops there, mostly Seventh Cavalry, with nothing to do and no place to spend their evenings except in the little town. It was a hell-roaring outfit, bragging about the Washita and the conquering of the Indians, the worst Indians of them all— the Cheyennes, with some Kiowas and Comanches too. And General George Armstrong Custer was on top of the heap.

There were some to question and resent this, and not

only those who remembered the miserable Cheyenne prison camp that was out at the post so long, full of the women and children that the yellow-haired commander had walked over the snow from the Washita. More were tired of the swaggering Seventh, particularly in a place where so many picturesque men wore long curls, fancy vests and the polished six-guns that demanded attention. The rowdiest of the troopers, the one that caused the most trouble, was Captain Tom Custer, brother of the general, even when Major Andrew, Mike Sheridan, Little Phil's brother, wasn't around to contribute to the disorder. The encounters between Tom Custer and his followers and the leaders of the buffalo hunters gave Wild Bill his chance. When Marshal Hickok arrested the captain there was a roar from the angry troopers that could be heard clear out on the buffalo plains. Bill knew he had run himself up a box canyon now, and more than ever kept to the middle of the street and to corner tables, but they finally got him, ganged in around him in a saloon. Plainly Bill was to be shot down as coldly as Black Kettle was on the Washita. But Wild Bill Hickok had been in saloon brawls before Hays City was born. He drew, and those who saw the fight in the smoky room reported that he was plainly the original two-gun man, the one who started the term. But there were around twenty-five, thirty troopers and Bill carried a lot of lead when he backed out of the saloon doors. He managed to get away from them all in the darkness, leaving five, some said seven bluecoats down, dead and dying. He escaped to the river ice, swam the narrow open channel and hid out in a buffalo wallow, his clothing frozen to his wounds. He dared not move while the troopers rode the night for him, whacking every bush and clump of grass, the gleam of their lanterns turned into every hole and hollow. Finally Bill managed to reach a friend, another hide man, who smuggled him into a loaded box car and got him away, although troopers were guarding every ridge, trail and train on General Sheridan's orders to bring Wild Bill in, dead or alive—marshal or no marshal.

But there were many who sided with Hickok. Tom Custer and Mike Sheridan, the brothers of the generals, were troublemakers. Both were often very drunk, Mike so full he had to be carried to his quarters. But many looked forward to the time when Hays would be rid of both the long-hairs like Hickok and the arrogant troopers.

When Bill was able to handle his guns again and his fingers had recovered some nimbleness, he went out on the town in Kansas City and elsewhere, so long as it was far from the troopers of the Seventh. Mrs. Cody was wintering in Topeka, with Bill in and out. Often the two long-haired, fancy-dressed plainsmen were together, Cody the story teller, Wild Bill the quieter man, as was becoming in a more dangerous one. But it was irksome too, even the admiration based on his claim as a plainsman, for the plains mark their own and hold him well.

The buffalo hunters were moving out upon the great Arkansas herd, commonly estimated at five million head, and as high as fifteen million by some, although this figure probably included much of the Texas herd. Wild Bill needed money but he had to keep out of reach of the Seventh Cavalry. The regiment was on wheels nowadays, likely to show up anywhere, and so Hickok decided to get out of the west entirely. Once more he went to the Republican in Nebraska but this time he hired three good lariat men, well mounted. Far southwest, up Beaver Creek, they struck a large buffalo herd. Bill knew all about hide hunting, but this was a new kind of deal and it took them two weeks of hard work to rope six buffaloes. They finally got them tied and to the railroad, not the K. P., which ran through Hays and past the Seventh Cavalry, but up to Ogallala and through Omaha, where Bill was met by the four Comanche Indians he had hired. Because they were going into an animal show, one brought a cinnamon bear and another a monkey. Bill shipped his outfit to Niagara Falls and set his show up on some vacant ground, but found he had no way to collect money for it out in the open.

Yet how else could he put on THE DARING BUFFALO
CHASE OF THE PLAINS as it was advertised, except in
the open?

He went broke as fast as any tenderfoot might sitting
in at his table in Hays. Finally Hickok had to sell the buffaloes to get himself and the Indians back to Kansas City. By
then Sheridan, the Custers and the Seventh had been transferred, so Wild Bill returned to Hays and was hired to clean
up on the outlaws and the new element that was appearing
—the roistering cowboys from the cattle trail.

The hide business too was taking on a new aspect.
John Mooar, the New Yorker who had worked up a booming
trade in hides for leather, had hired some of the best hunters for his outfits working the range. But he had his eyes on
the future and so he made a special trip to see Col. R. I.
Dodge. As commandant at Ft. Dodge the colonel's troops
were to guard the line of the Arkansas, keep out all hide
hunters trying to cross south into the treaty regions of the
Indians.

"What would you do if we went hunting down in
Texas?" Mooar asked the colonel.

Dodge, a hearty man, laughed aloud. "—If I were
hunting buffalo I would go where the buffalo are."

CHAPTER IV

BIG GUNS AND A ROARING BLIZZARD

THE winter drifts lasted into the spring of 1871, but finally they began to shrink, grey and dirty, and the snow water roared in the gullies. When the spearheads of geese came honking northward, they settled to rest a little, not only along the flooded Cimarron and Arkansas Rivers but on the many lakes out on the prairie and in the buffalo wallows brimming full. Every day there were more yellow calves to shy at them, and to run among the shaggy, ragged herds as they drifted north too, moving in small bunches with the spring.

By then another migration, more nearly an invasion, had started, this one of men, and from the east, the customary direction of their movement. Their coming was spearheaded too by the new railroad that crept up the Arkansas towards the gold of the western mountains. With the long continuous rise in unemployment and in wage cuts, there was a rush to the buffalo country on all the trains and trails and across the open prairie too, by wagon, horseback and afoot—a rush westward that was exceeded only by the 'Forty-niners for California. Out-of-work railroaders came, and teamsters, fortune hunters, trappers, guides, veterans of both sides, men from colleges

and from slums, and men escaping their families or one jump
ahead of the sheriff. Many hoped to work on the tracks, but
only if they failed at hide hunting. They got lost on the
plains, turned around, and in their panic, their frenzy to keep
moving, could wear themselves out running even without the
torment of possible skulking Indians, the heat dances on the
horizon and the shimmering, disappearing mirage lakes.
Some greenhorns threw their guns away and fled from anyone who would rescue them, perhaps had to be ridden down,
run down. Almost none of them remembered that the
streams all led eastward, towards the settlements, and that
the calm man can go for days without food if he must. Even
the buffalo gnats like dust clouds killed no one, although a
tenderfoot's eyes might swell shut from their poison, his inflamed ears grow large as saucers, his body fever-hot. More
died from fear than from Indians, rattlesnakes and thirst.

But others came, many others—anxious to tap the new
hide bonanza. If they managed to stay until they shot a few
buffaloes, they got buffalo mange and became sick from over-
eating on wild meat. Later they got more seriously ill from
the restricted meat diet. Unlike the Indians, the new white
hunters ate little but the choice muscle parts. They usually
roared the first time they ran into friendly Indians out on a
little hunt. In a buffalo paunch turned inside out and hung
from a tripod of sticks, the Indians cooked the choice visceral
parts—liver, heart, lights, some of the net, and so on, by adding a little water and then dropping hot stones inside for the
cooking. They even cut up the cooking paunch and ate that
too. Emptied of their contents the small intestines were cut
into small square pieces and with a droplet of bile from the
knife point on each piece, the small children ate them down
like candy. No, these were not fit ways for civilized man.

But when the mouths of the new hunters got sore and
raw and would not heal, they were glad to follow the advice
of the Indians and the old plainsmen to eat the tallow from
around the kidneys. That healed them right up.

If the green hunter did manage to get some hides decently dried, free from rot and beetles, he might lose them to hide rustlers, or hostile Indians might slit them to pieces. At the stations he found rotgut whisky, gamblers, dance hall girls, holdup men and the new garroters moving out from the cities. But there was also the wide and fruitful country that grew fat buffaloes and might grow fat cattle and fat crops. The land was free for any homesteader with the filing fee, around fourteen dollars, and the persistence to stay with the hundred sixty acres and sweat the sod into crops with the breaking plow and the hoe. Many who never made fortunes in hides became good settlers, brought their women to the dugouts and the grasshoppers and rattlesnakes, the hot winds and the blizzards.

But perhaps the green hunter could hire out to one of the merchants now beginning to organize and supply their own hide outfits, as Mooar and some earlier robe traders were doing. Each crew worked under the direction of an old hide man. Central depots were set up and corrals large as for remudas were built, anticipating an immense harvest. Some dug brining pits and lined them with hide to hold the salting tongues and sometimes the hindquarters and humps, the meat perhaps further cured in smokehouses built of poles and hides, easily knocked down and moved with the herds. There had long been meat sold during the winters, hauled frozen by the freight outfits returning light on the trails, later in the light east-bound cars of the U. P. For years there was a good trade in smoked tongues; even an old bull's was a delicate morsel to the continental gourmet. Brined tongues packed in discarded whisky barrels brought good side money too, particularly for the lone hunter who usually made the most of everything. Some even gathered the mops from the heads that were left unskinned on the prairie. The thick bush of hair over the head and eyes brought around seventy-five cents a pound. Bull hides were worth two dollars at trading points, cows and calves a little less, compared to the six-

teen-fifty that a Grade A Indian-tanned robe brought both
Bates and Durfee through their New York outlets. These
two firms were still the biggest collectors of good quality robes
and hides in 1871.

As the new hunters swept over the plains the prospects
for prime robes grew less and the average quality of the summer hides also dropped, with so many torn or badly dried.
For a while only about one out of every five buffaloes killed
produced a salable skin. Far too many were lost to rot and
vermin. Often the buffalo was badly shot and got away to die
in some draw or brushpatch. Now and then the green hunter
followed the wounded animal too closely into a narrow canyon or washout and was gored, even killed.

While the best of the professional hunters considered
summer hide-gathering wasteful, many decided to jump in
while they could, now that the whole country swarmed with
men chasing buffaloes. A few women joined the hunting too.
One of the best shots around the Republican herd was a Mrs.
Raymond from Nebraska, out with her brother. Later she
was credited with teaching a newcomer to the region, a W. F.
Carver, called Doc, to hunt buffaloes, bring down the big
bulls in the chase. Doc Carver took his marksmanship and
his stories over much of the outside world.

Buffalo leather was now frankly sold for what it was,
admittedly spongier than steer hide and more porous, but
also more elastic and very strong. It was excellent for all the
belting needed by the expanding industrial world, and for
the growing fashion in leather furniture and floor and wall
coverings. Most of the handsome leather panelings found in
the homes of the new industrial and financial barons were
buffalo, and for carriages, sleighs and even hearses it was the
best leather produced.

But the rush of hide men called for better guns. An
occasional plainsman could make a living with the fuke, the
sawed-off shotgun firing ball, and Wyatt Earp killed all the
buffaloes he wanted with an ordinary shotgun. Most hunters,

however, used old army rifles, ever inadequate for the inexperienced hide man, particularly as the herds grew wilder.
Some brought old muzzleloading Springfields converted to
breechloading, eight-and-a-half pound guns, .50 caliber;
others perhaps the Sharps .50 caliber breechloading cavalry
carbine of about seven pounds. The Henry and the Spencer
rifles were not powerful enough against the matted hair, the
thick hide and heavy skull. The marksmen, who liked the Bal-
lard rifle because of its exceptional accuracy, found the
caliber too small. Often it was less effective than a good Indian bow well handled—a good four-foot bow of hickory or
of elkhorn stripped into thin layers and carefully set together
with hoof glue, or perhaps one of *bois arc,* the Osage thorn,
driving arrows tipped with razor sharp points cut from hoop
iron, the hoops from the barrels of snakebite, rotgut whisky.

The first shipment of heavy rifles to reach Hays City
Soldiers were usually poor hunters. Too often they
were handicapped by sights that were too coarse, a trigger
that was so hard few could pull it with the first finger joint,
and, due to economy, seldom had enough target practice, let
alone at moving objects. Raw troops died on the prairie because they had never shot their weapons as much as a dozen
times before they had to face the crack mounted bowmen of
history, let alone those Indians with guns.

The first shipment of heavy rifles to reach Hays City
came in calibers .44 and .45. The hunters, still dissatisfied,
got Sharps to produce one to their own specifications—the
gun they called the Big Fifty or Old Poison Slinger, made to
load and fire eight times a minute and able to throw a bullet
about five miles, the early users bragged—the "shoot today,
kill tomorrow" gun as the Indians called it. With an occasional lucky hit, a scratch shot, the Fifty could bring down a
buffalo almost a mile away, but it cost eighty dollars to one
hundred dollars or more. The hunters used it without sling,
resting the heavy barrel on cross sticks or a tripod. Some fired
prone, some from a sitting position, which helped deaden the
boom of the gun a little. Unlike range cattle, buffaloes in the

1860's and even into 1870 scarcely noticed a man afoot if he moved with care.

Shells for the new guns were factory-made to the hunters' specifications too, and measured three inches in length, either straight or bottle-necked. The better hunters loaded their own. Mooar filled the shell with powder to about a half inch from the top, set it with a light blow of the hammer or the heel of the calloused palm on the ram, pushed a wad in on top and a little more powder and then rimmed in the bullet he had wrapped in paper. Others dipped the base of the bullet in beeswax.

Some hunters used heavier and heavier loads of powder, some never less than 100 or 110 grains. Mooar, like many other fast shots, preferred the lighter model guns. Years later Mooar said he killed sixty-five hundred buffaloes with a fourteen pound rifle and fourteen thousand with an eleven pounder. By then the Sharps buffalo guns had been made in different sizes, each bigger and heavier than the last, some up to sixteen pounds. If the hunters could have obtained cannons loaded with canister, or Gatling guns firing three hundred fifty rounds a minute, they would have bought them and exterminated great herds in the time they killed little bunches of eighty or a hundred.

With the hunter came the hide freighter. Coke, the skinner for Wild Bill Hickok back in 1867, was hired out to a freighting firm from Sidney, Nebraska. After old Whistler rescued him and Wild Bill from the Indians, Coke decided to work with an outfit of from ten to twenty men and a lot of heavy wagons to corral in an attack. In these long freight trains each unit was two wagons, hitched together, with six yoke of oxen, drawing two hundred hides on the tongue wagon and one hundred fifty on the trailer. At bad spots, whether snow drifts, mud or August sand, one wagon was drawn through at a time. By 'Seventy-one as many as twenty-five such outfits might be seen from a high point, coming across the range.

During the year of 1870 around two million buffaloes had been killed in Nebraska, Kansas, Indian Territory and Texas for the hides. The slaughter brought angry protestations in every legislature, with real alarm over the disappearance of the buffalo, and not only among those contemptuously termed "Indian lovers." But to many others any prohibitive legislation was undue interference with business. The protestors were called names in public and in the newspapers, mostly by men who had no knowledge of Yellow Wolf's prediction twenty-five years before that the buffalo would vanish, or a similar warning from the United States Engineers in the 1850's. Surely they had never heard of a much earlier complaint by Romans in his *Natural History of Florida,* back in 1776, against the wanton destruction of "this excellent beast for the sake of perhaps his tongue only." Most of the hunters would not have cared, and even more would not have believed that the buffalo could be exterminated. Wyoming, however, joined Idaho in legislating against the hide hunters and a representative from Arizona introduced a bill in Congress outlawing the professional hide men and all killing of buffaloes on public lands, which meant the banning of practically all hide hunting except by Indians on their treaty grounds or by white men on railroad lands. But the bill went into the congressional wastebaskets.

By the summer of 1869 Bill Cody had moved into a region he was not to desert entirely for very many years. He hired out as scout and guide to the troops at Ft. McPherson on the Platte. The Overland Trail had long been known as the whisky road to the Indians, who learned to look with concern upon the barrel-filled wagons in their villages. Very many fine robes that the women tanned were swallowed up by the firewater that made their men crazy. Many chiefs banished the whisky traders from their camps, much easier since most trade with the Indians was outlawed anyway. But the hide business boomed the liquor trade at the old road-

ranches, particularly around the army posts, which furnished
a steady base of customers in dull seasons. The Ft. McPherson
region was well enough supplied so even the quiet and sober
Charley Reynolds got into trouble with the drunken troopers.
Bill Cody did a little better with them, and although the
scout pay was poor for one with such flamboyant taste, he
tried to add to it with a little business of his own. On larger
expeditions he took along a wagon of supplies to sell to the
troopers: tobacco, candy, dried fruit, some air-tights, as
canned goods were called, and always a barrel of whisky with
a tin cup on a chain. The driver was often young Charley
White, who was called Buffalo Chips, perhaps because he was
almost a shadow of Cody, an admiring, stalking shadow.

The summer of 1869 Ned Buntline had come out from
New York looking for a real, a genuine western character in
the flesh. Around McPherson he saw the handsome Bill Cody,
who fitted the specifications as though he had made them.
The Broadway publicist talked a big future to Cody, who
would never again think of himself as anything but Buffalo
Bill.

Cody's troubles around McPherson were with civilians, although those who knew him generally treated him
either with idolatry or with tolerance for his arrogant showing off. He picked no gun fights with anyone, seldom had a
gun on him off the trail or the buffalo ranges. But many Hard
Cases looked upon the Platte region as their own and after
Bill had a couple of fights with some of them, Mrs. Cody
came west from St. Louis and set up housekeeping in a little
log cabin beside the post. She had trouble keeping her nationally known husband from accepting the hospitality of
every visitor and traveler who wanted to say he had set up a
drink for the scout so widely publicized, particularly after
James Gordon Bennett of the *New York Herald* hired him as
guide for a hunt, called the Slaughter of the Millionaires
around the Platte, although the number of buffaloes the millionaires killed was reasonably small. Afterward Bennett ap-

plauded Cody over and over in his paper. So now, dressed in fringed buckskin, great white hat, soft shining knee-high boots, and fringed gauntlets, it seemed unlikely that Bill Cody would ever hunt buffaloes commercially again.

But there were plenty of hide men, enough to arouse the Indians that Sheridan and Custer had considered whipped for all time, or at least so the newspapers quoted them. A surveying party of twelve men was killed on the Nebraska-Kansas border the summer after Custer's punishing, and every few days there was news of a hunting camp raided somewhere, horses driven off, men shot. The Sioux and Cheyennes from the agency on the Platte were only given hunting permits if a sub-agent was along, and even then the army officers sometimes turned the most reliable friendlies back to the agency, a very hungry place. So small parties slipped away to hunt for meat, angry enough to attack hunters and settlers both, and without a responsible old chief along to control them, or a sub-agent. It was, the old-timers complained, another case of the military forcing war on the Indians. But very few let themselves be caught by the troops, and once more the hunters began to work in larger parties, ready to shoot at the sight of a feather rising above a hill. The fringe settlements too, had to protect themselves as well as they could, and a so-called Buffalo Militia including some of the hide men, was organized in Kansas. They drilled, scouted, and built a sod fort fifty yards square, the walls seven feet high and four thick, as a refuge for the women and children.

But soon the buffaloes near the settlements were only bleaching bones and the sod fort grew over with weeds, for civilization was truly creeping up every river and creek. Already it seemed the only buffalo to be found in all the Hays region was the young one owned by the sutler at the post. By the time he was around two years old he had acquired the beer habit, with no limit beyond the generosity of the troopers. He was often admitted to the officers' room at the sutler's. Sometimes when he got drunk he cleared the place with one charging lunge, bluecoats flying out the windows and doors. Sometimes he climbed up on the billiard table, or tried to follow a friend, or a foe, up the stairs to the second floor, and then was afraid to climb back down and had to be pushed down backwards, blindfolded, with scarcely the space for all the men it took, and the ropes and planks. As his spike horns lengthened this fun grew dangerous. But many visitors came out to the post just to look at the one monarch of the plains still to be seen around Hays.

The approaching Santa Fe railroad was tapping a very rich buffalo region in southwestern Kansas. In May 1871, Col. R. I. Dodge drove in a light wagon from old Ft. Zarah to Ft. Larned on the Arkansas. At least twenty-five of the thirty-four miles was through one immense dark blanket of buffaloes—countless smaller bunches come together for their journey north. From the top of Pawnee Rock, Dodge could see six to ten miles in most directions, all one solid mass of moving animals. Others who saw this herd reported that it was twenty-five miles wide and took five days to pass a given point—probably fifty miles deep. Dodge estimated that there were about four hundred eighty thousand in the one herd; perhaps a half million that he saw himself that one day. With those that others observed beyond Dodge's sight but still of the same herd, it was estimated at from four million to twelve million counting fifteen head per acre for the former number. This was the great southern herd, coming north for the summer grass.

Nor were these the only buffaloes in the region. Two months earlier Colonel Dodge had camped over night with several wagons and a small escort on the Arkansas below Ft. Dodge. It was too early for rain but the weather was cold and blustery and they stopped close under the shelter of some low steep bluffs bordering a creek. Dodge selected a small pocket in a bend and crowded the tents and wagons in close together. Late at night, when the fires were out and the camp, all except the sentinel, was asleep, the colonel heard a faint roaring sound, far off but steady. He thought of water, a cloudburst up the creek somewhere, and hurried out to peer up the stream in the darkness for the faintly luminous line of approaching foam of a flash flood. But the sound was on the prairie wind and suddenly Dodge recognized it. He hurried the sentinel to awaken the corporal and two more of the guard, but gently, and then gave them their orders.

By now a faint but unbroken black line was visible in the darkness, buffaloes, bearing down fast on the camp. With his men Dodge climbed up the low bluffs to the prairie between them and the camp, and about fifty yards out. He knew the herd had to be split or they would all be trampled into the earth, the camp and all the men together.

The five of them waited until the advance line of buffaloes was about thirty yards off and then they fired their muskets in rapid and continuous succession and let out simultaneous yells, the yells of five badly scared men. One of the lead animals fell dead but the rest kept coming, the thunder of their running hoofs shaking the earth. The small row of men did not break; more buffaloes were brought down and finally, right upon them, they parted a little, then more, and swerved in the face of the red gun fire and the noise. The herd split, the wind of their running like a blizzard sweeping past on both sides of the men. They tumbled in confusion down the steep little drop and thundered off into the darkness. They passed within thirty feet of one flank of the camp and seventy-five feet from the other, the men in it roused out of a deep sleep, paralyzed by the roar and the firing. If Dodge and the sentinels had not been awake the entire camp would have gone down under the stampeding herd, which must have been four or five thousand head.

Buffaloes on the run were recognized as one of the real perils of the plains. Indians always had scouts far out from any village with women and children, whether camped or moving—men who could determine the distance and the direction of a large stampede from far off by laying an ear to the ground. But the railroads couldn't get out of the way, and sometimes whole trains were thrown from the tracks, for those in front could not stop with the push from behind.

Railroaders reported a curious aspect of the buffalo. If a herd was on the north side of the tracks they stood gazing stupidly and without alarm at the locomotive passing within a hundred yards. If, however, they were on the south side, even as far as a mile or two away, the train set the whole herd into the wildest commotion. At full gallop they made for the track as though it crossed the only line of retreat. If they got across ahead of the train they stopped, but if it was in their way each buffalo went at it with the desperation of panic, plunging against the locomotive or cars or between them as though blinded. Although numbers would be killed, those behind kept coming, and then stopped and stared as soon as the obstacle was passed.

After trains were thrown off the track twice in one week, engineers learned to respect the peculiarities of the buffalo. If there was a herd rampaging for the north side of the track, the engine was slowed or stopped. Whether this happened only when the train was passing up wind from the herd, or in the path of a migration was apparently never settled. The trainmen took no chances; they stopped.

Even in 1870 it was usually considered suicidal for a white man to hunt south of the Arkansas, in the region the Indians considered theirs, particularly when their claim was restated by the Medicine Lodge Treaty of 1867. Few traders except those with Indian families went down there except on the worn path of the Santa Fe Trail. Freighters for the southern posts, like Camp Supply, moved with soldier escort. Usually a few daring hunters did slip across the river for the fine furs and pelts when they were prime with winter and the Indians kept closer to their lodges. Still some failed to return. The men worked singly down there, for safety, slipping along with more stealth than the lynx cat, taking beaver, otter, ermine, mink and an occasional silver fox, using the big grey prairie wolves, which sometimes brought as high as six dollars a pelt, to fill out the load. A good load, if saved from the Indians, might bring up to one thousand dollars, good wages for two months' work, even dangerous work.

The country south of the Arkansas was also a sportsman's paradise, with no end of small game. Turkeys in great flocks roosted on the south confluences of the Cimarron and farther south. Spread to feed on grasshoppers and prairie seeds they blackened the prairie like buffaloes from far off, and the whirr of their wings in flight was like the roar of a tornado moving over the plains. By dusk the timber of the creeks was loaded with roosting birds, the branches bent and breaking, the earth underneath a grey guano. Sheridan's Roost on the fork of the Canadian was named for the turkeys slaughtered by the general's troops when they made camp there on the winter expedition to the Washita for Major Elliott's body.

In the summers the prairie was flush with grouse, prairie chickens, and curlews with their pink underwings lovely as a flash of sunset cloud. Then there was the dainty little prairie plover that rose singly, at forty, fifty yards and soared gently away, rising gradually, such ready and toothsome game for the hunter. Wright, an early hide man from around Dodge, once killed nearly two hundred in an hour for an entourage of eastern sportsmen.

Wild Bill Hickok had been out hunting with a couple of skinners for a while, making money but he wasn't very easy about it. Some of the Custer adherents were around talking big, and some Johnny Rebs who claimed that Bill was always laying for southerners, ever since he killed Mc-

Canles, the Virginian. Besides, the son, Monroe McCanles, might be honing for revenge. About twelve at the time he saw Hickok shoot his father he must be around twenty-two now, and probably even quieter, more brooding than when he whacked bulls to Denver in his middle teens. Not that Wild Bill was afraid of any man he ever saw, if he could see him.

Whatever the reason, Bill left the buffalo ranges and the next stories came from Ellsworth, Kansas. It seemed that a man named Bill Thompson was jealous of Hickok over a woman. One day he caught Wild Bill in a restaurant, sitting back to the door, and fired. But he missed and Hickok, one of the fastest men with a gun, shot Thompson dead.

But later there were other stories. Thompson hadn't died, hadn't even been hit. Maybe no such man had ever been in Ellsworth, although loafers around the saloons there insisted a Bill Thompson was in town all right but far from being killed by Hickok, Thompson had gun-whipped the Prince of Pistoleers like a dog. Bill's nose, however, was not broken down as it should be from any pistol-whipping worth the name, and by mid-April he was marshal at Abilene, selected for the job by McCoy, who was the new cattleman mayor, as was fitting, since Abilene was now the northern end of the cattle trail, the longhorn capital of the world. Often a thousand cowboys were camped around there at one time, and more of the wild and reckless breed coming and going. With the thirst of a season's trail dust in their throats and a season's pay ready to set their back teeth afloat, they were the men to make the professional hide hunter look like a psalm singer, as some were. The hunter had to be a steady man to keep at the hard and dirty work day after day, alone or with only a partner or two, and danger always just over the next rise. He had no gun-packing trail boss to look out for him, cuss him out like a mother, and keep him in line.

So now, when the cowboys rode, whooping and shooting, into Abilene, Wild Bill Hickok was to take over where the trail boss let go. In addition there were all the Hard Cases, the men drawn to the K. P. towns by the prospect of easy money, buffalo money. Many came from Chicago, Philadelphia or New York, the garroters among them swift and silent in the darkness of the border towns, a bit of whang or rawhide string easier to come by than a gun or even a knife.

It was a period fitting the Hickok reputation, and if Bill had his softer moments now and then, there was Susan Moore, who, some said, was at the bottom of the shooting match with Dave Tutt over in Missouri, with Tutt left to kick his life out in the dust of the street. Susan had moved into a little house at Abilene and for a while Bill was seen with fewer of the idolatrous boys and youths that his flamboyance and his reputation drew. Here, too, he met a Mrs. Lake, in town with the circus that she managed since her husband was killed two years ago. She rode a horse as Bill had never seen a woman ride before, not only in the little circus ring but out on the open prairie. Sidesaddle, she spurred her black mare beside him after the buffalo bulls, taking them over knolls and through bogs and across prairie dog towns, her horse zigzagging between the holes on a dead, a greyhound run. Her eyes were afire with excitement as she set the few shell pins left back into her hair and wiped the lather from the neck of her mare with a lace handkerchief. Truly it seemed that one could scarcely say where this woman left off and the fine black Kentucky mare began.

Sometimes Wild Bill was seen with a woman called Mattie, one of the handsomer young madames of the town, teaching her to shoot the little pearl-handled pistol she carried. "One meets such wicked men," Mattie said as she pocketed her warmed gun in satisfaction. But Mrs. Lake was not the woman to take pleasantly to such companions for her friends, and soon she was gone with her circus to other frontier towns; to be admired by other men, Bill accused, this once breaking from his usual quiet and gentle way on a matter that called for less than gun smoke.

At Abilene as at Hays City, Wild Bill never used the sidewalks but kept to the middle of the street. In times of serious trouble with the cowboys and perhaps a scattering of buffalo hunters in from the west, he carried a sawed-off shotgun, but even then he was still the jauntiest, flossiest buffalo hunter of them all. Once he pursued two men who had committed a murder and then skipped out to the open country. He ran them down and killed them both, it was said. Perhaps he was a little cocky over this, also his new frock coat with a white silk ruffle-trimmed shirt and checked vest. Or perhaps it was a genuine test for the new marshal planned to end in a gun fight with Coe, a professional gambler from down Texas way. Coe owned the Bull Head at Abilene and some said that Hickok had lost his hide money to the gambler. On a drunken spree Coe and a friend put on a big brawling and loud-mouth scene until the marshal interfered. Guns were drawn and the bystanders dove for any cover they could. Bill's gun brought both Coe and his friend down, as well as a man who came running out of the shadows of an alley. But the latter turned out to be Bill's deputy marshal, his beloved friend. Dramatically Wild Bill Hickok knelt beside the dying man, gathered the delicate form in his arms and carried him to a table, Bill's long curling hair falling about his tear-stained face as he bowed his head.

"I have killed my best friend," he sobbed. "I couldn't see it was him, and I killed him—"

So once more Wild Bill moved on. The Coe killing stirred up considerable anger among the trail drivers to Abilene and set the saloonkeeper's southern relatives gunning for Hickok. Many stories were told of Wild Bill this summer. By now he had become so romantic a figure that his appearance on the street of any border town started lurid tales of bloodshed and sudden death. He went back to Hays a short

time, where Mrs. Lake had opened with her circus. Then
he returned to Kansas City, often his refuge when the frontier
proved an uneasy bed. He was weary of his old stomping
grounds, he admitted, in one of his rare moments of self-
revelation, but he didn't add that a card sharper had taken
him for a thousand dollars, a man so crude-fingered that
Bill should certainly have detected his manipulations and
put the gun to his red-handed thievery.

But in the future Wild Bill Hickok would keep out
of the dark, smoky, lantern-lit frontier holes that passed as
saloons. He had money enough from a short hunting trip,
with a little credit, to buy the clothing that fitted life in the
city—new broadcloth, with the fine white shirts he liked,
ruffled and pleated very skillfully, and with a little more
elegance in his vests and gloves too. But Bill realized that he
should have been out on the buffalo ranges instead of working
as marshal. He could make at least five thousand dollars the
coming winter, and if he had gone out in the spring his good
friend Williams would still be alive. Yet he had only tried
to rest his eyes from the blazing summer sun of Kansas, or its
glare on the winter snows, as the doctor in Kansas City ad-
vised.

So the men who first brought the business of hide
hunting to public attention were scattering their pittance as
they themselves were scattering, the ones already called the
old buffalo men because they had hunted four years ago.
Lonesome Charley Reynolds still tried to make the fortune
he promised himself but he had moved to the upper Missouri. With both the troopers and the Indians gunning for
him, he decided to quit their country, go where he had no
enemies. Once more he became known as a quiet, pleasant
man to whom the term "little" would always be applied, although he was taller than most of the early frontiersmen,
such men as Kit Carson, the Bakers and Jim Bridger. He
was more self-contained and more dependable too, perhaps.

Lonesome Charley shot meat for the Missouri posts, drank no whisky so far as anyone knew, played no cards, bucked no crooked wheels. He kept his chin clean-shaven and his hair cut so that only those who looked beyond, to the deep bronzing of his skin, the squint that sheltered his quiet blue-grey eyes, discovered that this man had spent most of the years since his childhood in what was still called the wilderness.

Once he said, very quietly, "The railroad'll be pushin' through here soon, up the old Missou' and the Yellowstone, like down south."

The trappers and wolfers laughed. "Hell, man, this is *Indian* country!" they told him.

The fall of 1871 remained fine long after the eastern sportsmen were gone, but without the fragrance of earth and prairie ripening in the sun. Instead there was a stench beyond anything that the buffalo hunters who had fought under Meade and Lee could recall even on the portentous winds blowing from the slopes of Gettysburg. Then there was one swift little snow, followed by the warm drowsy haze of Indian summer, so warm the hunters slept outside of the tents and wagons as in May. But a blizzard came, suddenly, dropping the temperature ninety degrees in six hours, sweeping down on the hunters, many of them tenderfeet, some so new they did not understand that the buffalo chip was the only fuel on the prairie, the fuel that must keep them alive as the temperature dropped far below zero, and yet the first to be water-soaked in a storm, and covered by snow.

Three such tenderfeet from Wisconsin got off the train up in Nebraska and hired a team of mules and an open wagon to hunt hides on the buffalo ranges, to make a small fortune in a few weeks as the stories all promised. They were out only a few days when the blizzard struck, sweeping upon their wagon out on the tablelands, giving them no time to make camp. Before they realized what was happening they were shut in by the driving, blinding storm, so thick they couldn't see beyond the ears of the mules. All they could do was let the team drift with the wind. The snow deepened until the wagon stuck in every bank, the cold so biting they had to keep walking in their snow-caked town overcoats, to stay alive. With no sense of direction in the roaring blizzard they lost all idea of time and distance too, until the mules gave out. They unhitched in the storm dusk and fed them a little grain, holding the nose bags against the tearing wind, the animals humped up, ice-caked backs to the snow. The men tried to eat too, but the food was frozen and they could not find a bush or a tree for fuel.

The men knew they must get off the empty tableland, with the freezing wind so penetrating. They tied their bed blankets around them as best they could and tried to push the weary mules on, holding the wagon to keep from upsetting in the gullies and washouts lost under the new snow, the wind lifting it at the slightest tilt. The men kept moving beside the slow wagon, plunging into drifts waist deep, turning out for footing, slapping their arms to keep up the circulation, hoping to strike a draw or a canyon, a patch of brush, a buffalo hunter's camp, or even the Indians, dangerous as they had seemed until now.

The mules played out again, stopping, the men taking turns whipping them until they were so exhausted they had to keep each other from sinking down into the snow to rest. Then one of them stepped off the drifted edge of a gully in the blinding storm and sank deep into the soft, powdery snow. Too weak to pull himself out, his shouting lost in the storm wind, he crouched down and tried to put his hands inside his trouser belt to warm them, planning to go on as soon as he rested and warmed a little. But for just a moment he would surrender to the drowsiness that was soft as the snow all about him.

A long time afterwards the man awoke, coming out of a dark, deep valley, pulling himself up through layers of

foggy warmth. Some one was near him, an unclear face looking down, a hand holding him back when he tried to sit up.
He was in some dark, dirt-walled place, a settler's dugout
stable. Both his frozen feet had been amputated by a neigh-
boring homesteader who was a doctor. Even so he was lucky
to be found at all. His two companions were already buried.
Even the mules seemed to have frozen.

Slowly the man turned his head down, squeezing his
eyelids shut as he did the night of the blizzard, to keep the
water from running out.

Another new hunter, but one who had already seen a
hard winter out on the plains while freighting for Custer's
expedition against the Cheyennes in 1868-1869 was young
Billy Dixon. This fall he was hunting buffaloes with a partner and some skinners on the headwaters of Pawnee Fork,
drifting back and forth from there to the Smoky Hill River,
but with a permanent camp on Hackberry Creek. When the
blizzard struck everybody made camp but the supplies were
short and as soon as the wind went down a little Dixon
started for Hays. He took an empty wagon with four mules
and a saddle horse tied alongside. Mules worked more quietly in big drifts, were less likely to snap off the doubletrees
or break out a tongue. The horse was for escape if the wind
rose again and whipped the snow into another blizzard.

By keeping to the wind-swept slopes, shoveling when
he had to, walking in his clumsy buffalo coat and buffalo
pacs, made with the hair turned in, Billy Dixon got through,
although his hands seemed frozen and his nose swelled like
a lump of sore-finger bread just out of the skillet, except that
his nose was purple.

At Hays the express agent hired Billy at blizzard rates
to take a load through to the troops down at Camp Supply.
If he couldn't make it all the way, then at least as far as Ft.
Dodge. Billy agreed to try, wanting to look for richer buffalo
ranges anyway. With fifteen hundred pounds of express he

got to a roadranch the first night. The weather was bitter cold, so cold that his eyelashes were frozen inside the big buffalo collar. By ten the next morning it was spitting snow again, but he had agreed to push through, so he started, walking part of the time for warmth, floundering along beside the mules. The load was bulky and awkward, the road nothing but deep crusted drifts or icy slopes under the new snow, and the cold bit his lungs. At a long divide that dropped to a steep slope, the freezing mules, out of all control, broke into a gallop that nothing could stop. Billy clung to the lines and tried to keep the wagon right side up. When they got to the next roadranch the young freighter was scarcely able to speak. A crowd of storm-stranded men crowded out around him for news but Billy's jaw was locked like a vise, the lockjaw of dangerous freezing. Some of the old-timers understood what had happened. They hurried Billy into the dugout, piled wood on the fireplace and thawed him out, although it seemed he could never be warmed again, sitting at the fire for hours, shivering and burning at the same time. It was Billy Dixon's first experience with killing cold. It could very easily have been his last.

When he finally reached Ft. Dodge he heard that the storm had brought the buffaloes in by the thousands, all trying to take shelter around the walls of the post. Artillery pieces had been fired at regular intervals all through the storm to keep them from pushing the buildings and corrals down. Next day the wind had died and Billy got on his saddlehorse and struck up the Arkansas about thirty-five miles, keeping to the barer ridges, looking over the country for hunting prospects. There were signs everywhere of an enormous number of buffaloes, the snow cut and worn, the long bottom grass flattened wherever it was exposed, the willows cropped close by the weary, starving animals. In every direction were the thawed, brown, icy spots where buffaloes had bedded for the night, but not one was left in sight now. When, from a high point, Billy turned his eyes across what

might have been glaring snow, he held his breath at the
wonderful picture before him. As far as he could see the
wind-swept table was one solid mass of buffaloes, dark under
a thinning breath cloud. They were grazing quietly on the
curly grass called mesquite grass, its winter brownness laid
bare by the sharp moving hoofs.

The next day Billy Dixon started back to Ft. Hays
with his mules. Many hunters were there, driven in by the
storm. Some were uneasy about him and his express load.
A lot of stock and many men had died. A wagon train of
cord wood for Hays City had been caught in the blizzard, all
the cattle frozen and the men in frightful condition when
they were found. The storm had struck just as they were making camp for the night, the stock already turned loose to grass.
The men tried to hold the oxen from drifting and so many
of them were soon lost in the driving snow. One, the cook,
managed to find his way back to his wagon and died there,
frozen stiff. He had tried to build a fire in the bottom of
the wagon bed but the wind blew the flames out. The cook
had frozen to death surrounded by enormous quantities of
stove wood.

There was hardly a man in the outfit who didn't lose
a hand, a foot or a limb. Their camp was only five miles
from Hays City and the first clear day everybody who could
turned out to search for the lost men, gathering them up
to the hospital at the post. Some of the storm-driven freighters had wandered clear to Dixon's roadranch and found shelter there.

When Billy told of the black ocean of buffaloes that
he saw northwest of Ft. Dodge, most of the hunters set to
overhauling their outfits at once. But Dixon still had to go to
look after his camp, unreported since the blizzard. His men
were all safe and in good shape. The next day he scouted
west of the main camp on the Hackberry and found thousands of fresh buffaloes drifted in there too. It was plain that
the big herd had come a long ways into the wind during

the blizzard, at least from south of the Arkansas. When the weather moderated they worked back southward to their usual winter range. But by then almost eight weeks of severe weather had passed, enough to make this the hardest winter in years, so cold that even some Indians froze just walking from one camp to another.

By then it was known that at least fifty white men had died in the Arkansas River area, and there was no telling how many more unknown and unreported tenderfeet, who were working on their own or just on their way to the buffalo ranges as the Wisconsin men had been. Of those found alive many had to undergo amputation, mostly at Ft. Dodge and at Hays, or sent east for treatment. Over two hundred men—hunters, freighters, soldiers and settlers—had lost hands or feet. A winter like that put the bark on a man, if he survived the country.

The experienced frontiersman always carried a buffalo coat or robe to keep him dry. If he was caught out he could wrap it around him and dig in under a protecting bank somewhere before he was wet and exhausted. With his rifle set up, the barrel as an air vent, he let the snow drift and pile over him. In this way he could out-last a three-day blizzard as the Indians did, without food or fire if necessary. But the novice, the greenhorn, wasted his strength in fighting on in the storm as long as his panic could drive him and then fell in exhaustion anywhere. At the best he let himself get wet from the snow and with no fuel for fire, he chilled, perhaps into pneumonia, if he did not actually freeze. The tenderfoot had no chance without fool luck.

Yet in spite of the Indians and the blizzards, buffalo hunting drew men because it was almost the only business in the region and about the only one really booming in the nation. Typically it was being taken over by large organized outfits, outfits better equipped to buck the Indians and the elements, and to resist the pressures, local and national, against the wholesale slaughter of the buffalo. There were still some hunters going their own way, men like Charley, Buffalo, Jones, who shifted from rifle to rope, and a new-comer named Youngblood, who often hunted alone, but with-out the neatness, the orderliness of Charley Reynolds. Gen-erally he dressed the meat out and sold it to restaurants, to emigrants on the trails and to any land-seekers. For this reason he stayed closer to the trails than other hunters, but even if buffaloes were often scarcer there, he had a steadier income.

Then there were the real drudges of the growing business, the skinners and hide handlers who were seldom known by name, perhaps not even to the owners of the out-fits. The gold they were paid was as good at the gambling tables and with the Phil Sheridan Girls as though spent by a man whose name was known from sea to sea.

CHAPTER V

THE ROYAL HUNT

JANUARY brought a thaw, but before the snow cleared off enough to lay the dead bare for counting, there was news of more company coming to the buffalo country. This time it wasn't just a few millionaires who might be coaxed to help finance a lagging railroad or a senator with high-toned lady guests in sidesaddles, red veils flying, or some second string nobility out for a summer's gallop after a few buffaloes. This was royalty, big royalty—the Grand Duke Alexis of Russia—and as was fitting to a true man of Moscow, he was coming in the middle of the hardest winter most of the frontiersmen could remember.

The nation was indebted to the duke's father, Czar Alexander, because he supported the Union side during the Civil War. Just when it seemed that England would back the Confederacy, he dispatched a large section of the Russian navy on a visit of friendship to America. England took the hint. Now President Grant could make a gesture of appreciation through this gay but troublesome son of the Czar's. The handsome Alexis had married the daughter of the royal tutor and his father had the marriage annulled, it was said. Anyway, he was concerning himself only with wine, women and cards now—just the man for a western tour with Sheridan and Custer of the Seventh Cavalry, the regiment already called the Cossacks of the western world.

With his light hair, blue eyes, downy young side whiskers and mustache, and a high white forehead under his fur cap, Alexis made a fine picture in the parade at Omaha in the open barouche with gold trim and drawn by four fine greys. There was another parade out at North Platte, an early morning one in the cold clear air, with the duke riding beside Sheridan and Custer in an open carriage headed off towards the buffalo country, the duke's entourage a gay show of colorful Russian uniforms and gold braid following along behind, the newspaper men a drab contrast.

Out a ways they were met by General Palmer and an escort of well-drilled cavalry. Bill Cody had been drawn from his scouting at nearby Ft. McPherson—a fine picture in his fringed buckskin and broad white hat. There were half a dozen others to help scout and guide, mostly buffalo hunters, including Lonesome Charley Reynolds, hired back from the north because he knew the region as no other white man did, once trapped it and then hunted it all for buffalo hides, mostly afoot, ducking the skulking Indians who pursued him. The officers who had given him trouble were gone, and Reynolds was needed to make sure that no hostile Sioux or Cheyenne got near this Grand Duke Alexis.

Fresh horses waited a couple of hours out, where a company of cavalry greeted the party with a presentation of sabres to flash in the bright, unseasonably warm sunshine of January. From there on they saw an occasional lone old buffalo, the first few pursued in single-handed chase by Cody or some of the other hunters. Loud bravos and another passing of bottles celebrated the death of each one as the great animal thundered to earth and kicked his last in the winter grass.

After four o'clock, with the sun slanting low, the party reached a bluff overlooking a new encampment in a bend of

Red Willow Creek called Camp Alexis. The cavalry band played "Hail to the Chief" while the Negro troops who were in charge of the camp and the services for the guests stood at attention. Then there was a grand charge of feathered and painted Sioux whirling around the duke's party, with some fine dare-devil riding by the warriors as they clung to the far side of their running horses, hanging on by toe and mane-hold, shooting blanks over the straining necks.

Ah, these were real Cossacks, the red-skinned Cossacks of the American steppes!

Under the low bluffs lay the neat encampment—wall tents for the guests and the officers, hospital tents for the messes and long rows of field A's for the troops and the servants. Three of the wall tents were floored, the duke's carpeted in deep royal red, all heated with box or sibley stoves. Off to one side was an expanse of new pole corralling; on the other were the circles of painted, smoky Sioux lodges, with their great herds of ponies on the hillsides. All the Indians were out in feathers and beads, and their brightest flannel and blankets to greet the visitors. The camp had been established some days ago, with a supply train for the troops and guests, and twenty-five wagons of goods for the Indians, including plenty of coffee, sugar and flour, a thousand pounds of tobacco and many other presents. A hundred Indians had been invited, at the most two, but as the officers of McPherson knew, the Sioux loved any celebration or event and kept coming. Now around a thousand Indians were there under the long-time peace chiefs, Spotted Tail and Whistler, the latter the man who had saved Wild Bill Hickok from the angry warriors a few miles southwest of here a little over four years ago. But Wild Bill was nowhere around now, not with Sheridan and Custer, although Duke Alexis had asked immediately about this Wild One of whom he had read. The nearest Sheridan had was Buffalo Curly, the expert young hunter for McPherson, the curly-headed youth who, some said, was the brother of Wild Bill—a twisted-nose brother with the same fondness for guns. But perhaps that was a mixup, and occurred because Curly sometimes called himself Billy Barnes, the name that Wild Bill's brother Lorenzo used around Hays, the name that Wild Bill himself had used when he wanted a quick alias. Some had also heard of Buffalo Curly called Jack McCall, although here he used the name of Bill Sutherland.

"Ain't no wonder folks thinks it's safer to ask 'What name you travelin' under?' " Charley Reynolds said to another old hunter as they watched Curly showing off a little for the duke. Once Sheridan started to say something of the complication of names on the American frontier, when the duke brought up the Wild One a second time. It might amuse him to hear that even the Wild Bill of whom he enquired was really named Jim. But the general had struggled with interpreters during his observation of the Franco-Prussian war a while back, and before the interpreter here, whose medium was mostly Parisian French, the general gave it up.

After the evening meal an artist along from Omaha made a few sketches of the guests and the scene, and then Sheridan announced that this was an early night to bed, for tomorrow the hunt would begin. So on the duke's twenty-second birthday he rode out into the wilderness sunshine of a January morning. He was on one of the Cody buffalo horses, dressed in winter hunting garments, very quiet in color compared to the bright uniforms of his entourage, "his kings," as the Negro troops called them. But their awe turned to laughter as these kings, one after another, fell off their horses, which had been selected for their showiness and spirit from all the surrounding army posts and grained up for weeks.

With the scouts, the guides, and some Indians ahead, and an escort of troops, the duke rode out toward the Republican herd. Beside him were the plains heroes of Indian fighting, Forsyth, who still limped from the Beecher Island

fight, and Custer of the Washita. A few paces ahead of the
duke rode Cody in his buckskin, his hair falling over his
shoulders, shinier and longer even than Custer's, leading
them out to the herd that Lonesome Charley and some Indians had located yesterday, and watched all night to prevent drifting.

The duke had a rifle in the scabbard and at his side
the new presentation Smith & Wesson, one of the .44 Russian
model revolvers made on a large arms contract for the Russian government. Following the example and directions of
Cody, he brought down his first buffalo in grand style, Cody's
hunting horse carrying him up very close to a big old bull,
heavy and ponderous. Alexis was a masterly horseman if
not a practiced running shot against the great bison of the
American plains. Custer and Forsyth also distinguished themselves. The two-hour hunt left between twenty and thirty
buffaloes scattered over the rolling prairie, depending upon
who told the story. The butchers for the officers' mess came
in to take enough fresh hump roast for all around, leaving
the rest for the troops and the Indians. The duke supervised
the skinning of his buffalo and the cleaning of the head for
mounting. It should have a place of honor among the trophies
of his palace. When it was unloaded from the pack horses
in camp he was pleased to discover that the head was even
finer than he had realized in his excitement, the horns less
worn than usual for such an old bull—really the finest head
taken in the hunt, although on the range it had seemed that
Charley Reynolds had managed to shoot the best one, a very
wild bull that had almost escaped. There was much expressed
admiration and drinking of toasts, and much praise of this
wonderful plainsman, this Wee-am Codee, this Bison Beel
who led the hunt.

Later when Cody, who had celebrated a little too well,
was taken away for a while, it was revealed that the duke
and Sheridan, too, knew there was a woman in the party,
brought by her brother who had homesteaded nearby lately.

She had seemed sufficiently hidden in her brother's hunting outfit and by the forked saddle she rode, although the few settlers in the region already knew her as an excellent buffalo hunter. This Mrs. Raymond had taken a fine bull too, before the duke got his, but fortunately rather far from his run with Cody, so he need not notice it. But the young Alexis did notice that she was a woman, and when he discovered that she spoke French very well, he asked her to accompany him through the Indian camp to study the home life of these extraordinary aborigines whose children looked like some of their own Mongolian tribes at home.

Later there was great feasting and singing, Russian, Indian and then by the troops and the scouts, one of whom was a trained concert singer who had found times too hard and so came west to hunt the buffalo last year. In the morning the sun came out even finer and today Custer rode with the duke, Custer in his buckskin too, and General Sheridan along, but taking it slower.

Today the Indians, led by Chief Spotted Tail, made a neat little surround for the royal guest. They came up on all sides of a small bunch and started the running buffaloes into a frightened circling, winding it ever tighter and closer together. Bow-armed, with arrows ready for the strings, an extra one in the teeth, the quivers full, they brought them down, one after another, within a compact area not much larger than an acre. A huge bull broke for freedom and one of their noted bow men, a half-brother of the chief Whistler, sent an arrow clear through the buffalo, his horse thundering along beside him. The bloody arrow was left behind, to quiver a little as it stuck a moment in the frozen ground and then fell into the grass as the buffalo's running forelegs began to crumple under him. Then he went down, his head still outthrust.

The duke and his men gave the Indians a great Russian cheer and then another after the hunting dance that the Sioux made during the noon rest. In the afternoon Gen-

eral Sheridan took part in the shooting too, and watched the
duke get two more buffaloes, but it was good that it was the
final hunt, for too much recklessness was showing up. Mike
Sheridan, the general's brother, ran his fine horse down in
the chase, to be left flat as the buffaloes, and Custer's horse
fell dead after they reached camp.

There was another interval of unpleasantness during
the evening smoke when Spotted Tail rose to make a speech.
It was not in the tone of unctuous flattery of the rest of the
hunt. Old Spot looked grim and sober. His people were poor
in the midst of all this wealth and show that the whites
were making from the Indian's buffaloes. He was now allowed a trader, but one with few goods and they should have
two to make for competition and better prices. In addition
Spotted Tail wanted permission to hunt here south of the
Platte until the farming the white man promised to teach
his people fed them well. None of the things that the treaties
promised came, only soldiers to chase the Indians around
and kill anybody they could catch, particularly women and
children. Even he had to move many times and quickly the
last few years and none could doubt him as a peace man,
always with a white sub-agent along to see that his young
men made no trouble. Who watched the troops to see that
they killed no one?

Little of this long and customary complaint was in-
terpreted for the duke, although he inquired of Mrs. Raymond later. "The chief, he was of extremely serious mien—"
the young Alexis persisted.

Afterward the royal guest was serenaded by the cavalry
band, the Indians made a powwow with a little war dance
at a great evening fire built before the young duke's tent.
He gave the warriors fifty dollars in fifty-cent pieces and
passed out twenty beautiful blankets and many fine hunting
knives with ivory handles, made for the Czar's own men.

They returned to the railroad, still through the most
unJanuary weather the old-timers could recall. There Alexis

gathered his guests to his private car, the entertainment ending with a big dinner, complimentary speeches all around,
and the presentation of a large purse of money and a diamond stick pin to Bill Cody. Then the duke and his escort
of American generals went on to Denver and back on the
Kansas Pacific. In eastern Colorado they stopped for one more
hunt, this time guided by Chalkley Beeson, and without the
show of Buffalo Bill or Spotted Tail's Sioux. Chalk was a
former stage driver and hide hunter, in addition to being a
good musician who was also interested in ranching and in
investments along the new railroad coming up the Arkansas
River. The hunt was a good one, and afterward the royal
party stopped for a visit with the legislature at Topeka. A
fine picture was taken of the entire party, and one of the
duke with Custer, both in their hunting outfits and their
pistols, against a romantic backdrop. From Topeka the party
went on a brief tour of the south. By now the duke was
wearing a buckskin shirt like Custer and Cody, even with
evening dress. All these things were in the papers, and
plainly the young duke had made other conquests besides
those of the great American bison. Fifty years later there
were grandmothers who spoke wistfully of the handsome
warm-eyed grand duke they met in their budding days.

    Back up along the Platte the duke had scarcely got
away before the fine spring weather changed back to January and the first killing blizzard of 1872 hit the region, the
drifts very deep and the cold down towards forty degrees
below zero. In west Nebraska a train was stalled in the snow,
the people inside hoping to last out the storm somehow.
Then another menace appeared. Snow-caked buffaloes came
blundering out of the south, their noses headed into the
stinging, driving snow, their great heads butting the cars
blindly, jolting them, teetering them against the drifts and
the force of the north wind, the wood cracking. But the
deep snow slowed the force of the herd and they spread,

floundering, along the train both ways, packed in by those pushing from behind, huddling against this little wall against the wind. They wouldn't leave, not for yells, the whistle or pistol shots. They just drew themselves up under their whitened humps against the cars and waited for the end of the storm with their eternal patience. Many died there in the terrible cold but their meat fed the passengers and when the train was finally dug out, the cut through the snow was lined by the huge carcasses.

But for all the hard winter it was a time of easy money among the buffalo hunters, with nothing much to spend it on, no families, usually, no home to keep up, not even the real need for a pair of Sunday pants. So there was always tarantula juice and poker. Not even California Joe thought of playing at less than a five dollar ante. Joe and a partner were selling meat at six cents a pound to the contractors who got ten and twelve. Most of the southern cattle recently brought to southwest Nebraska died when a sleet storm spread ice over every spear of grass and then ended in deep snow and temperature that froze the wet and shivering long-horns. Some of them were charged to the Indians as depredations. The government accepted one claim against Spotted Tail's Sioux for ninety thousand dollars and took the sum out of their appropriations, a claim later proved fraudulent, as so many things were basically in those years. But this one got into court and repayment was actually secured. In the meantime these cattlemen had paid an old squawman forty cents a head to skin the frozen stock the Indians supposedly ate.

This was the year of rising protests against corruption in the administration. In January Hazen had reported to Congress that the post trader at Ft. Sill paid a bribe of twelve thousand dollars a year to obtain and hold his appointment. Nothing had been done but later in this election year of 1872 it was dug up as ammunition against Grant's reelection. This time Custer was on the same side as Hazen, making the same charges, but mostly as though he had initiated them, and with much more noise, to Grant's increasing anger.

Curiously, this was also the year of the war between the generals. Although much of the maneuvering seemed to be out on the plains, the feud had deeper roots, some perhaps even before Custer's days at West Point and his later suspension and Grant's swift approval of the sentence. Custer had a little revenge for West Point when he struck Hazen's Cheyennes on the Washita but later something more happened at Hazen's post, Ft. Cobb near there. It was when the headmen of the Cheyennes had come to surrender and talk about getting the white captives the Southerners held released. Sheridan happened to be there, and wanted to turn the cannon on the Indians, men, women and children, who were being held in the corral for the counciling. Hazen curtly refused, pointing out that he was the Indian agent here, and that this was his post and so he ranked Little Phil whose policy had long been: the only good Indian is a dead Indian. It was a good story and was told with the pleasure of a gooseberry sourball on the tongue, rolled and savored. Some who knew Custer bet he was laying for Grant too.

"Hell, Grant's his boss!"

"Custer figgers he's got to be the bigger man, by now—"

After all the publicity that Sheridan and Custer received from the buffalo hunts put on for James Gordon Bennett and his important entourage of millionaires and for Grand Duke Alexis, General Hazen lifted his voice in angry protest against this useless and wasteful government-initiated slaughter of the buffalo, the dissipation of a great public resource, a public trust. But Custer was the hero of the Washita and with his own romantic writings and the powerful newspapers that backed Sheridan, the protests of a man like Hazen were little more than the hoots of a burrow owl living among his rattlesnakes, as Custer characterized the complaints, the rattlesnakes presumably Hazen's Indians. It was true that General Smith, commandant up at Ft. Laramie, made the same protest, as did a dozen other old army men of the frontier.

Congress did start another move against the hide hunters, and the U. S. Biological Survey decided to send out a young man to make a survey of the herds left along the Platte. George Bird Grinnell, who had been in Nebraska two years before with a Yale expedition, was stationed west of Kearney when what was left of the great herd that wintered on the Republican crossed the Platte. He estimated it at no less than five hundred thousand head, but at the rate of the killing, millions a year now, these would not last long.

Nothing came of the talk of federal legislation, although Montana joined Idaho and Wyoming with a law against the buffalo hunters. In Kansas, too, the legislature passed such an act but the governor had many important reasons, it was said, some of them private, for not signing the bill. When figures on the number of hides shipped annually were requested from the railroads for Congress, it seemed their records either gave no numbers at all, as the Union Pacific, or incomplete ones, as the Kansas Pacific, with 13,646 hides billed out during the year 1871, when the general estimate of the buffaloes killed that year was around two million and when one large St. Louis hide dealer alone bought about two hundred fifty thousand buffalo hides and this was only one of many companies in the business.

Most of the railroad stations had large sheds generally packed with dry hides, a common sight in Kansas and Nebraska. The great shed up at Cheyenne and those at Sidney and the stations between were all on the U. P. which had no record of any buffalo hides shipped at all. The K. P. did admit carrying 1,161,419 pounds of buffalo meat, with no record for salted or cured meats, which must have been

much greater in amount during all the months except the
depths of winter frost. The wagon hauls were very long ones
and the freight cars had no refrigeration.

Certainly the railroads realized the pressure for legislation to protect the buffalo, and take away most of their
freight. Perhaps it did seem wiser to turn the cars over to
the shippers to fill as they liked, with no labeling.

No matter what the railroad figures indicated, the
chief industry of Kansas or at least three-fourths of the state
in 1871-2 was the trade in hides. It paid for the railroads, drove the Indians back, helped bring rapid settlement,
turned money loose locally. And as the market for farm produce vanished with the rising tide of depression in the east,
the hide business became almost the only one left, that and
the cattle that came up the trail. Because the longhorns were
suddenly worth very little, they were spread over the new
ranches along the creeping settlements, to be held for higher
prices—one more argument for clearing the ranges of the
dark herds that ate the grass, that drew the cattle to follow
along the wild buffalo trails into the wilderness, and not return. The feeling against any interference in buffalo hunting ran higher than ever, particularly locally against the
expulsion of hunters from Indian Territory and the immediate vicinity of agencies elsewhere. Officials who tried to en-
force such laws and treaty agreements were threatened with
mob violence, with tar and feathering and a necktie party.
In his annual report of 1873, the Secretary of the Interior
mentioned the complaints against the hide men but believed
that the end of the buffalo would bring the Indian to a sense
of the need to work. Some pointed out that the secretary was
a job-holder in an extermination administration. Still no one
but the Indian really balked. He looked upon the buffaloes
on his treaty grounds as his cattle, and the hunters as thieves,
rustlers, to be shot down as the white man shot rustlers down.

During the winter of 1872 the center of the great
herd of the Arkansas was west of Ft. Dodge, although many

still ranged east towards Wichita, the headquarters for a great many of the new hunters. This herd had once summered up towards the U. P. in Nebraska, but there was a swarm of hunters out in that region as early as seven, eight years ago, with the roar of their guns and the pursuing smell, pursuing insatiably. They were not like the Indian, who stopped to feast, to cure his meat and robes, to dance his successful hunt and make his ceremonials, to chase after horses, to loaf, make love and war. The white hunter was always there in the herds like a dreadful sickness, with its terrifying stink and death.

Slowly the buffaloes had begun to veer off westward from this northeastern encroachment, the Arkansas herd sometimes reaching almost to the summer foothills of the Rockies, scattered thin over more arid land. They went farther south than the Arkansas tributaries in the winter too, now, sometimes clear into the Panhandle and towards New Mexico. And when they returned to the river in the spring, they found a line of hunting camps waiting to shoot the thirsty buffaloes, shooting night and day.

Before the railroad tracks pushed out as far west as Ft. Dodge several traders had set up business at the post. Charlie Rath was paying two twenty-five a hide for the great fine loads that Mooar and his outfit brought in. Another hunter with an eye for trade was Emanuel Dubbs. A fire had swept away his little fortune last year and with his wife he moved west to Kansas on a grading contract for the Santa Fe railroad. What amounted to a western initiation was the battle he saw at Newton, Kansas, between the cowboys of the cattle trail and the track crews, with seventeen men left dead in the dust of the street as the wounded were carried away.

In June, while taking a long ride up the Arkansas with a couple of contractors, Dubbs was caught in admiration for the river, the broad stream, shallow and limpid, flowing through the wide valley, with the pleasant islands, the cotton-

wood groves, and buffaloes scattered along the bottoms like
dark browsing cattle, feeding, sleeping, the calves romping
and playful. He tried to run a buffalo with his riding mule
and was thrown, the earth hard as stone as he hit it.

But Emanuel Dubbs liked the country so much he
turned to hide hunting for his new start. He camped openly
south of the Arkansas on Bluff Creek, flowing towards the
Cimarron, and was a new kind of hunter to the region, one
who saved the hump, the hams and even the horns along with
the hide. He sugar-cured the meat carefully by an old recipe,
and contracted to ship it in carload lots to a Kansas City
wholesaler. Dubbs was a thoughtful, judicious man and he
considered hunting for hides alone wasteful, perhaps actually sinful. It took a while in the country before he realized
how many buffaloes were shot for perhaps the tongues alone,
the fine tongues whose blackness distinguished them as a
superior delicacy over the red of ordinary domestic cattle.
They brought around twenty-five cents each, a little more
if particularly well cured for the fancy trade, and they
made a money load in less time and bulk than the awkward,
often slow-drying flint hides. Although there was too much
danger in these Indian hunting grounds south of the river
for most men who knew Indians, a newcomer like Dubbs
could easily take a risk he didn't understand. A few more
newcomers followed him, but after several were left face
down in the grass, the crown of their heads perhaps naked,
most of the rest hurried back across the river.

The hunting north of the Arkansas was mostly taken
up by substantial business-like outfits now, men who guarded
against every danger possible. Billy Dixon had moved his
men from Hackberry Creek up to the Saline and the Solomon, encountering small bands of Indians. Generally they
were passing through, going north or south, supposedly
friendly, but always due for a close watch. Now and then
Billy heard about some hunter killed, or with a narrow escape, perhaps after taking an arrogant or terrified shot at

visiting Indians or a party passing by. Billy gave strict orders
that none of his men were to take such pot shots or to trouble
the Indians in any way so long as they didn't interfere with
the hunters. Sometimes a small party came to the camp, always hungry, and these he fed. They liked coffee with a lot
of sugar and were willing to trade anything they had for it.
The Kiowas, particularly, loved the sugar.

It was the year of the mad skunks. In addition to the
Indians and in summer the tarantulas, rattlesnakes and an
occasional copperhead in the south, there were the skunks
to watch too now, skunks that came out boldly in daylight.
The men might be attacked as they crept up on a herd or
pegged out the hides, while they sat around the big supper
frying pan sopping their sore-finger bread into the gravy or
while asleep, even up in the wagons. Usually the skunks were
harmless, even sociable creatures, moving in under corn cribs
or under houses in the settlements. They were always hanging around the buffalo camps like stray dogs, eating the beetles around the hide piles, showing up for the supper bones,
perhaps a mother marching in out of the dusk with a row
of the striped little kittens following, hoping not to be driven
away with thrown firebrands or a splash of hot grease.

But now suddenly the neat black and white, plume-
tailed animals were ragged and drooling as they came charging in, snapping at everything, the small teeth sharp and
deadly. Colonel Dodge, on a scout up the Arkansas near the
old Santa Fe crossing, was awakened by a commotion in
the servant's tent next to his. When the noise died down the
pungent smell of skunk crept through the camp. Evidently
someone had disturbed a garbage raider. In the morning
one of the men had his hand bandaged. A skunk had come
into the tent and grabbed his hand, he said. The ball of
the thumb was torn and lacerated where the prowler had
hung on until he was clubbed to death and then pried loose.

There was no caustic except fire in camp, and after

so many hours Dodge decided that such extreme measures would probably be more disturbing mentally to the man than physically efficacious. Instead, the colonel hid his concern and had the wound treated like an ordinary injury: washed thoroughly with castile soap, the mangled flesh cut off and the wound packed in water dressing. Soon it was healed but Dodge was still uneasy. Often these bites healed very readily and then were followed by hydrophobia months later. This case, however, turned out to be the only non-fatal skunk bite that Dodge heard about in all the Arkansas River region while he was there, although in Texas and up north along the Platte he had known of many men bitten without a serious consequence.

A few weeks after the soldier had his thumb lacerated a trader was bitten near Ft. Dodge. The man got his revenge by emptying his pistol into the miserable little skunk before he had the wound cauterized. He got the best care possible but he died of hydrophobia anyway. And those who carried madstones did no better, not even with the rare, egg-shaped stones said to come from the stomach of a white deer or white cow. It was said that the stone clung like a leech to the wound for hours if the bite was infected, and when removed, would turn milk a bilious green. With milk seldom available, warm water generally had to do, although one hunter killed a dozen wet buffalo cows to milk their bags, as Indians did for newborn babies who lost their mothers. But even with this buffalo milk to cleanse the madstone the man died. Hair balls from the stomachs of buffaloes were sought out in long-dead carcasses, and also proved useless. The believers in the madstones insisted that they failed because they had not come from white buffaloes, probably true, for the albino was a rare and sacred animal to the Indian, and sought out.

There were sixteen fatal cases of hydrophobia in the region and of the eleven up around Ft. Hays that came under the observation of the post surgeon, all but one were fatal.

For a while there was a sort of panic among the hunters and freighters. A hunter with a little knowledge of Latin camped out on a sandbar of the Arkansas, surrounded by water. In the night his cheek was torn. He tried to cauterize the wound, using a still pool as a mirror to direct the hot iron, and then rode as hard as he could for Ft. Dodge, but he died too, after his cheek had healed with no scar that his beard wouldn't cover.

All this time parties of men went out to kill the skunks, scouring the prairie around the towns and posts, the brush patches and the breaks, but the country was so large and wild and the bitten dogs had to be destroyed too. Indians trading at Ft. Dodge told of times when mad wolves came right into the lodges, wolves from whose bite no one ever recovered. Old hunters tried spreading poison, dubiously, saying they would probably kill mostly wolves and coyotes, the summer hides worthless. And dogs too. Finally the skunks disappeared, a dead one found here and there, perhaps no more than skin and bones, some of them right up around buildings or in the buffalo camps.

Along in the spring a number of hunting parties had ventured into the Texas Panhandle and south, toward the Canadian River. But the Indians, particularly the fierce Comanches and the Kiowas, were ready and gave them a running fight every day, despite the troops in the field down there. So the hunters retired to the Arkansas, swung around up the river and approached the southern buffalo ranges from the west. But it was too long a haul for profit and was given up, all except from below, the hides sold at Fort Worth, which had a thriving buffalo business ever since the war, when leather for the marching grey troops was a pressing need.

There were more hunters making meat up in the Republican region now. Youngblood still saved much of all he shot. Near Sappa Creek he ran into Shadler and a partner,

traders for whom he hunted a while, averaging eight buffaloes a day, for which they paid him fifty dollars for the hides
and the well-handled meat. This took longer but with the
thinning herds a man could still send money home as Youngblood did, put aside something towards a ranch when the
buffalo grass was clear. Or to buck the tiger in some hide
town.

Lonesome Charley Reynolds had drifted back up the
Missouri after the royal hunt, scouting for the army engineers running a railroad survey up the Yellowstone, where
there were great herds of buffaloes waiting for cheap transportation. This was pure Indian country, where no white
man could legally go, but while there were a few little raids
against the escorting troops, most of the Indians were busy
with their hunts, usually by arrow, and making robes.

In the meantime Bill Cody had taken up James Gordon Bennett's invitation to visit New York. There the long-
haired buffalo hunter watched a play with Studley acting
the part of "Buffalo Bill Cody, the Beau Ideal of the Plains."
Afterwards Bill was called upon for a speech. But he was
an outdoor man without much education and with no experience in oratory. Besides he had celebrated a little. The
speech was a failure, but the incident awoke the talented
showman asleep under the fancy trappings of the border
dude. It changed Cody's life. He would not make a failure
of the show business, as Hickok had with his six buffaloes
and a handful of hungry Comanches.

At Chicago, where Sheridan had taken him, ostensibly
to judge some horses, Cody met Ned Buntline again. The
New York publicity man talked about Wild Bill Hickok's attempt at a buffalo show. What such a venture needed was
a manager who knew the ropes and had an eye for publicity, to work with a good flashy frontier character—namely
Ned Buntline and Buffalo Bill Cody. But it would take
money.

Wild Bill was back hunting buffaloes again. His un-

easy camp was near the forks of the Republican where he
had to watch out for the Cheyennes and the Sioux. From
Hays he had gone to Kansas City, but after a little trouble
in a saloon there in mid-August he went to Cheyenne for a
couple of weeks, and, out of money, returned to the Republican, always the hide hunter when he was flat.

An eastern newspaperman wrote a story about the less
profitable but more picturesque hunting of a man called
Buffalo Jones. Charley Jones had filed on free land up the
river from Ft. Dodge, put in his sod corn and gone out for
hides. He drifted north from the Arkansas with the herd,
keeping near the head of it so in a run or a stampede the
movement would be towards him instead of away. At each
creek he got two, three days of hunting before the buffaloes
started to string out over another dry tableland. He left
his hides pegged down to dry and moved his wagon ahead
of the herd to the next water, clear up to the Nebraska line
before they turned back. By then he was taking some of the
calves alive, roping them from a good buffalo horse. He got
a dozen and sold them for seven-fifty each and glad to get
it, with the hide market falling fast as the depression spread.

The summer of 1872 had been wet, with the grass
heavy, even the local buffalo grasses sending their seed-
stems higher from the short, tight-curled mat. Then the hot
dusty winds of August had dried out everything, followed
by a fine blue haze of fall over the prairie. The cottonwoods,
the ash, boxelder and the willows stood tall and golden in
the thin air, with the red of the creepers like patches of buffalo blood along the brush. Then one evening late in October
the gentle wind from the southwest that was tolling the
buffaloes back toward the warmer country increased to a
gale.

Far off in the dark Buffalo Jones and the other hunters
could see a red reflection on the clouds. They paid little attention to it except to admire the fine color. But the next

morning the sun rose red in smoke, the air stifling, and by
night the whole sky was a lurid orange, from the east
around the entire south and far into the west, the whole
horizon a burning red. The hunters drew together in groups,
and in the little stations and settlements no one slept except
the children. The second morning all the prairie remained
dark as dusky night, with only an occasional rift in the black
clouds of smoke, the sun a thin disk, cherry red as from a
forge, but without light.

The few settlers were out breaking fireguards, but
the earth was dry and iron-hard, and the wind so powerful
that no one dared start a backfire that could outrun any
horse. The hunters still out tried to flee to any barren,
gravelly breaks, for none of the fall streams were wide
enough for protection with the bottoms long-grassed and dry
as tinder. The air filled with flying ashes and around noon
the roaring of the fire was like a racing express train. Buffaloes thundered past, antelope ran panting, and deer
bounded over washouts and gullies until their sharp hoofs
fell short and they went down, exhausted. Wolves with their
tails between their legs stopped to look back on the ridges
and fled on, bewildered, perhaps finally to slink under the
wagon of some hunter, or into some creekbottom mudhole
with rabbits and skunks and a dozen other small creatures
who had no burrows, all cowering together. Then more
buffaloes came, from farther off, exhausted too, their black
tongues hanging out a foot. Cottontails crept into any shelter,
even between a standing man's feet as the ashes sifted over
everything, and smoke burned the blinding eyes, choked the
lungs.

Men caught out on the prairie covered their heads
with coats or robes and tried to cling to their plunging horses,
keep their wild tossing heads covered too, as the fire roared
over a rise and perhaps past. And all the while the smoke
rolled high overhead on the bending wind.

Then the air was suddenly cleaner, brisk instead of

burning, with only little streaks of blue smoke blowing along the ground from the buffalo chips and clumps of bunch-grass and brush left smoldering on the black prairie. The hunters hurrying to find grass for their horses saw buffaloes piled in draws and canyons, broken and burnt, dead and still dying, and antelope scattered over the prairie, now and then one with the hoofs roasted off from running over burning grass, but perhaps still alive, the soft eyes like a stricken woman's.

Many of the older buffalo hunters who were far out had risked setting their own little fires, letting them run, and then retreating to the cooling black swath that had spread and raced over the prairie as killing as any blaze. Buffalo Jones, who got his small herd of captured buffalo calves home safely, always had his matches handy to set a backfire, but there were many tenderfeet in the path of the great wind-driven blaze, greenhorns to the prairie trying to hunt buffalo, and many new settlers too. Several times the next year word came of someone found dead, clothing burned off, perhaps a wagon charred to the iron, or even two. Usually the newspapers blamed it on Indian depredations, but those long in the region knew what had probably happened.

Although the Indians of the agencies along the Platte River still had their hunting rights on the Republican, the government's hand was becoming very firm. More and more the hunts were restricted to entire bands, with an acting agent along and perhaps a dozen other white men, and troops always close by. This year Grinnell, who had worked on the buffalo count, went out with the Pawnees on their fall hunt. In a single great surround the eight hundred Indians got a thousand buffaloes in one day. They went back to their earth villages loaded with meat and robes and many fine stories of exploits with bow and gun. There were plenty buffaloes left for everybody.

The old hide hunters with their heavy, long-range

rifles, men like Wild Bill, Charley Reynolds and California Joe, were feared and hated by the Indians, but such friendly Sioux chiefs as Spotted Tail and Whistler often stopped at their camps, partly to shed a kind of protection from wilder young warriors, to keep them from attacking the camps and getting hurt or, worse, bringing trouble upon the Indian women and children. It would be foolish when there were so few things that they could get from the buffalo camps— a little powder, but not much when divided among hundreds of men who owned a gun or perhaps a share in one. Sometimes there might be a little sugar and coffee too, but not enough to risk the bullets from good and far-shooting guns like those of the hunters, or to bring armies marching against them as happened to the Cheyennes twice in four years. This must not be done to the Sioux. They made no depredations against the settlers, harmed no women and children, and hoped to keep their own families as safe.

It was true that chiefs like old Whistler went to the buffalo camps for more than to show their friendship before the warriors. They went for a little coffee too, and perhaps a plug of the sweet tobacco to shave into their pipes with the fragrant willow and kinnikinnic. Whistler had known Wild Bill several years before the time he saved Bill from his angry young warriors, back when the young men still thought that these whites could be driven out, the whites who controlled the guns and the powder that the Indian must buy.

The fall of 1872 Hickok was hunting with Newt Moreland not far from several other camps, including that of California Joe, Bill Street and Yamo, the big, jovial story-telling preacher who cramped the speech and the jug-passing propensities of no one. Wild Bill's camp was near Whistler and his band. The Indians were hunting peacefully, with an agency representative along to see that no whites were harmed. One winter day the chief stopped in from a visit to Spotted Tail. He had a nephew along and one of his sub-chiefs, just the three men—not enough to make the hunters uneasy, he knew. So they rode over to Hickok's camp for a friendly *Hou!* and perhaps a little to eat besides the pounded meat they carried. Because Whistler had been to a tribal council he rode his spotted ceremonial horse, his chief's horse, and carried the fine blanket he was given in Washington in the spring.

But as the Indians approached, just the three men, the hunters ran towards their tent and wagon. Both of them were surly, even after Bill saw who it was, neither of the hunters laying down his gun although Whistler, as befitted his position, was unarmed and the others left their guns in the scabbards.

They made the signs of hunger and were given a little cold fried buffalo steak that they ate with their knife points, munching dry hardtack with it, while the two white men sat together at the other side of the fire, silent. Then Whistler spoke his few words for coffee, and when no one seemed to understand, he motioned towards the coffee pot of hospitality that had been filled very well for him the time he charged in to save Bill's camp and his life five years ago. But today the white men seemed unfriendly, perhaps not understanding, so the old Sioux arose and went to the pot and started to make the sign of pouring and of lifting the grub box lid, as for a tin cup perhaps, or for sugar. Swift as in a barroom brawl Wild Bill drew and shot Whistler down. The subchief, seeing the movement, tried to spring forward to protect his old friend and was killed by Moreland as Bill dropped the nephew. The three men died much as McCanles and the two with him died back in 1861, only easier, neater, for eleven years are a long time of learning.

No other Indians were around in sight, but Hickok and his partner realized that everybody of Whistler's village would know where the chief had been and could trail him here as easily as a greenhorn might follow the path of a prairie twister. The two hunters worked fast. Together they carried the bodies to a canyon west of camp and covered

them with trash and weeds. The ground was frozen and there
was no time to kill, with Whistler's band near and Spotted
Tail and all his warriors not much farther. The white men
in the region must be warned to get out before the frontier
burst into a flaming Sioux war.

The two hunters rode their horses and those of the
Indians in relays, spurring from one buffalo camp to another,
and stopping at every freight outfit, until wagons and riders
were streaming both north and south out of the Republican
region, heading for the railroad, the army posts and the settler sod stockades. Night and day they hurried, leaving their
spread of hides, even the great stacks of dried ones that were
ready for the haulers, sweeping the more exposed homesteaders along with them in their flight.

The next day the Indians came riding on Whistler's
tracks to the deserted camp and found the bodies. They carried them home in great mourning. Before the keening of
sorrow was well started, a war council sat in angry deliber-
ation. At first even the grieving and furious Spotted Tail approved a revenge party for his friend—a powerful party of
several hundred warriors to fan out against the settlers over
eastward beyond the Red Willow Creek region, where there
were many. There they would strike a hundred times, make
the heart good again in the flowing red blood, with fires
burning high and plunder sacks weighing heavy.

But by morning Old Spot had calmed, become once
more the judicious man he had learned to be. There were
many troops over that way, he knew, troops with not only
Bill Cody, but with Jack Stillwell along, a very good young
scout already famous before the Beecher Island fight. Jack
would find any village and none could hide the women and
children from him. Besides, even if they could all flee afterward, troops swarming like grasshoppers would surely follow
if any white women and children were hurt. The warring
would bring death to many good people, Indian and white,
and then there would still be the running, running for the

Sioux. And their good man Whistler shot by this Wild Bill who killed people like a mad wolf kills—this good man would not be brought back.

"Once the heart of our people had to be made good!" a young warrior taunted, in protest. "Spotted Tail has become afraid! He is remembering the time he was put into the white man's chains in the stone prison of Leavenworth!"

"Yes, we see he is afraid! It is time we had a new man, a strong one to lead us!" others roared out.

At this Spotted Tail admitted slowly that they spoke the truth. He was afraid, for he knew the power of the white man. That was why he was talking for peace now, talking against all the wind of their noise. And he would make them hear him if he must say it a hundred times. He spoke deliberately and quietly, making it last for hours, until it was too late to start that day, promising over and over that he would ask the White Father to catch this Wild Bill. Hang him up for this killing, in the way that the white man avenged himself.

"Hung up for shooting an Indian?" some of the Sioux shouted in derision. "Let us kill this man ourselves, then it will surely be done."

But the White Father had promised Spotted Tail that he would punish all who shot peaceful Indians. Yet if the young men here could find the two hunters who had brought down Whistler and the others, he, Spotted Tail, would not stand in their way.

With this permission, a big party of Sioux rode to seek out the two hunters. Old Spotted Tail watched them go, shouting after them once more that he would break the man who smoked his gun against any other whites. But by then the two hunters had gone far from the buffalo country. Moreland was seen riding the chief's spotted horse up in middle Nebraska, safely away from all the Sioux. Hickok had gone back to Cheyenne.

Some young men who had slipped away from Whis-

tler's camp for a little raiding were met by the troops set
between the Indians and the settlers on Red Willow Creek.
In a few days a runner came from the Indian agent. The
President was very angry that one of his great friends, the
chief Whistler, had been killed. He was sending an inspector
out and the murderer would surely be found and punished.

So not a shot was fired. But there was very little hide
hunting in the upper Republican region the rest of the fall
by anyone not well known to the friendly Indians. Wild
Bill, squinting over the dusky cards in his hand, felt the region of his free movement closing in around him like the
shadows of the saloon. First Illinois, then Missouri, the Abilene and Hays country, then anywhere that Sheridan, Custer
and the Seventh Cavalry might be, and now the southern
Sioux country too.

In a while Bill Cody came to Cheyenne with the
idea of a show, a wild west show, but with a manager, a
promoter who knew the business.

"What do you say—?" he asked, swinging off his hat
in the gesture he had been practicing before a full length mirror in a Denver house, shaking out his long curls, the smile on
his tawny face carrying the excited sweetness of an adventur-
ing boy.

Wild Bill hitched his holster around to an easier position and nodded. "Might as well, Bill," he said slowly.
"Our country is getting too damn small."

BOOK II

THE CROSSING OF THE
ARKANSAS

CHAPTER VI

DODGE CITY, THE DAUGHTER
OF THE HIDE MEN

WHILE the boom of the Big Fifty cut down the buffaloes in the Republican region, the Santa Fe was moving steadily up the Arkansas, another railroad following one of the great frontier highways that the east-flowing streams of the trans-Missouri country had long ago become. Charlie Myers set up a little trading post on the trail west of the Ft. Dodge military reservation, near a lone cottonwood that towered over the soddy of a government teamster and a collection of hide wagons. In 1872 a railroad construction gang pitched their tents not far away, and by August a little settlement called Buffalo City was started, in what was the heart of the great Arkansas herd, now the true heart of the buffalo country. By then Hoover, the wholesale liquor dealer, had his tent up, and a couple of the traders followed his lead by making liquor a side line, the bar perhaps a board or an iron-hard buffalo hide nailed over the top of short posts driven into the dirt floor. One evening two whisky wagons groaned to a stop. With their wheels sunk to the hubs, the hinged sides of each high wagon bed was dropped to make a little ramp to the bar under the lifted bows. Buffalo City was booming.

Dugouts and shacks came next, and town lots, perhaps

measured off with a lariat. The gamblers and the women had started to arrive with the first tent, some from the Kansas towns like Hays and Newton, left very quiet now that the frontier was moving on. Usually they came in the big bowed wagons that would do for business for themselves and their employers, their protectors, a while. One such outfit moved down from Hays with ten mule-drawn wagons, bringing all the equipment, the refreshments and the inmates for an establishment, two frock-coated gamblers, five, six girls and some roustabouts for the work. The owner sent a messenger ahead and so the hunters, freighters, soldiers and railroaders, and several of the gunmen from Hays too, went out from Buffalo City to meet the girls, to escort the wagon train into town.

They made a fine show as they came up the dusty street that was not quite two blocks long, between buildings that were mostly dugouts or half-and-half. Some of the wagon sheets had been rolled up to show the wares arriving, the barrels and the cases of bottles for the fancy trade, and then the girls of course, all dressed in their best, fans moving in the heat as they sang a gay little song, one of them picking a mandolin very sweetly. There was a fine display of calves too, as the girls clambered out over the wheels, holding their billowy skirts up away from the grease of the heavy hubs. They were led on a tour of Buffalo City by their employer. A whole bunch of dirty, bearded, gun-packing men pushed up around them as they went from one bar to the next, as many as possible crowding inside. It was considered very good for business, although hardly necessary in a town where there were only five other women, counting old Mexic' Mary doing business in a dugout that she made herself against the river bank.

Before the leaves in the brush patches began to yellow two of the new girls were dead, one from galloping consumption, the other from wolf poison she stole out of a hunter's pocket. By then Buffalo City had big pole and sod corrals piled full of hides waiting for the railroad, and great white ricks of buffalo bones that stretched almost a mile along the right-of-way. When the railroad came through, once more a mob, a really large one this time—hunters, troopers and railroaders—went out to welcome a new asset to the town. They pushed and crowded like buffaloes at a water hole down the track. They emptied their guns into the air and, setting a precedent for many later occurrences, shot the headlight out of the engine as it drew up, shattered the glass that had shone as bright as from a flame in the lowering western sun.

The men who started Buffalo City and tried to keep it orderly enough to do business, but not too orderly to sell whisky, were mostly old-timers, as old-timers went in this new country. Charlie Rath, a freighter and hunter, had learned to speak passable Cheyenne and Arapaho. He had been running a trading post at Ft. Dodge, five miles down the river, for trappers, buffalo hunters and Indians, particularly those from the region to the south. Rath's old friend Bob Wright, an early freighter too, was sutler at the fort and scouted for the Seventh Cavalry under General Sully the summer and fall of 1868. He hunted buffaloes too, but in the old way, preferring to ride up alongside with a sixshooter, bringing them down on the run, to rock the earth in rising dust. He had killed many from the corral walls at the post, to keep them from rubbing the place down when the great herds passed, and he knew their ways.

Charlie Myers moved his trading post up from Ft. Dodge, and the Mooar brothers and others came to settle, until at least a dozen traders and old hide hunters were set up at the young town. There was no government, no law except the sixshooter, the buffalo gun and the long knife. Some kept an old fuke heavy with buckshot or ball around the hide yard, under the counter or behind the bar as a sort of riot gun. Old-timers were a little contemptuous of the pistoleers, whether they packed their guns butt pointing back, or forward in the army crossdraw.

"Ain't no peacemaker like a load of buckshot in the belly," one of Rath's hands agreed. Still, you couldn't imagine Wild Bill Hickok or Buffalo Bill Brooks with a sawed-off shotgun for dress wear, although Hickok had used one as a trouble soother when he was marshal.

Representatives of the large hide companies at Leavenworth, St. Louis and New York were sent out to sleep a few nights in the dugouts and to drink their forty rod out of tin cups while they sized up this new bonanza. It was true that the plains were overrun by more hunters than ever, with a larger percent of eastern city greenhorns, real tenderfeet. But they were wasteful of buffaloes, let too many wounded animals get away to die, and spoiled more hides in the skinning and drying, particularly those lost to maggots and beetles in the warmer climate, which demanded much more vermin poison.

In spite of the growing unemployment in the east and the longer ride between free drinks almost everywhere, many of the newcomers still seemed to be plain Hard Cases, lawless, violent men, contemptuous of work, drawn to the frontier because there was no law beyond the fast draw and the ambush, whether for profit or revenge. Mistaking the conspicuous Bad Men of the saloons and gambling dens as representative of the region, the newcomers robbed, shot, killed and were killed.

Yet right from the start the backbone of the hide business was the percentage of responsible, industrious men bred by every frontier, men whose temper was slow, and their word better than any bond. They were trying to work out fair rules for the hunting, including the division of the ownerless buffalo ranges. By this time the chief shooter was the undisputed head of a party, even if the outfit was an informal one of four, five hunters working together. They camped where he pointed, moved when he moved. To the discoverer of a herd belonged prior occupancy rights. The later hunters could choose the best positions left but always without interference with the shooting and the supply of camp water of those already located.

Not that the hide men were dudes in conduct any more than in appearances. Usually shaggy and bearded, their clothing stiff with dried blood and tallow, their talk was also rough and loud, from perhaps weeks and months almost alone or from yelling against the wind. Sometimes they scratched a shoulder with one hand and a leg with the other while they rubbed a side with an elbow, easing the buffalo mange or interrupting the linebacks, the bed rabbits that could have been cleared out by laying their sleeping robes on an ant hill some warm day, as the Indian women did. While the hunter scratched he might be telling all who would listen how he had crawled up on a bunch yesterday and killed at least forty or sixty or a hundred at a stand, and ended up by hamstringing an old bull with his skinning knife.

Many of the newcomers hanging around to listen were young sprouts, sixteen, eighteen, seldom twenty. Usually they were drawn away from the hard-working hunters to the more romantic figures in frock coats and checkered vests, living by their nimble fingers, or to the surly, dark-minded men already known as killers. Some of these youths would end up slumped to the sawdust in a frontier bar or swinging from a cottonwood before they discovered how little differ- ence there was in the acceptable conduct of say, Bedford, Memphis or Troy, or even Pleasant Center, and this place called Buffalo City.

Four years ago Billy Dixon had freighted for Custer's expedition to the Washita and the Panhandle country, the winter of 'Sixty-eight and nine, and often at night since, he thought of the great herds he saw down there on the Indian hunting grounds, the buffalo, so tame they had to be driven aside with hoots and yells at nooning time, unafraid of the smell of man, almost undisturbed by the boom and stink of the big guns. Finally Billy got his five-man crew talked into chancing it down there across the river. Even Cranky McCabe, who was always blowing up and quitting as these lone men of the frontier often did—even he was going. As always he had taken his pay to the card tables and, pockets empty, had returned, smiling, no longer on the prod.

With his reliable, experienced outfit and the best of guns and ammunition, Billy went up the Arkansas River, thoughtfully out of sight of the troops, and crossed into what was still legally forbidden territory. The Indians were becoming more and more hostile the last two years, insisting that the whites must observe the Medicine Lodge treaty. If not, the Indian would soon face starvation and before that they would drive out the hunters themselves. The Arkansas was still patrolled now and then, but the soldiers were very few, the vigilance lax, and Mooar and others recalled Dodge's remark that if he wanted buffaloes he would go where they were. That was increasingly south of the river.

Once across, Billy stopped to cut and stack a lot of the long grass for hay so they need not turn their stock out to graze and risk the Indians sweeping them away. There was so much Indian sign, with some warning shots from war parties as they passed. Billy decided to turn back. He wanted to take one good look around before he had to give up entirely. He took one of the men, and well mounted, with a skinner following in a light wagon, they started southward, knowing they must keep on the move but hoping they could stay long enough to get the feel of the country and locate some good buffalo grounds for the future. At Crooked Creek they ran square into the Indians. They skirmished a while, shouting friendly greeting to them between shots over each other's heads, but evidently none of the party understood English. The chief just kept motioning Billy back northward, back across the river. He was an old man with a long brilliant feather fastened under the skin of his left cheek and all his warriors were painted in red and yellow and ochre patterns. Billy withdrew.

But young Billy Dixon was not the man to be driven out by just a few motions of a hand. He swung around and headed south again until they struck more hostiles, and knew from the sign that the country was crawling with Indians, and so the hunters decided to head back for camp in the dark, get out while they could. But Billy miscalculated by about three miles and they had to bed down in hostile country, three men alone. They were up at every squeak or stir all night, and next day Billy called his hunters in. They would have to kill more time standing off the Indians than they did hunting if they wanted to keep alive. But then suddenly the buffaloes came, trailing in by the thousands, so Billy decided to try it two, three more days, load up with all the hides they could get and hit for the river, laying on the whip. They were so successful that a week slipped by and a half of another, with hides still pegged all around the camp, most of them too green to haul and too heavy. Then they ran out of meat. Dixon rode out to a small bunch of buffaloes grazing about two miles off, mostly young stock. He found them restless, ready to run at anything as if the Indians had just been chasing them, probably roiled up for hours, even days.

Getting as close as possible, Billy dismounted and began his crawling. He picked a young bull and fired the Big Fifty. The herd stampeded at the first shot, raising a thick dust. He fired as rapidly as he could into the blurred, flying mass and brought down several more before they were out of range.

This rapid firing alarmed the men at camp. A herd of about fifty antelope came up on a ridge half a mile off, stirred up, running in swift, wide circles like Indians do to signal that an enemy has been seen. Then they dashed to the top of the hill again and stood there, rigid, gazing off towards where

Dixon had been firing. Billy's men were so excited they took these antelope for mounted Indians, certain that Billy had been shot and scalped, with the camp next for attack.

Planning to make a run for the river if possible, they rounded up the horses, got the camp equipment loaded and were ready to pull out. While one of the men argued that it was wrong to leave without getting Billy's body, at least knowing if he was really dead, Cranky McCabe loaded a few more shells, so nervous the primer rattled in his hands. But he was ready to fight the whole camp over the joshing he took when Billy came riding in a few minutes later with his scalp still on and meat across the back of his horse. Once more McCabe quit, but this time he didn't strike out across the country alone.

When they got back to Buffalo City, they found the first real buildings going up where only dugouts and tents and a few shacks had been. The hotel was open, and as a special treat Billy took his outfit to the one big room for dinner. It turned out to be salt pork with beans and black coffee with bread and pepper sauce on the side—seventy-five cents each. They could beat that a mile any day at camp. But the hides brought two-fifty to four dollars, the most they ever got, a total of one thousand, nine hundred and seventy-five dollars. Billy received a check for a round two thousand, the twenty-five dollars difference too inconsequential to bother with an uneven figure in this booming new city of the hide men.

But the lusty little town didn't last long, not as Buffalo City. The government rejected the name for the post office because there was already one Buffalo in Kansas, and a Buffalo City. Instead, the department substituted the name of the fort down the river and called the post office Dodge City. The hunters drowned their sorrow in one wild evening and then swore unswerving loyalty to this daughter of the buffalo plains whatever her name. And she was still a dutiful daughter. Even with hard times rising high as a thunderhead in the east, whose hail and lightning would certainly shake the prairies, the hunters were doing well. To be sure the railroad creeping westward from the new Dodge had a hard time raising the money to pay the track layers but if they didn't reach the west border of Kansas by the end of 1872 they would lose the federal land grant, the great subsidy of free land from the government. Although hides were going down, the hunters still averaged around one hundred dollars a day in the Great Slaughter Pen, as the region was now called, and some did much better since the winter was bringing the buffaloes back to the river into tight little cold-weather bunches, slower and tamer as the snow deepened. Rath and Wright shipped over two hundred thousand hides out of the town this first fall and winter, and two hundred cars of hindquarters, mostly frozen, with two carloads of tongues. The other traders handled at least as many hides.

This was a lot of loose money in a new town in unorganized territory, without court or sheriff or law. A secret vigilance committee was organized by the better, the more responsible men, and all Hard Cases and troublemakers were warned to leave town. Unfortunately the vigilantes weren't gunmen and to back up such orders, they had to take in a few known killers who wore 'em low, just a few. Immediately these gun toters took over the town, and the young daughter of the buffalo hunters became the sweetheart of the Bad Men before she grew into pigtails.

Although the town was known as Dodge to everybody now, the business was still buffalo. One herd of cattle had come in during the early days. A nineteen-year-old youth with a trail crew of eight men had driven the two thousand cattle up from Texas. Fearing the Indians of both the Territory and the Panhandle he swung around west up through New Mexico and down the Arkansas. But there were no loading pens at the new station and he had to take the herd down to Great Bend. There would be loading facilities at Dodge before next season, if the cattlemen had to build them, provided that the Santa Fe didn't go broke and let the rails turn to rust, become sun-warmed roosting places for grasshoppers and rattlesnakes.

The railroad made it to the state line and then stopped. New Year's Day, 1873, found a great knot of out-of-work trackmen moving into the Dodge region, the entire road gang of immigrant Irish, Swedes and Germans, and many veterans of both the Union and the Confederate side. Every one of them who could rustle up a team and wagon, or a partnership in an outfit, started after buffaloes. The noise of the guns could be heard in every direction, booming and thundering hour after hour, like another Gettysburg. A line of camps was set up along the river from Dodge City to Granada, Colorado. One saloonkeeper from Dodge kept several outfits going with so much profit that a few more such winters would have qualified him for the highest social and political honors of the state, some Kansans complained sourly. His trade included the Indians too; a gallon of watered whisky was worth a pony or five Indian-dressed buffalo robes. Buffalo hunters in the region regarded a keg or two as a necessary part of their outfit, adding to the number of hides their outfit made and all they could get illegally in trade from the Indians. It did bring friendliness towards the hunter who had the whisky but endangered all the other whites. Drunken warriors were a particular menace to the emigrants on the trails. Not that responsible Indians were more drunken than the whites, men long in the region had never seen a drunken Indian woman, but a bad Indian roaring with firewater was a very bad Indian.

There were rumors of depredations up north lately. There was a newspaper report that the famous hunter, Ame Cole, with a couple of others, was standing off a pack of Indians somewhere in a draw near the Nebraska line. An army supply train was plundered, the captain shot, and the Royal Buck surveying party wiped out. But the dead came in, captain and all, surprised to hear the news. Buffalo Jones, bringing in a load of meat from that region, said the only Indians he saw were four Sioux looking for Pawnees. It was all a complete canard, perhaps started by unscrupulous hunters who wanted to turn back a new enemy, the settlers moving into the shrinking buffalo ranges with gun and plow.

Down on the Arkansas it was estimated that about seventy-five thousand buffaloes were killed within sixty, seventy miles of Dodge before the town saw the green of its first springtime and the warming sun came to bring a stench that no amount of scent in the lace handkerchiefs of the town's girls could dispel. Then the spring that brought a roar of wind strong enough to raise a dust storm was suddenly gone. Even the elk had been fooled. The great herd of them that centered between Camp Supply and Dodge usually stayed in the deeper southern canyons until all danger of blizzards was past. They were already up as far as the low breaks of Crooked Creek, the deer out in the buckbrush of the flats, the geese gone north. The buffaloes too had started to move early, many across the Arkansas and to the wide tablelands that few of the green hunters had even seen. Then the Easter blizzard of 1873 struck.

Billy Dixon had swung his outfit around to Pawnee Fork, changing camp often as the buffaloes scattered, until he was back to Silver Lake, out on a bare open plain. There was another camp near, and both were caught without wood and with very few buffalo chips.

The storm started with a grey drizzling rain that soaked everything, changed to sleet and then to fine, sharp snow, driven by a wind that roared out of the bare northwest. The horses had to be doubletied to keep them from breaking away with the storm. The buffalo hides they fastened from wagon to wagon to give the horses a little shelter ripped loose. Their flapping scared the horses more, enough to break their hitch ropes. The heavy wagons were tipped over, and, loose now, both the hides and the horses were gone into the storm, almost as swiftly as the fires of the camp stoves had been sucked out and lost, and the flaring smoky light of the kerosene lanterns.

The tents had blown away with the first blasts of the storm, and the temperature dropped so it burned the breast even under the canvas of the upset wagons. The men worked hard to secure extra robes over the bows and fasten them with hurried strips of rawhide. Billy and his men crawled into the pile of bed robes together and shivered with the rock of the wagon, their heads covered so they did not see the lightning flash pearly white through the snow. Although they were hungry, nobody tried to dig around for anything to eat. Most of their grub had blown away with the cook tent out into the drifts of the prairie.

Finally the wind dropped, the sun came out and the men crawled from under the robes to stand together on the hard drifts, their heads in the cloud of their breath. They looked over the gleaming white of the plain, empty of everything except the frozen lake, and the drifted wagons like small snow-covered knolls. Not a horse was in sight anywhere. They were afoot, without fuel, and the temperature far below zero and still falling. But they got through the night with the tiny Indian fires of tallow that Billy had learned to make.

The next day they struck out early to hunt their stock, following an occasional frozen track on a wind-swept knoll which led to a roadranch twelve miles south. They stayed in the dugout there, with the gathering of buffalo hunters out of the storm, until the snow thawed enough to get their wagons. They told stories and played cards, poker, and black jack mostly, with pitch for those with Methodist feet. They wrestled and shot target, Billy Dixon admittedly one of the best with the rifle, although a three-hundred-pound blacksmith formerly with the track crew talked a real bull's eye; never missed, he said. But he didn't prove it.

Finally, in disgust, the hunters tried to push a rifle

into his hands. "Put up or shut up!" one said, the others standing around to see that it was done.

But instead of firing the man drew back like a bronch from a cold bit, and all the fat of him shook. "Don't make me touch it," he begged. "I been marked! My maw was scart by a gun what blowed up in my pappy's face—"

Gradually news of less fortunate men caught in the blizzard came in. One man was found face down across the railroad tracks, frozen to a rail, and Johnny Riney, one of the first settlers in Dodge, had lost both feet. All the hospital space at Ft. Dodge was full of the frost-bitten, with around seventy major amputations performed on civilians by the post surgeon. There was one tub case that everybody stopped in to see, staring at the poor greenhorn as at some circus freak— a man with both arms and legs cut off, leaving only short stubs, like some rugged old cottonwood stump left to weather on the prairie, roots and top all lopped away. At least a hundred men died, mostly hunters but some settlers too. Newcomers with covered wagons had scarcely an animal left to them if they themselves survived. Ox teams, some as large as sixty, seventy head, drifted and died in the snowbanks, perhaps not even the heads out.

When the sun warmed and the drifts began their busy little spring songs in the spreading fans of water, the hunters pulled out for the ranges again. But not even Billy Dixon could find enough buffaloes, although he traveled in a northern circle of almost two hundred miles, going as far west as Sand Creek, where Chivington had massacred the Cheyennes almost nine years ago, their bones still scattered over the battleground, whitened and bleached. One of the hunters gathered up a wagon load of them, small and large, piling them into his hide rack. At least he would make that much out of the spring's work.

There had been new rumors of Indian trouble off in the Republican region. It seemed a couple of troopers from

McPherson with bob-tail discharges were killed by the Indians. The army patrol of the Republican valley was struck by a cloudburst that washed away twenty-six horses and six men. Only great bravery kept the number of dead this low, for the valley of their camp was suddenly a roaring river that swept everything away, tents, wagons, horses and all.

But the rumors were never of buffaloes any more, and so Billy Dixon's partner quit to go into the saloon business. Some of the other hunters left their outfits near Sand Creek and shagged off to Denver for a look at a real town, maybe do a little prospecting for gold. They found some other old hunters from the Republican region there, including Bill Cody. As usual Bill was talking big, but about show business —going to take a lot of buffaloes and Indians east, give New York a taste of the gen-u-ine west. Cody and Texas Jack, another hunter from McPherson, had been put on the stage by Buntline last winter and now the hunters heard Bill blowing about it around the saloons. "Old See-Me-Bill," they called him as he leaned elegantly on this bar or that one, considering his handsome new goatee and his beaded buckskin in the mirror behind the bar, as he recounted the events that Buntline had cooked up for their play. He told them as though they were true, had actually happened, and all to him.

"Aw, come off, Bill," one of the hunters yelled to him. "Remember me? I shot that old bull what was chasing you back to Hays, time you got your monicker Buffalo Bill."

The others laughed, but Cody and Hickok did make an ornamental pair in the fancy saloons, both in new buckskin, Cody's beaded, Hickok's fringed with red banding, their long curls over their shoulders. Cody had brought Hickok from Cheyenne. Now he was telling a fancy story of being attacked by fifteen, twenty Indians on the way. It was a great fight with much derring-do, and Indians bit the dust all around the two lone plainsmen.

"Just workin' up a little turn for that wild west show you been tellin' about?" an old prospector asked.

A couple of hide men in the Republican country a couple of years ago nodded to Buffalo Bill's story of the Indian attack. "Yeh, guess them Indians was some of old Whistler's outfit, tryin' to get Wild Bill's curly locks fer a little scalp dance, eh Jim?"

But Wild Bill no longer acknowledged the name of Jim, and he seemed not to hear when somebody said he saw the two Bills lead their horses out of a boxcar down at the tracks before their grand parade together up the main street of Denver, drawing a string of followers as they came. They had probably done what any sensible man would—rode the cushions down from Cheyenne.

Wild Bill didn't talk and drink big like Cody, like some handsome boy testifying to his fights with the devil for his mother's missionary society. Wild Bill found little satisfaction in loud and bragging words, and the general untidiness of the drunkard offended the pride that was like wild flesh growing in an old, old wound, the wild, proud flesh, which, when touched, brought the swift jump of the gun, the thud of the bullet.

But now the two Bills stood together under the glittering crystal chandelier of a Denver saloon. The evening was still young and for the present their credit was good. Unfortunately Bill Cody was robbed of two thousand dollars worth of jewelry at Larimer street where a man could expect this. But he had lost the diamond-set buffalo head pin from Duke Alexis, his favorite show piece.

It was just as well that Hickok kept out of the Republican country. The federal Indian inspector had been going around gathering evidence on the killing of Whistler, and sat in a long conference with the Indians at Sidney. There were many complaints against the encroaching whites, the buffalo hunters and railroads. The Sioux were told by their relatives up on the Yellowstone that Charley Reynolds had been seen up there with Custer, going along the Yellowstone with many other whites. They did not know that this was the survey for a railroad through the northern Indian country, but they were angry and suspicious.

The new head chief of Whistler's band said that the buffaloes here would not last more than the rest of the year, meaning the white man's 1873, and they hoped they could stay on the Republican unmolested until fall. There was nothing to eat up at their agency and here they had their sub-agent to see that no one harmed the whites, even though there were still some whose hearts were bad from the killing of their peace chief.

But the Sioux had said nothing about their traditional enemy, the Pawnees. Early in August the Pawnees came to hunt near the Sioux camps just above the Republican. There were not enough buffaloes left to divide with these enemies. And besides there were many old scores to settle, even with white men along. The Sioux struck the Pawnees and killed many of them at a place that was called Massacre Canyon afterward. The victory did not restore Whistler to them but this was one revenge that could not bring the soldiers falling upon their women and children. To be sure, there was much scolding talk from the whites afterward, talk like from a shrewish wife sitting in the lodge. But to this every Sioux had learned to close the ear.

This summer there was another story of a great buffalo shooting match like the one Bill Cody liked to tell to the tenderfeet, the one supposedly held over near Ft. Wallace in which he claimed he took the title away from Buffalo Bill Comstock. As the sod thickened on the grave of Comstock the story grew from its early planting by Ned Buntline. But the new hunting story was told about another man who grew his hair long since he hit the plains, about Doc Carver, shoot-

ing against Buffalo Curly, the Jack McCall of the many
names, down towards the Republican. It seems there was a
five hundred dollar purse, with many side bets and eight hundred spectators. Carver won, it was said, by shooting one
hundred and sixty buffaloes in sight of the whooping crowd
of whites and Indians. It wasn't for the shooting, although
Mrs. Raymond, the lady hide hunter, had taught Doc a lot
about running buffaloes. Curly was certainly the better shot,
just about as good as Wild Bill Hickok and some said better.
But with a cast in one eye and a broken nose, there was no
future in show business for him. The story of the hunt was
planned to build up the handsome Doc Carver as a daring,
reckless plainsman, Doc the come-lately but who looked the
part, towering over Wild Bill, Cody, Custer, Sheridan and
most of the others.

Before the town once called Buffalo City had reached
her first birthday she was known all over the nation for her
wildness and her violence. Men were killed in the saloons
and dance halls, in the street and on the prairie, twenty-five
that first year, shot or knifed in drunken brawling, in anger
or in robbery, or merely as bystanders. Afterward the body
was perhaps laid outside until burial was more convenient, or
in the heat of the south Kansas summer, put quickly away in
some draw or washout where the covering was easy. Some
protested that not all these twenty-five were *bona fide* killings, that this included at least two buffalo hunters frozen in
the blizzard and counting them was plainly to brag up the
wickedness of Dodge and as unsporting as branding mavericks
when there was marked stock to rustle.

William Brooks, another latter-day Buffalo Bill, one
who had been marshal of Newton back in the wild brawling
days, was appointed marshal of Dodge that first winter. Four
brothers tried to gang up on him, avenging the death of a
fifth over a card dispute up at Hays. Dubbs was in town with
two wagons of buffalo meat and happened to see the brothers

come looking for Brooks. He shouted a warning to the marshal and got a wild shot or two in his direction, which he returned, but shooting into the lenient sky of Dodge. Brooks took care of the four brothers. Standing in the plain light of a doorway he drew and killed two of the men and wounded the others so they died later. He got only a shoulder wound, but a girl in the room behind him was struck by a stray bullet.

Dubbs finished up his business and hit back across the river where everybody told him it was very dangerous.

From the start there had been roaring battles between the hide men and the railroad gangs that made them feel crowded. Sometimes the two threw in together against the troopers, particularly just after the paymaster had made his round and most of the post rode into town looking for redeye. The soldiers had been in the region first and said so in language that all understood but few liked, particularly not the southerners. Many of the troops were Negroes, Freedmen. A polite industrious Negro who had been the servant of Dodge, the commanding officer, ran a hack over the five miles between the post and town. Early in June while he was in town gathering up a list of purchases, some drunks drove his wagon off. He ran out to stop them. They shot, and he slipped down into the worn dust of the little street, a look of surprise on his broad, gentle face.

A trooper spurred to the post with the news and returned with a detachment of Negro soldiers led by three white officers. A rumor got out that they were coming with orders from Washington to burn the wild and lawless town off the face of the earth. It came straight from the telegraph office, someone said. The dispatcher had picked up the message.

"Then, by God, it must be true!" a buffalo hunter yelled, and ran for the big camp of hide men beside the town. The excitement spread like a prairie fire in an April wind, with much dust and galloping back and forth. Afterward it was told that Tom Nixon, a crack shot and one of the best of the hide men, got together forty of the hunters with their Big Fifties and met the troops at the edge of the military reservation. Anyway the soldiers never showed up at Dodge, only some officers with warrants for the killers, who couldn't be found.

General Dodge wired the governor and was told that until the county was fully organized he was authorized to hold, subject to orders of civil authorities, all persons notoriously guilty of violation of the criminal laws of Kansas. With this letter and enough cavalry to block the streets leading out of town, Dodge had a search made and not a buffalo hunter lifted a gun against it. The corpse was still there on the sidewalk under a buffalo hide. One of the murderers walked up boldly to the dead man and jerked the hide off. Pointing to the bullet hole, he said, "I shot him there!" bragging, big as a hero, some Wild Bill Hickok. But the other man hid in the icebox of Peacock's Long Branch saloon and was helped to escape during the night.

With falling farm prices, drouth and grasshoppers, the fringe settlements were so near starvation that the troops considerately went to the Republican to kill meat for the hungry families. But they found the great ranges almost bare. Even most of the older, the whitened bones were gone, picked up by settlers perhaps a hundred miles east, bone pickers whose experiences grew into a song that jolted along like a top-heavy bone rack hurrying over the old buffalo trails:

> Wagons pull in from the prairie dry,
> To ricks of bleaching bones piled high.
> Four dollars a ton—but not for Sed,
> A rattler was watching that buffalo head.
> One settler less to tear up sod
> And pray for rain from a deaf old God.

Some claimed there was a man named Sed, the one found dying near Sheridan, Kansas, his arm swollen to the shoulder, two small fang punctures in the wrist.

But the buffaloes weren't gone for good, the old-timers insisted. "One a these days they'll start comin' out along the breaks, heads down, gruntin' like they do, runnin'—"

And perhaps it was true. A little over a year ago a hunter called Kentuck had made a small fortune out of just such a situation. He had found only scattered buffaloes for months. Then, when he was camped on a small stream south of Ft. Wallace, the lead cows started to come in, traveling fast, noses to the ground, headed into the wind. Luckily he was camped under a little hill that split the herd, for in one day he was surrounded. The buffaloes were worn and hungry as from a long, long migration and they stopped right around him to rest and feed. He shot from one knoll, then another, day after day, never far enough so he had to move camp. Finally one morning every buffalo was suddenly gone but he had shot enough to raise his harvest of hides to ten thousand dollars for less than one year.

And over at Greeley, Colorado, a buffalo hide tannery was starting up, to be the largest ever built anywhere.

The last Hunters Jamboree of the Platte and the Republican, the one of the fall of 1872 and that winter, had left the prairies dotted with rotting buffaloes. Spring came and the redbud made a rosy smoke along the Kansas slopes. Clouds of white and orange butterflies hovered over what was usually the sharp metallic sweetness of the wild plums in snowy bloom, the perfume of the creamy chokecherry blossoms. But all the fragrance had been lost in the stink of the rotting, maggot-filled carcasses.

The spring of 1873 had seen even more hunters, at least two thousand hide men worth the name and spread far over the plains, the federal land surveyors reported. One party of sixteen had killed twenty-eight thousand buffaloes during the summer. The next session of Congress would hear about that.

In the meantime money was getting tight, dollars big as the wheels of a Murphy prairie wagon, and hide prices falling. Time to bring in everything fast. Single outfits with a string of nine-yoke ox teams, each team drawing a big lead wagon and two trailers, might bring in as many as four thousand hides in one haul. Some used racks big as those for hay and loaded the hides flat, and drawn down tight with chains or rawhide over the top. Others folded the hides down the middle and stacked them on wagon frames. A few rolled them in bundles like carpet and hauled them standing inside high sideboards. Sometimes the buyers went out upon the range but the first year in Dodge the hides were usually sold on the streets.

With no bank in Dodge, the buyers had to carry plenty of cash on hand. One of these was LeCompt, working for Lobenstein, the great Leavenworth hide dealer who hired nobody but Irishmen. LeCompt used to stand out on the street at Dodge, both overcoat pockets stuffed with greenbacks in rolls of different denominations, thousands of them, to buy hides. One afternoon Mooar's hide train rolled into Dodge looking for LeCompt. But that day some gamblers had tolled him over to the wrong side of the tracks where it was not safe to go at night. Mooar wouldn't sell to anyone else when LeCompt was in town, so he hunted around and found him at a poker table with four men, a big stack of chips in the pot. He had around one hundred dollars in chips, besides the pile of greenbacks at his elbow. Mooar didn't like the looks of the men so he walked up to LeCompt and acting pretty mad, whacked him on the shoulder and shouted, "By Godfrey, if you want them hides of mine, get out there and count them. I want my money and go home."

The buyer looked up and Mooar roared even louder that he wasn't waiting around. There was another man on the street with a pocket full of money, ready. LeCompt got up, folded his hand, left it beside the chips and the greenbacks and got away from that table. "By God, you saved my life right there," he said outside, patting the hard tight rolls of bills in his pockets, seldom less than ten, perhaps even thirty, forty thousand dollars. As soon as he sat in on the game he realized he had been framed, and prospects weren't good for getting out the door alive, so he played on, helpless until Mooar came along.

A buffalo hunter might be cleaned out in a few minutes by the sharpers that hung around town. It happened even to old Dirty Face, who, unlike the other hunters who usually washed up a little when they brought their hides in, never washed his face at all. He was known as saving and close, even stingy. He never gambled, never set up a drink, just stood around the back of the saloons in his dirty jeans, his feet wrapped in old hide and wire, warming himself on cold nights. But he did it once too often. With two thousand dollars in his pocket and a lot of hides to sell in the morning he let a black-curled little girl from across the Missouri talk him into taking one chance at the roulette table. He won, and a thaw of excitement began to creep into his little grey eyes. But his luck turned and he lost everything before morning, money, hides, wagon, rifle, everything except his horses. In disgust he sold them and left the country without taking time to sleep or wash his face.

But to strangers from the east the startling thing about Dodge was that with all the gamblers, tinhorns, roadagents, horse thieves and gunmen, not a door was ever locked. A man could lose his wad or his life any night or day but never have his pocket picked.

Many of the hunters and some traders too, considered the buffalo an eternal source of revenue, one that would replenish itself forever—not out of a hole in the earth as the old Indian legends said, but replenished. Not Emanuel

Dubbs. After a year in the Dodge region watching the herds retreat southward, he decided uneasily that he better spread his bets. So he filed on a homestead south of Dodge and he and his wife went into dairying, in addition to the hide and meat business. But almost at once Dubbs had trouble, not from Indian raids, but horse stealing, the easiest kind of robbery on the frontier, one that required no courage, no particular intelligence, not even much initiative—the perfect solution for the man who was too lazy to follow the buffalo. Often it brought swift and fairly extreme punishment. One night every horse was swept off Dubb's place by men that he had often fed when they were hungry. Although some tried to blame it on the Indians he knew sign when he saw it. He walked the five miles to Dodge, got thirty-five determined men together and caught up with the thieves in the hills west of Hays City. In the gun battle the leader, Dutch Henry, was hit several times. All the gang were either killed or wounded, but some of Dubb's men died too, and more were hurt. The stock stolen around Dodge was all recovered and one desperate outfit destroyed. Some of their guns and their hats and coats, bloody and full of bullet holes, were tacked up in the saloons and dance halls of Dodge.

"Tacking up a dead owl to drive the rest away?" some of the eastern loafers asked.

But that night several more horse herds disappeared. Ruefully Dubbs admitted it looked like horse stealing was becoming the second industry of the region. And from the look of things many others might be taking it up soon. Last year a scouting party from Ft. Dodge to Indian Territory had never been out of sight of buffaloes all the way. This year they saw only empty prairie, dark-spotted where carcasses had fed the grass, the bones not yet bleached. They saw no buffaloes until well into the Territory and then the poorest scattering, but the Indians were plentiful and angry. Eastward from Ft. Dodge thirty, forty miles along the north bank of the Arkansas, there was a continuous band of putrescent carcasses, the air stinking, and to the west it was the same. The hunting camps along the river banks had done it, the guns bringing down the buffaloes night and day as they came to drink. In one place there were sixty, seventy carcasses on a spot of not over four acres—a great loss of good wholesome animal food.

A year ago the buffalo herds interfered with the pleasure of hunting, whether antelope, deer or game birds, even with hunting the buffaloes themselves. Now the hunter had to go perhaps a hundred miles south and west to find respectable shooting. It was true there was still the great Texas herd but there were Kiowas and Comanches down there. Compared to them the Sioux and Cheyennes sending a few arrows and bullets into a camp as they loped past were like sky pilots spouting hell fire on Dodge's Front Street of a Saturday night. But now it was go south or pick bones, and fight off the hungry settlers to get them.

And then Dodge City received the news of Black Friday, and the crash of Jay Cooke's railroad empire.

CHAPTER VII

SOUTHWARD INTO INDIAN
COUNTRY

D ROUTH, grasshoppers an' hard times go together like lice an' the itch," an old-timer said sourly. He guessed he ought to know; starved out back in Iowa in 1857 and been scratching ever since.

He put what he could get for his load of buffalo bones into an old tobacco sack and went to listen to the sky pilot over on Front Street. Black Friday and the crash of Jay Cooke's railroad empire had been followed by the rapid failure of five thousand businesses, and by a flocking to the gospeleers, the devil skinners, in the west, while larger and more genteel crowds gathered to hear Moody and Sankey preach of the comforting mercy of God.

In the east other crowds gathered too, this fall of 'Seventy-three, loudly protesting the capture of an American ship for running arms to the Cuban insurrectionists. "Clean out them Spanish bastards!" they shouted, many hoping that war would bring back employment and markets, loosen up the American dollar, set things to booming again.

But the war scare cleared and once more there was a great surge to the buffalo country, men walking, riding or on wheels, more with families along because there was nothing to eat at home. These came with perhaps a crate of chickens at the tail of the wagon and a cow tied behind, the fox-faced children peering out under the old wagon sheet. Some even tried to take their families out to the moving herds where the meat was, and the Indians, as well as every other kind of buffalo killer, from the English sportsman to the latest crop of Hard Cases. Everyone still wanted to shoot and few were willing to do the other, the dirty, stinking work.

As usual the newcomers were losing wounded animals and spoiling hides. But more and more of the hunting was by organized and grubstaked parties, usually from six to sixteen men or more, the leader a cool and experienced shot, with perhaps other hunters in addition to the skinners, cook, hide handlers and the reload man who kept ammunition up. For a good hunter and his party the trader supplied the weapons and cartridges, the wagons, horses, blankets, knives, steles for whetting, and the cooking equipment: two water kegs, a big coffee pot, dutch oven, a big frying pan, tin plates and cups, with each man using his knife point as cutlery. There was flour, salt pork, a few pounds of coffee, sugar and beans. A tent or two or a whack-up of hides provided the shelter, par-ticularly as the party moved southward. The men were paid in proportion to the buffaloes taken. Central depots were es-tablished to receive the hides and supply the hunters with necessities and a little more, sometimes.

The pretence of keeping the hiders from crossing south of the Arkansas was gone like a breath cloud in the sun. A toll bridge to lift the great hide wagons out of the quick-sand was thrown across the river. It made a gate-keeping job for Riney, who had lost both feet in the blizzard of 1873, one of the few amputees to earn a living in this country of ac-tion. No one knew what became of the washtub man, with only stubs for arms and legs.

With the Republican herd thinned out and the traffic in hides about done, the K. P. railroad was truly the Keep

Poor now, even before the scourge of grasshoppers ate up the farm produce for which there was little market anyway. The Santa Fe, called the Jerk Water route because they "jerked" water from ponds and wallows for the engine, still frayed out at the Kansas line. Cooke's Northern Pacific headed up the Yellowstone was stopped dead by Black Friday, far from one living buffalo. There seemed only one possible solution for the Northern—to verify the old, old rumors of gold in the Black Hills, to start a rush of prospectors, and of financing. Naturally the Hills were Indian country, where, by treaty, no white man had the right to go, but why should a handful of dirty, treacherous savages suddenly be permitted to stand in the path of the white man's progress?

With an eye to attracting the romantic American investor, General George Armstrong Custer was selected to open the way to the new bonanza that summer of 'Seventy-four. With 110 wagons, 1200 men, Gatling guns and artillery, a large contingent of scouts, both Indian and white, a staff of scientists and newspapermen, and a party of gold-seeking hangers-on, he left Ft. Abraham Lincoln and led the way straight into the Black Hills, his trail another spear driven into the heart of the Indian country, this time that of the proud and arrogant Sioux who had thrown the United States Army and their three posts out of the Powder River region in the Bozeman Trail war, six, seven years ago. The Indians buzzed angrily along the Custer trail and set fire to all the country so the general's stock went without grass and his men without meat on the way back, but they were helpless with their few smuggled arms against the bristling power of the expedition.

From the Black Hills the general reported the gold he sought, a great deal of gold to be found from the grass roots down, and it was Lonesome Charley Reynolds who carried the news out. He might have stayed behind and with his frontiersmanship safely hidden himself to locate a rich placer strike. He might have stayed behind and made the fortune

that was to last his lifetime. But he knew the country southward from the Hills better than anyone else with Custer. So
he was given the best horse of the command and, with the
general's hearty grip of best wishes, he started away into the
darkness, through the rough Hills and out upon the flat
empty prairie that was alive with angry Sioux. But nobody
caught the dodging Lonesome Charley. In two days he
reached Ft. Laramie on the Platte. In his saddlebags were
dispatches that brought men running thick as fall ants hurrying before the threat of winter snows. But the men were running to the call of gold and to back the Northern Pacific,
which many somehow believed was heading straight into the
Hills. Soon they would be stepping off the train into pockets
where gold waited for the pan and the rocker, where streams
ran over rapids with yellow pebbles glistening in the sun. To
be sure there would be also shipping points in the heart of
the great buffalo country, for the fine, thick-furred robes
grown against the long winters with cold that dropped to
forty below.

After the great slaughter of the Arkansas herd, the
remnants scattered into the breaks of the Cimarron and the
wilder country southwest. Almost no buffaloes had come to
cross the Arkansas in the spring. Together the railroads admitted hauling 1,378,359 buffalo hides in the 1872-1874 period and no telling how many more in unlabeled car lots,
also 6,751,200 pounds of buffalo meat and 32,380,050 pounds
of bones. General Nelson A. Miles said 4,373,730 buffaloes
had fallen in the three years since the hunters moved down to
the Arkansas. The army here did what it could to carry out
the actual if not expressed government policy by overlooking first the penetration across the river and then into Indian
Territory and the Panhandle. When the Texas legislature,
alarmed by the news of the decimation of the Republican
and the Arkansas herds, was finally about to pass a bill outlawing the hide hunter, General Sheridan hurried to Austin

to protest. They were making a sentimental mistake, Little Phil insisted. They should give the hunters a unanimous vote of thanks instead, and appropriate sufficient funds to present a bronze medal to each one, with a dead buffalo on one side and a discouraged Indian on the other. "These men have done more in the last two years, and will do more in the next year, to settle the vexed Indian question than the entire regular army has done in the last thirty years. They are destroying the Indians' commissary; and it is a well-known fact that an army losing its base of supplies is placed at a great disadvantage. Send them powder and lead, if you will; but, for the sake of lasting peace, let them kill, skin and sell until the buffaloes are exterminated. Then your prairies can be covered with speckled cattle, and the festive cowboy, who follows the hunter as a second forerunner of an advanced civilization."

The Texas legislature acted on Sheridan's advice. Apparently President Grant was of the same opinion, for he pocketed the bill to outlaw the hide hunter in the territories. In the meantime the Indians of the southern plains, the Kiowas, Comanches and Southern Cheyennes, called a council of war against the buffalo hunters. Back in the spring of 1874 the President had promised one of the Cheyenne chiefs to keep the hide men, whisky peddlers and horse thieves out of Indian Territory—the same President who pigeonholed the bill outlawing the hide hunters. There were still men in Congress who, while approving the expansion of empire, thought it might be attended with a little moderation, a little decency. They objected to starving the Indian into unequipped agrarianism; they spoke up for the preservation of the buffalo, and for maintaining the honor of the government and its agreements. But their voices were drowned out by oratory and the boom of the Big Fifties.

When he returned to the Territory, the Cheyenne chief found that his son had been wounded chasing horse thieves who ran off most of the tribe's horses and sold some of them openly on the streets of Dodge. He was not wounded by the thieves but by soldiers. And in addition the whisky wagons and the hunters were both working deep into the Territory and the hunting grounds to the west.

Outraged by the government's failure, the Indians determined to expel the buffalo hunters themselves. It would bring troops shooting against the villages, and they needed the heavy long-range buffalo guns to protect their families, and plenty of powder and lead, but perhaps the arrow had not forgotten its soft little song of death.

So the war parties rode out, some clear up to the Smoky Hill region. Some watched the Kansas line for the hunters pushing in, some raided the encroaching settlements and the surveyors who were measuring off the land for more whites. White men died, some found only by wolves. Now and then the killing was really done by white men in moccasins, particularly around the new ranches over east, with Texas cattle that needed a great deal of feed. They hired buffalo whoopers to clear the herds off their grass, and often gunmen to discourage other competition for the range, from other cattlemen or settlers. Often the greenhorns out picking bones fired the prairie so the old carcasses would be easier to find, fires that burned the range and stock and buildings before they swept on down into the Territory, destroying the grass and the game of the Indians. So bone pickers too, were often kept off the range.

In the meantime the Indians were hungry. The agent for the Cheyennes and Arapahoes reported that he had no rations except beef to issue from New Year to mid-April, no flour, coffee, sugar and other items promised in the treaties. There was even very little of the beef—poor, winter-thin longhorns for Indians whose teeth had been sweetened by a lifetime of fat young buffalo. Enough to eat would have held most of the troublesome Cheyennes on the reservation. Instead they were out raiding. Now that the hunters were pushing down into Kiowa and Comanche hunting grounds there would be trouble with them too, and their coffee and sugar and other treaty goods did not come either.

Last fall, in 'Seventy-three, the Mooars had gone down into the Texas herd, and Billy Dixon made one of his big swings around that way. While he hunted below Wagonbed Springs in the Cimarron country, small parties of Cheyenne warriors kept coming through for three full days. They were going to fight the Utes, they said, acting friendly enough, but Billy got uneasy and stayed close to camp. His little outfit was only four men, and even with the Fifties that killed at seven hundred yards or more, there was always the danger of surprise or ambush in this Indian region.

When the Cheyennes were past Billy moved south to the Beaver in No Man's Land between Kansas and the Panhandle. They found only scattered bunches of old bulls. He stopped to take their hides because the big ones brought the best prices still being paid. He was there when the Cheyennes passed on the way home, making friendly signs that told how they had run the hunting Utes clear back into the mountains. Encouraged by this friendliness Billy kept moving, telling his men of the fine tame herds he saw when he freighted for Custer the winter of 1868-9. That winter they had to whoop the herds out of the way. But now it was hard to find more than an old bull hidden in a draw.

Once more Billy had run into a blizzard, a real Texas norther this time, full of dust and sand that greyed and sharpened the snow. It came up like a dark wall, shutting out everything. The men jumped into the wagon, with Dixon on horseback alongside quirting the mules. They made it to camp in the daytime dusk, nearly frozen. But it was too far south for a sustained cold snap and the drifts were soon going, leaving little grey ripples of blown earth on the grass.

Billy moved to Cold Water Creek, where the early Mexicans used to hunt buffaloes with lances from their swift horses. It must have been a fine sight, but today there were

only some old bones, very white and crumbling. At Buffalo
Springs they found the earth dark with buffalo chips and not
even a broken-down old bull around; at the South Canadian,
fish and deer and turkeys, with nothing for a hide-making
man. Below was a region of dry creeks with no water except
from the last of the thawing snowbanks, so they turned back
in a wide bend, without seeing one man, red or white, since
the Cheyennes up near the Beaver. That was the advantage
of winter hunting; the bucks sat at home around their fires
and talked big summer war.

By February Billy Dixon was back at Dodge. He had
seen very few buffaloes in all that wide circle, and yet there
were great herds down there some place, from all the bedding spots and the miles of browned chips. Unless the Indians were right and the buffaloes really were going back
into the ground to escape the white hunters—

The next few weeks there had been much uneasy talk
around Dodge, with the hide sheds and corrals all empty, the
stores piled high with goods ordered for a big winter that
had brought in very little. Bones instead of hides had become the legal tender of Dodge now, bones at six to ten dollars a ton, for bone china, carbon that the sugar refineries
needed, phosphates for the soil, and for industrial phospho-
rus. Although more than a million pounds of bones went east
on the Santa Fe last year, this would be multiplied many
times this 1874. Often hundreds of tons were piled along the
right-of-way in ricks taller than the box cars, to be hauled out
in trainloads when it was worth running a train through.

But this was the tail end of a business, the bedrock for
the buffalo town. Slowly the hunters and their hangers-on
had begun to drift away, some to work at cowboying, although the trail bosses already had a hundred volunteers for
every saddle, some into the cattle business, perhaps with rope
and running iron. Some returned to their earlier careers,
outlawry, mainly as roadagents and horse thieves, and with

plenty of recruits without the asking. A few of the gunmen who worked protection for the early saloons and other businesses of the buffalo towns joined their friends loafing around the new ranches starting up all along the cattle trails to the Platte. Smooth-palmed, these men worked no rope and rode no range except to see that it was clear of any settler who might try to plant shirt-tail patches of corn and beans.

Then the Mooar wagons came in to Dodge, piled high with prime winter hides. Last September their big hunting outfit had also crossed the Neutral Strip. They had taken eight hired men, some of them hide-outs from the law. The Mooar brothers preferred these for skinners, cook and wagon men. They were usually happy to get paying work and regular meals far from both sheriff and possible avengers, and not tempted to quit and tear back to town as soon as they had a little time to draw, or the weather got raw and cold. But the outlaws had to be kept from stealing the horses of any hunting camp or ranch they might pass, and from pulling out with Mooar property. Still the country was mighty big, and the Comanches were known to be out. The men stayed close to camp.

In November the Mooars had moved from the Canadian to Palo Duro Creek until spring, with the buffaloes plentiful and as tame as up around the Republican in 1867. They had the whole region to themselves except for a couple of hunters six, seven miles up the creek. Then towards the end of February the Indians killed one of these and, fearing a general attack, both camps hurried in to Dodge—a long, long ways to refuge, and to even the smallest item of supply, but the loaded hide wagons looked mighty good.

With the new hopes stirred by the Mooar success, A. C., Charlie, Myers began some planning. He was a general merchant now but as a hunter he once ran a smokehouse on Pawnee Fork. He used to divide the hindquarters into three chunks, each about the size of an ordinary ham, boneless, sugar-cured, smoked, and sewed into canvas for fancy

prices. Charlie looked at his piles of unmoved stock and made
the venturesome hunters of Dodge an offer. If the Mooars
and another outfit or two thought they could stay down south
with the Texas herd through another winter's hunt, he would
bring supplies to them, establish a trading station down
there. He would pay the hunters going down for all the
freight they could haul, and sell them their supplies at Dodge
City prices. They might as well load their hide wagons instead of traveling light. But there would be no whipping
away for the troops of Ft. Dodge at the first Indian feather
that showed over a ridge. This time it would be stand and
fight, fight Kiowas and the howling Comanches.

A new enthusiasm swept the dusty little March town,
started less than two years ago by the hide trade and already
like an aging belle, clearly past her prime, with business dying and her population, the men and their women, moving
on. Now suddenly Dodge had a second blooming, almost
everybody wanted to join the move upon the Texas herd.
Myers was firm: nobody who couldn't shoot his own way out
would be taken in. He ordered a huge stock of goods in addition to the surplus on hand. They were just about ready to
start when Emanuel Dubbs came through from disposing of
his winter harvest of cured meat at Kansas City. For the first
time Dubbs broke his rule against hunting the thin, poor
summer hides and joined Myers. He added a six-yoke ox
team with trail wagons, a four-mule team and his buffalo
horses. By then, Rath, a strong competitor of Myers' for the
hunting trade, was getting ready to join too. Jim Hanrahan
had brought his large hide outfit in because it wasn't paying.
Instead of breaking it up, he decided to join Myers' train too,
with enough whisky wagons for a saloon. Finally a blacksmith, O'Keefe, loaded up his equipment. There was enough
ammunition along for a small military force, enough whisky
to supply a desert post, and enough of everything else needed
for building and maintaining a trading center, not for settlement but for money, buffalo hides. They knew they were vio-

lating the treaty obligations of the government when they crossed the Arkansas, but it was only a treaty with Indians.

"They's a lot a them Kiowas an' Comanches down that way," Amos Chapman said quietly when he heard about the expedition. But he was scout and interpreter at Camp Supply and married to a Cheyenne and suspect on every count.

All of Dodge was out early to see the departure of the big expedition that would restore the buffalo trade to the town. It was a fine little show, with about a hundred teams, mostly bulls, strung out, grouped by outfits, and separated into units for camping and grass on the way. The heavy wagons, piled high under the wagon sheets, were followed by many little herds of riding stock that raised a dust as they tried to break away in one direction or another. There were well over a hundred men, mostly experienced in the business —enough to shoot their way through the Texas herd clear to the Brazos, enough to shoot their way through all the Indian nations of the southwest.

At a shout the bull whips cracked like the pistols along Front Street, and a roar went up from the watchers. But some were silent, some who thought the expedition would never get back to Dodge. Many felt it was too risky, this going with such a clumsy force into the Kiowa and Comanche hunting grounds. Smaller, more maneuverable outfits—that would have been different. Some who needed work very badly, like Warren, the buffalo skinner whose wife and six children were almost destitute, were afraid to go. But a tenderfoot called Fairchild managed to talk his way in. Billy Dixon shook his long black hair back and itched to finger a trigger when he saw the man in a shining broadcloth suit, plug hat, flowered vest, cravat like a mountain sunset. He had hired a horse and a muley saddle and rode up and down Dodge as if he owned the town, to much laughter and spitting into the dust as he trotted by, bobbing like a monkey on his flat saddle. For the expedition he showed up in a dudy suit of brown ducking, high-heeled boots, spurs with rowels big as tin plates, sombrero, sixshooter, and a Big Fifty that cost him eighty-five dollars. He was ready to scalp Indians too, and flashed a new butcher knife as long as any the squaws carried in their belts.

At the evening stops there was usually a good time. Bat Masterson, the youngest of the outfit, was about twenty and Dixon still only twenty-four, but the whole outfit sang and danced, made music and told stories, when they could stop the veterans among them from fighting the Civil War all over again. There were two fiddlers along, an accordionist, and a dozen who could play the French harp. Sometimes the men danced alone or in couples as the early mountaineers did, on a dry buffalo hide pegged to the ground, a good slick one, full of tallow.

They made the crossing of the spring Cimarron safely enough, although it was a red turbid flood instead of the usual flat and briny little stream crawling over the glistening, salt-filled sand. But in the spring it was a dangerous river, three, four hundred yards wide, brimful, the current, more sand than water, full of underflow and notorious quicksands that were like a vise. Countless buffaloes had died here, and men, wagons, horses too were drawn under. In flood time a man's clothing got weighed down with sand and those who had to swim it crossed naked. But a good buffalo pony could ford the stream in short, quick steps, never pausing, whether walking or half afloat. To stop was to sink. Saddle horses were usually ridden back and forth several times to settle the sand a little and then the wagons were plunged in, one at a time, without the trailers, the stock doubled up on them, the teamsters whipping and cursing to keep the heads of the teams turned up stream and the wheels going.

Myers had called a conference about the Indians. It was decided that since this was Indian country they would be left alone if they left the hunters alone. Friendlies treated friendly, others as enemies. Everyone agreed, although plainly the tenderfoot Fairchild was spoiling for a fight, and

if the expedition never got back to Dodge, he would be the
man who caused the massacre. He would certainly fire at the
first friendly Indian who stuck his head over a ridge. He
popped away at everything that moved. At a night camp
they decided to give the tenderfoot a little scare. Three men
slipped out secretly to build a fire in a cottonwood grove full
of roosting wild turkeys, then a turkey hunt was proposed,
with Bat Masterson to guide Fairchild, Myers follow close
behind. They crept along until they saw the fire through the
thick timber. Bat stopped. "Indians!" he whispered hoarsely.
"Indians around a fire!"

But Charlie Myers put up a little opposition. He argued that Bat was mistaken, yellow. He better go back to
camp if he was afraid. Charlie and Fairchild weren't afraid.
Just then there were shots from the fire and Myers hit for
camp, yelling at every jump. Fairchild came too, firing his
sixshooter and running. Younger than Myers, he made it into
camp first, half a mile ahead of the other two. He stumbled
in, fell on a bed roll unable to talk, out of breath.

"Indians!" he finally gasped.

"By God! Mebby he's wounded!" someone yelled. He
ripped the tenderfoot's shirt all down the back, poured the
coffee pot on him and convinced him he was wet with blood,
probably dying. To questions about Bat and Myers, Fairchild
could only guess they were dead. The whole timber was full
of blood-thirsty redskins, their bullets and arrows had whistled past him all the way back.

Even when the two men came in, alive but apparently
winded, gasping, to hide their laughing, that they were surrounded by Indians, the tenderfoot didn't catch on. Of course
extra guards must be stationed. The obviously unwounded
Fairchild was set to walking guard along the river bank in
the darkness while the rest crept back to their bed rolls. He
did sulk when he discovered the joke, but it cured him of Indian hunting, and made a good buffalo skinner out of a
tenderfoot with a fancy vest.

The expedition stopped not far from some old ruins called Adobe Walls, in the Texas Panhandle where Bent had established a trading post for the Comanches and Kiowas almost forty years ago—not for robes, so far from a market, but for horses and mules, mostly stolen from the Texans. When peace was made between these Indians and the Cheyennes, they had come to trade at Bent's Fort on the upper Arkansas. Ten years ago Colonel Kit Carson was attacked here by a strong force of Indians. Surrounded and outnumbered ten to one, the fight lasted from forenoon to nightfall. Then the Indians, with their usual aversion to night fighting, withdrew. Carson was glad to get away.

The location, however, was still a good one, still in the heart of buffalo sign, with a small stream of sweet water running to the Canadian a short distance below. Dubbs and some of the other outfits stayed a few days to help start a new post near the old adobe ruins. Myers and Leonard put up a sod house twenty by sixty feet, with a stout ridge log and a roof of poles, fine brush and earth on top to shed the rain and any fire arrows from the Indians. They put lookout bastions at opposite corners and hauled cottonwood logs six miles for a picket corral, the twelve foot logs set three feet into the ground solid against each other, making a nine foot wall with a log store house in one corner. Jim Hanrahan's sod saloon was twenty-five by sixty feet with a long, straight ridgepole to hold up the dirt roof. Rath and Wright built their big supply house of sod too, and a hide yard. More houses went up until there was a little town with even a restaurant run by Bill Olds and his wife, the only woman there. Other outfits were drawing in over the new trail from Dodge, and word came of more hunters on the way down, working the little herds they found scattered over the prairie as they came.

But although it was time for the Texas herd to be moving up this way, there wasn't a buffalo around. Dubbs, Dixon and some of the others who had gone out soon after

Map Showing How the Buffalo Herds Shrunk
and Were Eventually Exterminated
Prepared by W. T. Hornaday, the Famous Naturalist

Bison Family
Courtesy New York Public Library

*Indian Hunters Driving the Buffaloes over
a Precipice, a Method Commonly Used
by the Indians
Courtesy New York Public Library*

*Print of Famous Primitive Indian Painting
Known as* The Buffalo Hunter

FACING PAGE — ABOVE
Indian Hunting Buffalo with Spear

BELOW
*Indian Buffalo Hunt
All Courtesy New York Public Library*

Easy Hunting. Hide Men Shooting Buffalo from a Train

FACING PAGE — ABOVE
Life on the Prairie, *an Old Lithograph*

BELOW
Bison Hunting, *an Old Lithograph*
Showing the Hide Men at Work
All Courtesy New York Public Library

*Praying to the Great Spirit for the
Return of the Buffalo
Courtesy Bettmann Archives*

their arrival had no luck either. Dubbs crossed the Canadian to the great tablelands where turkey and quail were thick along the creeks and prairie chickens in the sandhills. The whole prairie was unmarred by any trail except buffalo. These ran in every direction, some a foot deep, with sign of a great herd around recently, but not one left now.

Billy Dixon made one of his wide swings around the region, riding along the higher ridges, scanning all the country not only for the buffalo but for Indian sign, perhaps a thin column of smoke from some creek bend or the far-off flash of a signal mirror. Behind him came his wagon, lower down, signaled around arroyos and washouts by Billy's waving hat. Back, and to the right, rode another horsebacker, rifle in scabbard too. And sometimes for a whole day there was not another movement over all the wide plain.

They struck a hundred buffalo trails worn by the southward movement of fall, and sighted an occasional bunch of perhaps four to ten. All the hunters were discouraged. They must find the big herd or go bankrupt. Those older in the buffalo country got uneasy for another reason—the absence of buffaloes might mean there were Indians around. April passed into the heat of May. Lambsquarter in great patches furnished greens for Billy's kettle with scraps of salt pork when they should be eating roast hump ribs.

Back at Adobe Walls the new buildings were done by May Day and Mooar, Hanrahan and several others with big outfits hit the ranges. Many more hunters had come in over the one hundred and fifty mile trail from Dodge and were hopefully outfitting too. It was impossible to believe that the great Texas herd had vanished, but there was no hastening the strange impulse that sent the usually phlegmatic buffaloes hurrying across the plains twice a year. The hunters played cards, drank whisky, raced their horses, shot target and growled that Myers and Rath would permit no women, none of the Dodge Girls, at the Walls. There was fiddle playing and dancing for anybody who wanted to step around a little with a bearded, stinking hide hunter (although not stinking enough this poor spring) instead of the powdered and perfumed girls that had come to Dodge recently, some pretty fancy ones driven west by the hard times.

Everybody cursed the contrary buffaloes. By the end of May the whole venture looked like one great losing bust for Myers and Rath and the others who had built up the new Adobe Walls. Then early one morning, when Billy Dixon and several others were camped below the Canadian, the wonderful sound started to grow out of the earth. It swelled, came rolling in over the prairie, deep and moving, not unlike the rumble of a far train on a bridge. Everywhere hunters sought out high points to stare southward. There was nothing to see, but the herd was coming. Everywhere the news was on the wind. By the time breakfast was done, Dixon had his horse saddled and was heading south at a gallop. Five miles out he began to strike small bunches of young cows and bulls, all moving northward, heads down, grunting nostrils wet, into the wind.

Alone, not hunting, but with his rifle ready in the scabbard, the ammunition heavy and ripe about his waist for there would surely be Indians with such a herd, Billy rode on. Up on a high point, where he could see in every direction over the table, Billy felt his muscles harden and grow warm. The east, south and west were all one solid mass of buffaloes, thousands upon thousands moving northward. The bellowing of the bulls was a deep steady roar that seemed to reach to the clouds. Happy, Billy turned his horse and rode hard towards camp. When he got there the first of the lead bunches were coming in. He picked out thirty-five or forty, all bulls, and then fell to with the skinning. By night the herd was passing within rifle shot of the camp fire. Yesterday there was not a dark hump in sight anywhere, today he could kill enough from his tent flap to keep ten skinners busy.

When Billy had a couple of days work ahead for his men he went to the Walls to hire more help. Only one man

was footloose and that for only a few days, until his partner
brought in their final load of hides and they could start out
again. All the other hunters were working the rich herd in
close now. The Walls was deserted except for the merchants,
a few clerks and Mrs. Olds, who was training a morning glory
vine up along the door. Billy hired the man to skin for a week
or ten days at twenty-five cents a hide and guaranteed to
bring him back. It proved a costly venture, for when they returned the Canadian was so swollen that Billy lost part of his
team and his big buffalo gun in the crossing. Both men were
almost drowned.

They found the Walls alarmed over the Indians,
enough to outweigh the joy of the herd's coming at last. Two
hunters had been killed up on Chicken Creek. Plummer,
partner of the men, found them scalped and mutilated, a
heavy stake driven through one. Plummer cut the harness
away and rode one of the horses for the Walls with his warning and to get help with the burying. But the post was almost
deserted, most of the guns sold. Billy Dixon bought the best
rifle he could get and was starting back to warn his camp
when another hunter brought news of two more killed.

Now the hide men came hurrying to the Walls from
all directions, bringing stories of depredations through the
entire region of the spreading herd. Apparently the Indians
had been following the buffaloes for hunters as well as for
meat. There were some killings up around Dodge too—not
just the usual number of men kicking out their desperate
lives in the dust of the street; that did not concern the people
of Adobe Walls—but hunters dead on the prairie. One they
all knew: Warren, who had the wife and six children and
wouldn't risk coming out on the expedition because of the
Indians. He and two other men had hired out to Fleming for
a hunt south on the Cimarron. In a day or two Fleming returned afoot, carrying his sporting buffalo gun. He said their
horses had been swept away in the night down at Crooked
Creek. He and the unarmed Warren had walked east on the

trail of the thieves, leaving the other two men to watch the
wagon. Fleming found one of the horses, broken down and
abandoned, but a party of five Indians appeared and killed
Warren. Fleming had stood them off with his gun.

A small detachment of troops went back with the
hunter, who seemed a little shut-mouth about what happened. They found Warren's body all right, shot three times,
the entire scalp gone, leaving scarcely any hair or skin on his
head. But the young officer wasn't entirely satisfied, and after
Fleming was questioned at the post, he was taken out again.
Still reluctant, he changed his story a little, saying that they
had seen a loose pony far off and while Warren was cutting
across some breaks to it, five horsebackers, Fleming couldn't
tell whether Indian or white men, stopped to watch a while.
Then they rode off and Fleming hurried in to Dodge, apparently without looking for the unarmed Warren at all.

The troops found no Indians and, perhaps because of
a rain, no Indian sign, but some woodchoppers working
nearby all this time had seen none. Lieutenant Henely
seemed to doubt that the thieves were Indians. A photograph
of the dead and scalped Warren was tacked up in the saloons
of Dodge, and his son went to work for the Long Branch saloon to feed the family. Within a week the boy showed real
talent around the gaming tables.

Down at the Walls it was a hot June to be worried
about Indians. The spring flowers were dying under the
drouth of summer, and the buffalo herd splitting up into
smaller bunches. The yellow calves were playful now as the
young antelopes and the deer were playful, and the young
wolves and coyotes who lifted their thin, sharp voices in the
night, the bright-faced young coons who wandered along the
creeks, and the little skunks like bushy-tailed kittens. Birds
too, were everywhere, the mother fluttering to draw the enemy from her small ones, her cry a warning to freeze to the
ground, or to scatter in grass and brushpatch.

With all the alarm about Indians, nobody had actually seen one around the Walls, and yet the dead men were surely warnings to leave, to get back north of the Arkansas. Some of the hunters far out knew nothing about the Indian scare at all. Emanuel Dubbs' outfit, around the Salt Fork of the Red River, had found vast herds at Lelia Lake, with many water fowl and fish—a lonely, coolish, pleasant place. Good hides were still worth around two dollars and they worked fast in the heat and the dust. At the end of the third week they had over a thousand hides dry and ready to go.

They loaded all the wagons would hold and ricked the rest. The first night on the way back to the Walls they camped up a little creek not far from a high bluff, in a cottonwood grove. They had heard of an Indian outbreak, but rumors were always flying thick as magpies around a good hunt, and carelessly they turned all their stock loose except Dubbs' best saddle horse. At dawn he climbed to the top of the bluff to see which way the horses had wandered. Not a head was in sight. He saddled and went to look for them, scouting the strange country for hours. Around noon he found the trail, an Indian-driven trail. Dubbs followed ten, twelve miles and saw that he couldn't catch up before dark, so he started back towards camp. At the high bluff he left his horse and crawled carefully to look over the top, down upon his camp about three hundred yards off. It was torn to pieces as by a tornado, with the body of a man sprawled naked over the tongue of one wagon. A knot of Indian ponies was hidden in a pocket and under a low bank of the creek Dubbs could see the tufted heads of Indians, watching for his return. He glanced around quickly, his hand clenched on the grip of his rifle. He was alone and afoot, yards from his horse down there, grazing, head held sideways.

The sun had set, the prairie was greying. He made himself go quietly and leisurely down to his horse, feeling watched all the way. Mounted, he got his gun ready, pulled his sixshooter around handy, and started out at a casual jaunt,

as though to make one more search for his lost horses. But
the Indians rose with a whoop and began to fire. Dubbs shot
back with the Big Fifty and set his spurs to put his tired horse
into a run. He made it to a draw that led out on the tableland with a six hundred yard lead. The guns of the Indians
were shorter-ranged and he managed to drop a pony or two
every time they got close, but they kept coming, knowing his
horse was giving out. Only the darkness of the new moon
saved his scalp. He kept headed in the general direction of
the Walls, the Indians still coming somewhere behind but
having to follow him by sound. Finally he heard one last
whoop and yell far back, and then no more. It was time, for
his horse had been stumbling and finally went down for good.
The hunter packed the saddle on his back, knowing he must
be near the Canadian River, with the Walls somewhere beyond. Towards morning he got in and found everybody
asleep as though a thousand miles from murdering redskins,
but ready to wake up and listen to this new attack. One of
those listening closely was John Mooar, for his brother was
still out with their hunting outfit. They had all wanted to
work as long as they could, now that the buffaloes finally
came, three, four outfits moving together for protection.
Hide hunting had always been dangerous for the lone man,
and the outfit of only two or three, they reassured each other.
Even up on the Republican. Everybody had to stand off an attack sooner or later.

  Then suddenly a small military detail came riding in
from Camp Supply—a sergeant and several troopers with
Amos Chapman, government scout at the post. Chapman was
married to a relative of the Black Kettle killed by Custer on
the Washita, and some of the hunters stood away from him
and the troopers. It seemed they could have only one errand
here: spying out the camp of the hunters so a force could be
sent to drive them out. In addition, those who knew Chapman's connection with the Cheyennes of the Territory were
certain he was spying for the Indians.

The sergeant said they were looking for horse thieves and the hunters resented that too, particularly when the troopers scouted up the river the next day, where some of the Wall's herds were grazing. Chapman stayed at the post in the meantime, talking to the traders over at Rath's store. The hunters and drunks loafing around Hanrahan's and the other whisky traders were getting madder with every drink.

"It's that Amos what's brought the troops here!"

"Yeh, let's string 'im up tonight!"

"I say he's a spy fer them red devils. String him up!"

Hanrahan knew that Chapman had brought a warning that the Indians planned a concerted attack on the Walls when the moon now growing neared its fullness, with light for the travel and the morning pale. Probably the twenty-sixth or seventh of the month, if clear, and certainly at dawn. The Kiowas had carried the warpipe to the Comanches and the Southern Cheyennes to drive all the hunters from the Panhandle. A Kiowa medicine man claimed he had a bullet-proofing ceremony so they could walk right in against the most powerful of the buffalo guns.

The post trader at Camp Supply, doing considerable business in dressed robes with the Cheyennes and Arapahoes, was connected with Wright, now a partner of Rath here at the Walls. Chapman found out about the planned attack from his wife's relatives, and the trader had sent him here.

But Hanrahan couldn't tell this to the drunken men planning to lynch the scout, or all the hunters would head in a bunch for Dodge and desert the traders and their goods to the Indians. Yet Hanrahan had to save Chapman from at least a shooting scrape. He told the scout to slip away to one of the Mooar wagons behind Rath's store, and sleep there. The drunks tried to follow and lost him in the dark.

Soon after dawn John Mooar went to his brother's camp. After a couple of brushes with the Indians, they got back to the Walls and started for Dodge with their big hide wagons right away. By the time news came of a couple more

hunting camps destroyed, and more men killed, Rath and
Myers had their wagon train ready too. One of the Mooars
had tried to get Mrs. Olds to go along to Dodge when they
left. "You better come and get that tooth taken care of—"
John said quite casually. "Didn't I hear you complaining last
week?"

But the woman shook her head. "If it gets too bad Bill
or somebody'll yank it out with the pliers," she said. "Better'n that drunk of a dentist at Dodge—" She smiled a little,
her sunburnt face gaunt and leathering in the hide camp,
and it was impossible to tell whether she knew about the
threatening Indian attack or not. Anyway Mooar hadn't felt
he should urge Rath's hired help to leave if Charlie didn't
think she should go.

When the big wagon trains were gone the four, five
men who knew or suspected their danger sat together in the
shade of the low buildings wiping the sweat away with their
sleeves in silence, wondering what they should do, short of
letting out the whole story and bringing on a stampede. Deserting the goods here to the Indians would bankrupt at least
the newer businesses, besides, all these men, except Hanrahan, and Leonard were hired help left on guard.

Still there was too much uneasiness now, and so Billy
Dixon and many others decided it might be better to hunt
farther north, at least keep up beyond the Canadian that
flowed just south of the Walls. They stopped in for more supplies and the news. Jim Hanrahan asked Billy his plans and
suggested that the young hunter throw in with his outfit.
Jim had trouble getting a man who could keep his big crew
of skinners busy. A bargain was struck, Billy to get half the
profits. The wagons were lined up and loaded, ready for an
early start the next day. There were plenty buffaloes up towards the Neutral Strip, the No Man's Land, the Shadler
brothers told the waiting hunters. They had just brought
freight down on the Dodge trail through there and were

heading back in the morning, if anybody wanted to join up for safety. Their wagons stood in the bright moonlight near the Walls, loaded, the tongues down but ready for a start at sunup, the twenty-seventh of June.

CHAPTER VIII

ATTACK ON ADOBE WALLS

I T WAS a hot moonlit night at Adobe Walls, with now and
then the booming sound of an arrow hawk as he dove
upon the mosquitoes, the call of a ground owl along the
creek, or a young grey wolf's thin little bark. But mostly it
was a bright, still night, so bright the buffalo hunters who
came in that afternoon spread their blankets out of reach of
the moon in the black shadows of the buildings. Billy Dixon
had stretched himself behind the blacksmith shop, near his
wagon, ready for an early start with Hanrahan's outfit in the
morning. He had his saddle horse up as close as on the range,
tied with a long picket rope near the wagon. He put the new
gun, a roundbarrel Sharps, at his side between the blankets to
protect it from rain or dew, and reminded himself not to
forget his case of ammunition in Rath's store.

Every door was wide open, the lights turning out one
after another, as the Walls gradually quieted for the night.
It was a little later than usual because, instead of the six or
seven men and Mrs. Olds around lately, tonight there were
twenty-eight men, and much Indian news to trade with the
latecomers. Finally everybody was settled for a short sleep
and an early morning start, so still that the shy little white

192

jumping mice had already ventured out into the moonlight that made them almost invisible to all but the soft-winged owls.

Then, about two o'clock, the two men sleeping in Hanrahan's saloon were awakened by a report like a rifle shot. They jumped up in their shirt tails and looked out, although it seemed to be a cracking in the long cottonwood ridgepole that held up the dirt roof. Probably the entire top would be down upon them next, so they stirred out some of the others to help make repairs. Leonard, the only one of the traders still at the Walls, came for a while, and even Mrs. Olds looked out of Rath's and then around the bright moon-lit prairie. The only disturbance now was from the pet crow, awakened and cross, so she stroked his neck in the darkness and then went back to bed.

Over at the saloon some of the men were throwing dirt off the roof to lighten it, while others went to the creek to cut props for the ridgepole. By the time it was reinforced, the sky was lightened in the east. Most of the hunters crawled back to bed, but Hanrahan suggested to Billy Dixon they might as well stay up and get an early start for the buffalo ranges. He sent young Billy Ogg for the horses grazing a quarter of a mile off, down along a creek. Dixon had thrown his bed roll into the front of his wagon and was turning to pick up his gun when something made him look in the direction of the horses. Just beyond them, at the edge of a little timber, a large mass of something was advancing slowly out of the grey of dawn upon the herd and in the direction of Adobe Walls. It didn't seem to be dark enough for buffaloes. Then Billy was thunderstruck as the mass suddenly fanned out, gave one single solid yell, a warwhoop, and broke into a charge, the horses thundering on the baked earth, the yells of the Indian warriors, hundreds of warriors, thin and high.

Without stopping to think Billy ran for his saddle-horse, lunging this way and that at the picket rope. He got to the peg just as one more run would have jerked it out. With

the horse tied securely to his heavy wagon, Billy grabbed his
gun to get in a few good shots before the Indians could turn
to run. He started towards them, his rifle ready at the shoulder, to meet their swerve with a bullet. But this time the redskins kept coming straight on, straight for the buildings,
whipping their horses at every jump, and whooping. It was a
splendid sight, hundreds of the finest fighting men of the
southwest plains, the finest horses—all coming like a roaring
wind, warbonnets flying, the bronzed, half-naked, painted
bodies of the riders shining with ornaments of silver and
brass. And around them stretched the morning plains, the
sun striking its first rays over the horizon.

Billy fired one futile shot and ran for the nearest
building, Hanrahan's saloon. It was closed tight, the men
inside preparing for a siege. He shouted to be let in as bullets whistled and thudded all around him, knocking dust
from the sod walls. Just as the door opened Billy Ogg ran up
from the horse herd and fell inside, unable to stand from the
long flight, his clothing full of holes, an arrow through the
shoulder of his shirt, but untouched.

By this time the buildings were surrounded in the roar
of battle, every window pane gone, the hunters hugging the
sod walls as they tried to return the fire. Hanrahan and the
rest had brought down three warriors. The others, seeing
them fall, hesitated and swerved sideways, keeping back,
shooting as they circled the Walls, while inside the men tried
to barricade the openings with sacks of flour and grain, in
the saloon with barrels and sections of the bar up-ended,
while the pet crow flew in and out in alarmed cawing.

The surprise had caught the defenders in three separate parties. There were nine men at Hanrahan's saloon,
eleven at Myers and Leonard's store about fifty yards north
with the protection of the stockade. Seven men and the one
woman were in Rath and Wright's store south of the saloon,
the yard behind them piled with buffalo hides that could
shelter the attackers but were fortunately too tightly stacked

to burn. No party knew where the rest were or how many lived, and everybody had forgotten about the Shadler brothers, out with their loaded wagons, probably caught asleep, for there was not one bark from their Newfoundland dog before the fighting could drown him out. The other dogs of the post hadn't barked either but fled silently at the first whoop of the Indians, heading out the back for the brush of the creek, all except the one locked inside at Leonard's.

In the saloon the men had been awake, but some of the others, those who lived at the Walls and usually undressed to sleep, were still fighting hard for their lives barefoot and in drawers and undershirts. It took time to realize the situation and to barricade the door and windows, punch holes through the sod walls to stand off the Indians. There seemed at least four hundred out there in the smoke, some thought a thousand, and an additional dark mass over on the hill near the creek, their blankets and mirrors making signals for the fighting men, with couriers tearing back and forth.

In their first attack the Indians were completely reckless, as though they were actually as bulletproof as the Kiowa medicine man had promised, and could come right up to the Walls and knock the hunters on the head with clubs. Not even the bullets of the Big Fifties would break the skin. To the blare of a bugle among the Indians, they came charging in a whirlwind of dust and smoke, right up to the buildings, looking for the holes from which the hunters were shooting now, and shooting carefully. As one horse went down, and then another, those behind leapt over them, the rush coming on and on. But then men went down too, and after a little hesitation, as in unbelief, they were dragged away, those up close under the buffalo guns lying still as they fell, so none could tell whether dead or alive.

After the first telling volley from the hunters, the Indians reformed and many slid from their war horses and prepared to fight afoot, crawling over the bare prairie, up behind weeds and wagons and hide piles as best they could, moving like snakes of the desert. But the expert marksmen inside the buildings drove them back, only to see them mount and come through the dust and the sharp blue smoke in another charge. Three abreast they struck the heavy hand-hewn cottonwood doors of the buildings with the butts of their guns, whirled their horses and reared them backwards against the wood. They hurled lances and shot arrows and bullets in at the cracks where the bulwarking sacks were pushed back. They dared this even now that the hunters had cooled down and were firing very carefully, hitting everything they could see from their gun slits and the corners of the barricaded windows. Horses went down or were emptied of their riders and finally the Indians were driven back, inevitably driven back by the longer range of the buffalo guns. Once a lone young warrior in beaded buckskin and long-tailed warbonnet charged out from his force, clear to the gun holes, thrust his sixshooter into one and emptied it. He started back as bravely, and was hit, one more dead.

In the first lull of the fight it seemed to the defenders that the Indians had little to show for their warriors lost— nothing but the two Shadler brothers killed at the very start and scalped. Their big Newfoundland dog, who slept at their feet, had fought so hard when he finally awoke that the Indians scalped him as a brave enemy, taking skin off his sides. They ransacked the wagons, lugging away the provisions and the guns and ammunition. The twenty-eight oxen of the Shadlers were nowhere in sight, dead or stampeded. The horses of the post had all been swept away, all except the five in the stockade. These the Indians shot by poking their guns between the cottonwood log pickets. The one left crippled and suffering Leonard finished from a window. They had killed Billy Dixon's fine hunting horse first of all, the head still held up awkwardly by the short rope that was tied so securely to the wagon. The two teams tied around a wagon near Rath's were dead too.

During the lull the dust and smoke began to lift in

the rising west wind, but not inside the dark, hot and stinking
sod buildings, although cracks were opened in barricaded
windows as much as they dared, the smoke creeping out as
from a fire. One hole was wide enough to let the cawing crow
fly in to sit on the bar and scold. During the quietness
the hunters began to talk a little, almost the first words
spoken since the alarm, so naturally had these men worked
together, each understanding exactly what must be done.
The attackers were mostly Kiowas and Comanches, with a
few Southern Cheyennes that Hanrahan and even Dixon
knew. Several men over at Leonard's store, particularly Old
Man Keeler, recognized the bold young Comanche, Quanah,
the son of the captive white woman Cynthia Parker. It was
Quanah who led that fierce attack and had his horse shot
away under him. He was pitched to the ground, his gun flying
out of his hands, but he crept up behind an old carcass in
some weeds and then to a brush patch until another Indian
could ride in to carry him away on his horse. Even the hunters whose lives he sought had to admire the courage, the cool-
ness of this Comanche breed.

Two of the Indians brought down in that first wild
charge were Cheyennes that Old Man Keeler knew, one the
son of Stone Calf. The death of such a warrior could not go
unavenged.

"Looks like we sure run ourselves up a box canyon,"
Bill Keeler said mildly. He worked his jaws uncertainly as
he wiped the sweat out of his eyes in the lamp lit against the
darkness of the barricaded store. "An' hot as a dutchoven
with the biscuits burnin'."

One of the younger men hopefully recalled the fight at
Beecher Island. Keeler snorted. "Hell, ain't no troops comin'
tootin' to get us out, like they done for that aide of Sheridan's,
that Indian-hungry Forsyth," he said. But at least nobody
here was going to bawl and dig himself in the sand, not
even, a man could safely bet, Bill Olds' wife over there at
Rath's.

No, but it was a hundred fifty miles to Dodge. Camp Supply was nearer yet with hardly enough troops to protect the post in an uprising, and even Supply was a mighty long ways afoot through the Kiowas and Comanches howling out there. These were wilder Indians than up on the Republican, Indians fighting the first real invasion of these hunting grounds. They still thought they could win, so it was for all the chips today, and eager to rake them in. Still, the warriors were a little more cautious, circling the walls again, but hanging behind their horses by a toe hold over the galloping back, a wrist in the mane, shooting over the necks as the horses ran, as low to the ground as fleeing coyotes. The Indians spied out the loopholes of the buildings, and shot so accurately that the hunters feared for their aiming eyes and had to hug the walls inside.

Up at his store Leonard, with Billy Tyler, slipped out into the stockade in the back to protect the well. Some daring young warrior might decide to come over the pickets, or get up on the dirt roof of the store and chop holes to shoot inside. But the Indian fire through the cracks between the cottonwood log was so hot the men were driven back. As Tyler was slipping in through the half-open doorway, he turned to send back one last bullet and was struck in the lungs. Frothy blood gushed from his nose as he slowly settled to the dirt floor in the doorway, going down like a well-shot buffalo. The men pulled him inside and laid him out of the way while they stood off the new attacks, left him to gasp out his lungs in the stinging powder smoke of the room.

Outside one lot of Indians fired while another raced up horseback to get the dead and wounded away. Fallen warriors suddenly came alive and jumped up behind the rescuers. Rifles cracked, perhaps blood spurted down the horse's leg and both Indians whipped him on, lurching and staggering, to get away.

At Rath's place, Langton, left in charge of the store and the great piles of hides, had taken command. Mrs. Olds helped keep the barricades up as they were shot down, and a supply of ammunition handy for the men. Between times she made coffee, and once, when it seemed they would be overwhelmed, took her place at a gunslit. Her hand shook on the trigger, but she pulled it, the kick of the rifle sending her shoulder around. Once there were tears beyond those of the smoke in her eyes. She caught a glimpse of her pretty little mustang colt with a feathered arrow deep in his bloody back. A hunter had caught the colt from a wild bunch, and all spring he followed her over the prairie, nudging her for attention, rubbing her face with his soft nose as she stooped to pick the spring flowers. Now the colt was too gentle, too affectionate to run away.

Once too, the woman tried to coax the crow in, but he kept flying through the dust and smoke, settling here and there, rising in chattering protest as bullets came too close. An Indian who tried to catch the bird on top of a pile of hides got a squeaking peck in the face.

The hunters had noticed a pony with calico braided into the mane standing quietly near the corner of the hide stacks. It must be held there, Billy Dixon thought, and took a side shot at it from the saloon. The horse fell and the Indian behind it was exposed. Shots from all three parties fogged him good, made him dance to get behind the hides. Billy was almost out of ammunition for his new gun, the case he bought yesterday still at Rath's. The excited bartender had been banging away with Hanrahan's Big Fifty at everything, and Billy got him to trade weapons. With the powerful Fifty that would shoot through the corner of the hide pile, Billy aimed on the Indian. The brave leapt into the air, and howling, ran zigzag for thirty, forty yards and dropped in tall grass.

After that the Indians settled to an intermittent firing, creeping up, running back. In this comparative quiet the men at Hanrahan's wondered about those in the other buildings. Nobody in the saloon had been hit so far, although they had to hug the walls like gophers. The wounded Indian horses were crowding the walls as close outside, drawn to them for protection in their pitiful injuries.

By now those in the saloon were running short of ammunition and so Hanrahan and Dixon decided to make a run for Rath's store, with thousands of rounds in stock. They crawled through a window and hit the ground running, bullets striking like summer hail all around them. The door frame of Rath's made a very good target but they got inside unhurt, only winded. Everybody there was in good shape, but the saloonkeeper had to get right back to his liquor store, which must not fall to the Indians, nor be sampled too well by the hunters there. Every man would be desperately needed before this was finished. Because there were fewer men at Rath's than at the other places, and with Mrs. Olds here, Billy Dixon was begged to stay. He opened the door for Hanrahan, loaded down with a sack of ammunition, and covered the man's heavy run through the open space, keeping the Indians busy ducking the lead of the Big Fifty.

In Rath's restaurant the openings were barred with sacks of flour and grain. The Indians' guns were not powerful enough to carry through from a distance but they kept trying. Billy crawled up on top of the barricade to look out the transom and saw something crawling in the edge of the grass. Balanced on one knee he shook the black hair out of his eyes and fired. The recoil knocked him off backwards against a washtub and a lot of Mrs. Olds' cooking utensils, everything crashing to the floor around him. Everybody thought Billy was hit, but he crawled back up and fired a couple more times, finally one that struck.

By two o'clock the warriors had divided into two forces, east and west, riding back and forth to dare the buffalo guns, the bugler with them, the sun glinting on his instrument. Although pretty far, the hunters tried to pick some of them off, thinking about all the dark scattering of Indians over around the hills, watching, enough of them to overwhelm the Walls in five minutes—any five minutes if they wanted to take the losses—sweep over them like a gully washer striking a buffalo camp. Even if that charge never came and the ammunition held out, the only hope of the Wallers was troops. Perhaps through Amos Chapman, who knew of the coming attack, or through some hunter or freighter who might have approached near enough to realize the situation and was able to get away for help. If any white man could get through—

Late in the afternoon the bugler was killed near the Shadler wagons. He was running, carrying a big tin can under each arm, the bugle bouncing on his back. The cans flew both ways as he went down from a Sharps Fifty in the back. But not this antic or several others drew the hunters out. They knew there were Indians skulking close up to the walls, particularly off behind the stockade, which they would have burned long ago if it hadn't been a protection. Luckily all the besieged buildings were sod.

Hours of fighting and anxiety made the mouth go dry, the saliva thicken, particularly with the Indians flaunting the scalps of the Shadlers before the eyes of the Wallers. The one well was under the guns of the Indians squatting behind the pickets. In one of the lulls young Bat Masterson heard that Billy Tyler was hit. He made a run for the store and found his dying friend moaning for water. Bat started out with a bucket, but Old Man Keeler stopped him. Keeler was an old-time plainsman and many of the Indians knew him. "Gimme the bucket," he said, and jumped through the window into the stockade, with probably half a dozen Indian guns on him. He was almost tripped by his dog, who ran out between his legs. The pump was old and squeaky, and volley after volley came from the Indians along the far side of the stockade, sixty yards away. The dog, scared, crept between Keeler's feet and was killed there. The pump finally produced water, and with his bucket full the old hunter walked leisurely back untouched, but roaring mad about his dog. Bat washed Billy's face and held a cup to the grey lips. The wounded man drank and died.

About four o'clock a young hunter ventured out from Hanrahan's to pick up some Indian trophies. He wasn't shot at, and so tried again, gathering up a couple of fine warbonnets, three painted shields and an armful of bows, arrows, spears and beaded quivers. Others followed. Now they heard of the death of Billy Tyler up at Myers and Leonard's, shot so early in the fight. Dixon went to see why a grey horse had stood for hours at the south window of the saloon, and found a dead warrior fallen across the rope. He slipped off the silver-mounted bridle adorned with scalps, the hair fifteen inches long, brown and soft.

Around the corner of the little sod house west of Rath's store they found a painted and feathered warrior sitting upright, legs crossed but with his neck broken, stone dead. The Indian Billy had seen crawling in the grass was dead too, naked except for a white breechcloth and a six-shooter in his belt. A short distance off, back on the bloody trail, they found a shot pouch and powder horn, a little farther on the Indian's fifty caliber needlegun and behind that his bow and quiver. They searched out among the dead horses and found twelve Indians and the Negro who had carried the bugle. They tried to count up the men they saw carried away, dead or alive, but there was no way to tell the number. Fifty-six dead horses lay scattered around the buildings, some with arrows, others with bullet holes. Ten of these had belonged to the hunters. The last one of all to die was the little mustang colt.

By now the sun was near setting and everybody knew that the Indians would attack again. Working as fast as they could in the hard dry earth the Wallers buried the two Shadler brothers and Billy Tyler, putting them into one grave together. Afterward, in the bright moon, they looked to the protection of the buildings for the night, ate and tried to sleep a little in the airless barricaded buildings, the relay of watchers getting the fresher air of the bastions.

Dawn came over the silent walls. Hanrahan rigged up his black silk kerchief on a pole above one of the lookouts, the black flag of distress. The sun rose hot on the prairie that was without life except the pet crow flying from one dead horse to the next. A stench that seemed unbearable even to the hunters rose from the horses and the dead Indians but there was no team left to drag the carcasses away. Finally the men laced several buffalo hides together, rolled the carcasses over on them and dragged them away, five, six men to a horse. Twelve horses had died in a pile between Rath's and Hanrahan's. For these they dug a pit close by and rolled them in. The others and the Indians they left far out, to collect the long-tailed magpies and the buzzards already beginning to circle the sky above the Walls.

Although the hunters knew the Indians were watching, they saw only one party of them all day, off on a far bluff to the east. They returned the long range fire of the Big Fifties and then disappeared. The situation was gloomy, with Indians all around, not a horse left and perhaps all the scattered camps destroyed. But late that afternoon two teams came up the valley of the Canadian as though there was not one Indian in all of Texas. Some of the hunters grabbed their big guns and ran out to do what they could to help the wagons make it to the Walls. It was Bellfield's outfit and when they saw the black flag they whooped at the good joke, but when they reached the dead horses they whipped into a run. They had seen no Indian sign at all, which was fool's luck.

Two more hunters came in from north later and now there were horses and enough men so they dared send somebody to Dodge. Henry Lease, a serious, reliable man, a good hunter, volunteered for the dangerous trip. With one of Bellfield's buffalo horses, and carrying two pistols, a Big Fifty and belts of ammunition, he shook hands soberly all around, with

Mrs. Olds last of all. Then he rode for a shadowy draw. Probably not one man there thought he would get through. But Henry Lease would pile dead Indians all around him before he fell.

At the same time two men rode out to make a circle of the remaining hide camps. It was well they did for the Indians were not gone. The third day a party of fifteen suddenly appeared on the edge of a bluff. Billy Dixon tried Hanrahan's Big Fifty on them, and although the distance was not far from seven-eighths of a mile he managed to bring one man down, surely a scratch shot if there ever was one. The others fled into a clump of timber and a few minutes later two of them ran out on foot to drag the down man away.

As the news of the Indian outbreak spread, the hunters gathered at the Walls like blackbirds to a corn patch until there were fully a hundred men there. Everybody had to hear the story of the cracking ridgepole that awoke the camp, and then climb up to examine it, solid as ever. There was a growing sense of safety now, although the watch was still kept in the bastions, but anger too, and impatience to hunt. One morning about dawn, when the night clouds were breaking away the lookout saw heads rising out where the dead Indians and the horse carcasses lay. He called out an alarm. Bat Masterson and a couple of others ran out to see, everybody immediately up and armed. But it was only the heads of wolves as they dragged the entrails out of the Indians. Mrs. Olds held her arm over her face when they told her, as she did when she discovered the heads of the dead Indians stuck on the pickets of Leonard's stockade.

"—To warn the other owls away," one of the men had said sourly as he helped nail them there.

They began to fortify the buildings now, make portholes. A little enclosed lookout was built on top of Rath's store and one at Myers and Leonard, with ladders up the inside. The fifth day Bill Olds was stationed in the one above Rath's. The other lookout shouted that Indians were coming, and everybody ran for the guns. Billy Dixon saw Olds coming down the ladder with his rifle in his hand. A moment later the gun went off, tearing away the top of the man's head. As Mrs. Olds rushed in from the adjoining room, the body of her husband rolled from the ladder and crumpled at her feet, a torrent of blood gushing from the wound.

Young Billy would rather have faced all the Indians between the Red and the Cimarron Rivers than witness this accident, and to the husband of the only woman there. Her grief was pitiful. The men did what they could. They would have died fighting for her but at comforting they were awkward as the cottonwood log pickets, stiff, standing around. They buried Bill Olds that evening, not far from where he died.

The Indians that caused the alarm were a party of twenty-five or thirty coming down the valley of Adobe Walls Creek, heading east. They fired a few shots and went on by. Billy gave Mrs. Olds the lance one of the warriors dropped; that was all he could do.

Henry Lease had been gone for days and still the hunters at the Walls were an isolated little bunch of whites surrounded by Indians. Perhaps the Comanches had got Lease and the freight trains long overdue from Dodge. Perhaps no one anywhere knew of their plight here, and yet every day that they remained increased the danger of an attack by the combined tribes, a fight to finish this spearhead into their ranges, avenge the warriors killed.

But there were difficult men, dangerous men penned in together at the Walls, hunters who got along with no one, outlaws who had fled the sheriff, and both used their guns as other men would say, "Go to hell—"

Uneasy about no word from Dodge, Jim Hanrahan got up a party of twenty-five men including Billy Dixon and Bat Masterson, to make a run through the Indians. But Jim had an opportunity to exercise his command before they even started. Guns were very scarce at the Walls now, and ammunition too. After the death of Olds, Bat Masterson had borrowed his big gun because it had a longer range than Bat's own. When Mrs. Olds discovered the party was starting for Dodge in the morning she sent for her rifle. Bat wanted to keep it overnight in case of an attack. But Mrs. Olds was unstrung and sent a hunter named Brown to fetch it at once. Hanrahan offered to be responsible for the gun's return, but Brown got abusive and the saloonkeeper grabbed him by the neck and the seat of the pants and threw him out into the dust. When the man picked himself up he went for his gun. Hanrahan covered him but for a moment it looked like bloody Dodge, with several dozen dark-faced hunters, hands on guns, taking sides for a slaughter bloodier than the fight with the Indians. Friends grabbed both Brown and Hanrahan and disarmed them. But with the raw nerves there was no telling what bloodshed one pistol shot might start. All night the men of the Walls watched each other and in the morning Mrs. Olds got her gun, but the growing animosity of a camp far too long shut upon itself was in the open now. Everybody was ready for a fight, with any word an insult, any insult a bid for death.

Hanrahan's party started for Dodge with his Irish temper not improved by the realization that the big hunting outfit and the outlay for the saloon at Adobe Walls would surely ruin him. Avoiding the main trail because of Indians, they ran into the buffalo camp of Henry Lease. It was destroyed, his partner dead at least a week. They buried the man and went on—the first party to get through to Dodge from the region of the fighting. Most of the town had cheered the expedition out in March but everybody came to greet their return, anxious to know more about the Walls fight, news of which had driven hunters in to Dodge from every direction. Everybody was anxious about the Texas hide business that was to restore Dodge.

Yes, Lease had come in and a relief party of about

forty hunters and residents of Dodge was on the way to the Walls under Tom Nixon. But this, and the army promise of certain punishment for the Indians wasn't enough for some. Several of the men just in from the Walls went straight to the depot and jumped the first train east. But hunters usually got locoed by the hide business, couldn't leave it alone. Drouth, scarcity of water holes, northers, rattlesnakes, Indians, not even the U. S. Army, could have driven these men east of the ninety-ninth meridian.

The Indians were bitter about the bullet-proofing failure of the Kiowa medicine man, their best hope for throwing the hide men and their long range rifles out of their country while there were still some buffaloes left. Because the small party of Southern Cheyennes were guests in the attack on the Walls they had been given the place of honor, the lead, and so they took the losses, six of their good men killed, including the son of Stone Calf, with only four Comanches dead, a fifth badly wounded, and, so far as was known, not one Kiowa. After the fight a Cheyenne had grabbed the bridle of the lying Kiowa medicine man. But one more killing would not bring the dead warriors back. Besides, the medicine man complained that although not a gun was to be fired on the way a Cheyenne had killed a skunk. He had suddenly appeared among the Indians, certainly mad. The boom of the pistol had been thrown back by the hills.

But now the hearts of the Indians were very bad, even the Kiowas, who had lost much face. Both they and the Comanches scattered into many small parties to raid deep into the Texas settlements. The Southern Cheyennes went into Kansas and up as far as the Smoky Hill River.

In the meantime the buffalo hunters cursed the slowness of the army. Tom Nixon and his outfit brought Mrs. Olds and most of the men back from the Walls, all except a few left to protect the trader property, and even Nixon wasn't sure he would ever see them alive again. His party brought back souvenirs of the Indians killed—finger bones and scalps with long black braids. They had tried to get some of the skulls from the pickets of the stockade to set up behind the bars of Dodge but they were nailed down too solid. There was much big Indian fighting in the saloons now, some from the hunters too. Even Emanuel Dubbs was angry, Dubbs, usually a soft-spoken man who liked to quote from the Scriptures. It had been over two weeks before he could get a party to go help bury his two men killed before the Walls fight. He found only their bones; his wagons and all his hides were burned.

Those left behind at the Walls were still unrescued, the Indians unpunished, the whole hide business bankrupt. Finally Charlie Rath loaded a small train of wagons drawn by mules for greater speed if attacked, although Indians valued mules even above horses, and the stringy work bulls not at all. Some of the men who agreed to go along didn't show up, and a couple more slipped back while within running distance of Dodge. But Rath went on with the remainder, all experienced men, his freight mostly guns, ammunition and supplies for the Walls. He wanted news of the men still there and of his hides and goods. Half-way down the train was attacked by a big war party. The hunters corralled the wagons, the mules inside, and fought the Indians off. Several of the Indian ponies stayed behind, dead on the prairie, but Rath's favorite buffalo horse was there too.

Nationally, times were still hard in 'Seventy-four. The war with Spain, which was to end the depression, didn't materialize, and so, with the hide business gone, Dodge City welcomed the next best thing, a war with the Indians. It made a little money for the contractors and freighters and in the gathering of a large force there was always money from the troops—not another buffalo bonanza, but something. While the hide men watched impatiently, General Miles took until August to work up his expedition, a force large enough to whip the Indians of the southwest to a standstill, perhaps even to extermination. Unable to hunt, Billy Dixon went as scout and guide for Miles, relieved that any Indians shooting at him would now be the responsibility of the U. S. Army. Half a dozen hide outfits waited to sneak along behind Miles, although the general warned them he was moving at striking pace, with no time to rescue besieged hunters.

Then news of Custer's gold strike in the Black Hills came and like snow the hunting outfits melted away. The next morning Miles started for the Panhandle with nine hundred men, while other forces moved in from New Mexico, Ft. Sill, and from lower Texas. This time the hostiles of the southwest would certainly be crushed.

Lieutenant Baldwin with Indian trailers and Billy Dixon and Bat Masterson along, was sent around by Adobe Walls. The scouts rode ahead to reassure the Wallers before the dust of the troops appeared. Baldwin camped about a mile out, up wind from the stinking Walls, and went with Dixon to look over the battleground. Two of the men cooped up for weeks there now dared to ride out towards the Canadian for some wild plums, ripe and plentiful, but beyond safety until today. As though to prove the wisdom of their caution, around a hundred Indians charged out of a sandhill to cut them off. One man guided his horse with his knees and turned his rifle back to hold the Indians off. He got away but the other one forgot he had guns and pounded the wind out of his horse to reach the Walls. Weak from too much post hay the last two months, the horse gave out and the rider got a lance through the body, right before the eyes of Dixon and the troops. By the time the Indians could be pursued they were gone into the hills again. So another man was buried and the next morning everybody left for General Miles' command. When Dixon came past that way in the fall, the Indians had burned the place to the ground. The stockade was still smoking. None of the provisions had been touched. Perhaps the Indians thought they were poisoned. Miles, still angry about the Indian heads stuck on the pickets, as by some savage Africans, the Indian bodies left unburied for the wolves, remarked that poisoning the provisions wouldn't have been beyond the hunters.

Those who had been tolled north by the stories of possible gold in the Black Hills early the summer of 'Seventy-four were unable to get in, or even very close, and so the valley around Dodge City was once more full of waiting hunters. Few washed or had their hair cut, coming into town in the evenings as though returning to their hide camps, so hard is habit to break, even a new one. They drank a little, those who still had credit, and cursed the government and the slowness of its army.

Emanuel Dubbs had lost his entire outfit but Peters, an old hunting friend, still had a good one. He suggested that they go in together, on equal terms. Hiring two good men at seventy-five dollars a month each, and found, they struck south across the Cimarron. Near Water Hole in No Man's Land, they found thousands of buffaloes and not one Indian. They camped out on a wide flat, difficult to approach undetected, and took turns standing night guard. In five days the skinners had two hundred hides pegged out. As soon as dry they were loaded, flat, and tied down casually with ropes. This carelessness cost the life of one of the hunters. On rough ground the loads kept slipping and when the wagons neared a little creek with cottonwoods, Peters rode out ahead to cut some boom poles to anchor the hides. He was gone too long and uneasily Dubbs rode out after him. He saw a letter blowing against some weeds—one of the letters Peters carried in an inside pocket, from the girl who had his promise that this would be his last hunting trip. Knowing that the Indians had got him, Dubbs and his two skinners threw off about half the hides from each load and struck out for Dodge, carefully, cautiously. They made camp in a rough, hidden spot and watched the Indians following them pass.

Next day Dubbs found twelve dead ponies in a wide circle where they had tried to surround another hide camp, but the Big Fifties had won that battle.

Back at Dodge Dubbs didn't know what to do. About ten days later Tom Nixon proposed they go to kill buffaloes with a really big outfit. They got twenty-eight men together and fourteen wagons, with extra teams and riding horses. Nixon was captain, Dubbs second in command. They found great herds on the flats between Wolf Creek and the Canadian, but with no water for the camp except a lake of rain water that was mostly mud and buffalo urine. They had to make coffee of it, very strong coffee. Unfortunately the party was too large for profit and so they divided, Dubbs moving to a new camp.

There were a lot of wild horses around, to be caught some day, but now Dubbs had other things on his mind. A man who claimed to be a scout and Indian fighter owned the lead team in Dubbs' division but at the first smell of the redskins, he got his team so tangled they couldn't move. The fight lasted into the light of the new moon and when it set, about nine o'clock, the hunters pulled out for the main camp through the darkness, without most of their stock.

Emanuel Dubbs was getting tired of this losing game. The next morning he rode out with a party on the Indian trail. Towards sundown they caught sight of a big camp with women and children along, about a mile off. Dubbs had a fine dark brown cavalry horse he found on the prairie. He let out on the reins. The Indians began dropping horses, camp equipment, robes and everything, but escaped into the breaks of the Canadian in the darkness without one shot fired on either side. The hunters picked up about forty head of Indian stock and from then on it was a turn-about chase, with the Indians following them and no telling how many others around, perhaps in ambush. The next day it was the same, the next week too—surely no way to make hides. With seventy-nine head of horses, mules and Indian ponies Dubbs went back to Dodge and joined Miles for the duration of the Red River war of 1874 too.

In September General Miles sent Billy Dixon and Amos Chapman from near the North Fork of the Red to Camp Supply with dispatches. Miles offered them all the soldier escort they needed but he was short of rations. Knowing Indians, Chapman particularly, the two scouts preferred the smallest party possible, to keep out of sight. Finally Amos agreed to take four enlisted men. Well-armed, with saddlebags of ammunition, they traveled most of the first two moon-dark nights, hiding out after dawn. But the second day the rising sun caught them still short of a good day camp, somewhere on the divide between the Washita and Gageby Creek. It was a hot morning; the coats were tied behind the cantle and the horses tired. Towards the top of an unprotected little fire-bared knoll they found themselves almost face to face with a large party of Kiowas and Comanches —trapped, surrounded, compelled to make a stand. Dismounting, they turned the horses over to a soldier named Smith and almost at once he was shot in the back, his gun knocked out of his hand as he fell. The horses stampeded and the warriors rounded them up with loud whoops, knowing they were taking the scouts' best chances for defense or escape.

Now for once Chapman and Dixon were really trapped and afoot. They hugged the ground, knowing the Indians could ride over them in one whooping charge. Perhaps they were so confident they felt the risk was foolish. Men like these scouts wouldn't die without taking some warriors along. It would be easier to pick the whites off.

Two more soldiers were hit, leaving three men unhurt. The scouts decided there was a better defensive position for their long-range rifles out on the wide bare flat several hundred yards off. But before they could move, Chapman got a bullet through the leg, shattering the bone. The blood spurted. Coolly he made a tourniquet, twisting his neck-erchief tight with a long rifle cartridge. Now, with only two whole men their situation was really desperate on open ground. Billy Dixon ran for a nearby buffalo wallow, his hat going, bullets whistling past as he zigzagged like an Indian. The wallow was only about ten feet across, but it offered some protection. He shouted for the others and held the Indians off a while so all but Smith and Chapman made it, the men drawing their knives as they fell in, digging, throwing dirt like frightened badgers.

It was about noon when they reached the wallow. It seemed a futile defense, but finally they cooled to their work. All afternoon the two wounded men sat up against the bank and kept firing, helped to hold the Indians off. But Smith, probably dead, was still out there, and Chapman too, with his knee shattered and bleeding badly, firing, his marksman-ship getting respectful distance from the Indians, who knew that the wounds and the bleeding would do their work. Several times that afternoon Dixon tried to reach him but the Indians were good at that driving back too. Finally he made a run for it, his black hair blowing around his face without a hat to hold it down. But he got Chapman on his back, which was difficult, with Amos the bigger. The Indians tried to charge them with their lances yet the two made it, due to the cool fire of the soldiers that Miles had picked, even though wounded and hopeless now. They brought down several horses and a couple of Indians doing it.

But already the ammunition in the wallow was getting short, the strength of the wounded going as their need for water grew. If they had the cartridges in their saddlebags they might hold out until dark, but now—

Around three o'clock a black cloud rose in the west. Thunder grew to shake the earth and the lightning reddened the sudden blinding sheets of rain. Water gathered in the buffalo wallow, water for the wounded, water red with their own blood. The wind chilled them in their shirtsleeves, until

Chapman's bearded face was drawn, his eyes sunken with pain, but with his leg stretched out in the water he watched for the last charge probably coming soon, to finish off the white men so the Indians could hit for shelter. He knew how they disliked rain. Still the Indians didn't come, and an occasional sharper bolt of lightning showed them out of range, hunched on their horses in the silvered rain, their blankets clutched about them.

As the storm settled into a slower, steadier fall and the scouts counted out their few rounds of ammunition, someone suggested getting Smith's belt and sixshooter. The one able-bodied soldier slipped out and returned to say that Smith was still alive. With Dixon they walked the man over to the wallow between them and not one of the Indians straightened out of his huddling blanket to lift a gun or a spear. Smith's wound was through the lung and the wind sobbed pitifully out of his back at every breath. In the burnt country there wasn't even wet grass but they did get a few tumbleweeds to ease the man's lying.

The drizzle lasted to evening and by dusk all the Indians were gone. While Dixon cleaned the guns and tried to help ease the wounded in the cloudy darkness, it was decided that one of them should go for help. Dixon and the unwounded soldier volunteered but it was more difficult to leave now, with Chapman stiffening from his leg wound and Smith in great pain, begging to be shot. They eased him as much as they could and finally he slept, and died quietly there on the wet ground beside the water-filled buffalo wallow.

Now even Chapman seemed unwilling to have Dixon go. With the frontiersman's contempt for soldiers he argued that they would surely all be killed at tomorrow's dawn without Dixon, ignoring the fact that they had only half a dozen cartridges to be shot by soldier or hunter. What would be the use to bring help if nobody was left alive Amos demanded. Yet plainly the soldier couldn't be sent out. New to

the country, and without stars he would be lost in five minutes.

It was the tightest hole Billy Dixon was ever in and
made the Adobe Walls fight look like a Dodge City jamboree.
In his impatience he fought back his long black hair, wet and
heavy, blowing over his face. It was his pride, left from his
first year as a youth on the frontier, in the heyday of Cody
and Hickok. But now he was tempted to whack it off with his
knife to keep it out of his eyes during the fighting to come at
dawn. In the end nothing was done about that either as they
shivered like freezing buffaloes crowded together at the edge
of the brimming wallow. Morning came, without an attack
and now it was decided that Dixon must go for help. He
should have gone at dark last night.

"Maybe them Indians won't come back—" Chapman
said. "An' if we keep down in the waller, ain't no others
likely to see us, off the trail like we are—"

Billy started without looking back, carefully stepping
on the harder sod to leave no sign. Half a mile out he struck
the plain road to Camp Supply and, watching for Indians all
the time, he hurried as fast as he could, warm enough now in
his shirtsleeves that had been so thin last night. Then suddenly a big party appeared up ahead, Indians or troops, he
couldn't tell as he hid in the weeds. But they traveled two
abreast and so he wanged loose with his rifle and saw the
whole command come to an accordion halt. His second signal shot brought two soldiers to pick him up. It was Major
Price with Miles' supply train, on the way from Supply to the
field headquarters. The same Indians had held the train
corralled four days, when Price luckily came along and raised
the siege. The Indians had just given up the attack when
they found Dixon.

At the wallow the surgeon did very little. The men
were given a little hard tack and dried beef, but Price refused to leave any of his men with them and would not even

give them firearms, even though his ammunition was the wrong caliber for their guns. He had no authority to do these things, he said.

So they were no better off, with Chapman's knee swollen thick as a nail keg, and the wounds of the others inflamed, still alone in a buffalo wallow in hostile Indian country with only one handful of shells.

But midnight of the second day after the troops passed they heard the faint call of a bugle, a wonderfully sweet sound over a dark plain. They fired their guns in reply. At Camp Supply Chapman's leg was amputated above the knee, but he was soon back in the saddle, his crutches hitched to the saddlehorn. The only man lost was Smith, buried in the wallow. Eventually each man was voted a Congressional Medal of Honor. But they never forgave Major Price for exposing them to possible further Indian attacks and needless suffering, particularly for Chapman.

When Miles first started southwestward, the Indians had swung north around his left. Before he was out of Kansas the Southern Cheyennes had killed a surveying crew on Crooked Creek. The five dead men were left in a row on the ground, the oxen in their yokes, the hindquarters cut off, even the camp dog killed. There were twenty-eight bullet holes in the wagon, the water barrel like a sieve. The Indians had ammunition.

While this was south of the Arkansas, where the Indians believed their treaties forbade all white men to go, there were atrocities farther up too. On the old Smoky Hill trial, Medicine Water's Southern Cheyennes killed five of the emigrant Germaine family and captured the four daughters, ranging from sixteen down to four or five years. With the four terrified girls they hurried down across the Arkansas into the wilds of the Texas Panhandle. Seeing these white captives in their village cheered those cast down by the losses at Adobe Walls, and their hearts were good again.

But they would not be good for long, not with the soldiers marching everywhere, determined to punish the Indians thoroughly this time. Later in September Mackenzie captured the villages of the Kiowas, Comanches and Southern Cheyennes in a canyon near the Red River. The camp of Cheyennes at the upper end managed to get to their horses and escaped with most of them. There had been talk about going into the agencies because the hunting life was very hard without ammunition and the buffalo so wild, the troops marching everywhere. But when such a large force of bluecoats appeared, these Cheyennes, who had been attacked at Sand Creek and the Washita, were alarmed. They fled back to the Staked Plains as fast as they could pound their ponies.

But the troops followed, and when the trails scattered good scouts went out in wide circles as determined Indian hunters did. Early in November, Lieutenant Baldwin, with Bat Masterson as one of the scouts, surprised a camp that fled but left the two smaller of the Germaine girls in the path of the troops. They were together on a buffalo robe that they drew over their heads in alarm when the strangers approached. The children were tattered and worn by the two months with the fleeing Indians but otherwise unharmed.

By now it was known that their two sisters were in the camp of Stone Calf, the Stone Calf who had lost his son at Adobe Walls. But they were alive and Miles, in close pursuit, sent a messenger demanding the immediate return of the Indians to their agency and the release of the two girls unharmed or to face extermination. Stone Calf's starving camp was overtaken at the Texas-New Mexico border in a blizzard, the people almost frozen, starving, most of their horses dead. The chief began his last return to the reservation. On March 1, 1875, the four orphans were reunited.

Now the Indians were thoroughly whipped; the men assumed to be their leaders ironed and sent to prison in Florida. Now the Texas herd was free for all comers.

CHAPTER IX

TOWARD THE BRAZOS

THE year 1874 had been a really momentous one, from the Indian defeats in the Panhandle to the discovery of gold in the Black Hills and beyond. Somehow the great Republican herd and the season of 1867 seemed a hundred years ago instead of a meager seven. Its hunters were scattered. Some were dead, many gone into cattle or homesteading, and some into horse stealing and similar activities as easier and more compatible in this time of unemployment.

Much of the winter Bill Cody stood at the footlights and lifted his fine western hat from the cascade of yellow hair that already seemed of another generation. Most of the time he had the center of the stage unchallenged, for the uneasiness that had driven Wild Bill Hickok out of the Sioux country made him uneasy in the show too. Early he discovered that at least one of Cody's Indians was not a New Yorker in sepia paint but a blood relative, by a Siouan capture, of Chief Whistler and Whistler's nephew that Bill and his partner killed two years ago in their hide camp near the Republican. Friction arose. Wild Bill thought the redskins were biting the dust a little less promptly upon the report of his white-handled pistols. Now and then the Indian among them made threatening gestures toward him, bringing the nearly closed right hand sharply down and across from the shoulder, stopping it with downward extended fingers in a little rebound—the sign for "Kill! Kill, kill!"

And all the time the black eyes were watching him. Evidently the Indian had heard the story of the chief shot down on a friendly visit to Bill's camp. Perhaps Bill was remembering that no angry Whistler would ride in with his saddle quirt striking left and right to save him from the angry warriors as back in 1867.

Slowly the story of Wild Bill's departure from the show came back to the buffalo country. At Rochester he had obtained some of the sand shot cartridges Cody used to break the glass balls on the stage. With these Hickok peppered the bare legs of the Indians, real and pretended, making the warning sign to them that the next shot would carry a bullet. They ran howling through the audience and Wild Bill quit the show. Perhaps this happened just now because the Mrs. Lake that Bill met in Kansas was in Rochester with her circus, and she had such a pretty, motherly way about her.

But the Lake circus moved on and so Wild Bill came back west to Kansas City and finally to Cheyenne, where there was little to do, everything hanging like a hail cloud on the horizon, waiting for the Black Hills to open. He tried gambling again, at the saloon now called the Gold Room for the gold dust and nuggets along the back of the bar, apparently brought down from the Hills by Charley Reynolds when he carried Custer's news of gold from the grass roots down.

But something happened there to make Wild Bill leave. The stories varied, yet all agreed that whether he lost squarely or was swindled by the faro dealer, Bill did knock him over the head with the billiard cue he used for a cane and walked out with the contents of the cash drawer. And once more, as down in Hays and Abilene, it seemed best that Bill take to the open country, so he went trapping up in the Yellowstone region with California Joe. Wild Bill Hickok of the glossy curls upon his shoulders, the rose-embroidered vest and silk-lined cape, partnering with Joe of the ragged red beard, the man who never washed and who used a piece of mule rope to belt his ragged old cavalry coat.

Down around Dodge City and with Miles' column the buffalo hunters wondered if Bill wouldn't be showing up for a venture into the Texas herd to make a new stake. They didn't know that he stopped at Topeka for eye treatments and that not even the glasses so scorned on the frontier could make a buffalo herd look like more than a smudging of brush in a darkening haze to Bill now, unless straight on, just before him, like a poker hand. Certainly he would not venture south into the region of the Johnny Rebs, his sworn enemies, not into Texas, the home state of Coe, who died of Bill's fast draw, some said; of the old-fashioned drop from behind, others insisted. Not when Bill could see little more than the outlines of a man if he stood to the side or in the shadows.

Some news was brought back by the Kansas hunters who had been turned away from the Black Hills. It seemed that Coe's brother Jim showed up at Cheyenne, saying he had come a thousand miles, from the west coast, to avenge his brother. The story, which sounded like Ned Buntline, was that Wild Bill got caught with only the small double-barrel souvenir pistol Cody gave him in New York, with only one cartridge in it. But Bill saw Coe and a partner in the bar mirror, drawing down on him. He whirled, killed Jim with the one bullet, threw the gun in the face of the other man, pushed him backward against the bar, and broke his neck.

A hunter who had seen the fight with Thompson, one of the several men who survived being shot dead by Hickok, heard this neck-breaking story. "Guess Bill better go trap skunks with Californy Joe!" he remarked.

Bill went, perhaps because he was down to frayed linen and didn't even own a horse any more. He rode California Joe's extra one while Joe sat on his favorite, the mule.

Charley Reynolds was gone from the Platte country too. He went back to the upper Missouri with Custer out of the Black Hills and was trapping and hunting meat for the army posts. He seemed permanently identified with Custer and the Seventh now and while he did no bragging on them, he never said right out that the general's hounds could not catch an antelope who did not have at least one leg broken. Charley was untouched by the animosities and connivances that shook the regiment, or by the gold fever rising fast. He worked, saved his money and kept his hair neatly trimmed around the ears, his chin close-shaven under the drooping but moderate mustache, his steady blue eyes reddened by no more than the winds of Dakota Territory.

There were many depredations in his old stomping grounds in northern Kansas. But it wasn't the Sioux. They were on their last buffalo hunt in the Republican region, under the guard of an alert detachment of troops. When Spotted Tail and the other chiefs objected to the soldier escort they were reminded of the massacre of the Pawnees last year, and the protesting ones fell silent over their guttering pipes.

Not that it would matter now, Old Spot and the others knew. The hide men who came down from Sidney this year found more hunters than buffaloes. Yet there were still some scattered bunches in the wild region between the South Platte and the farthest reaches of the Republican, always sparsely watered, particularly after this summer of drouth that killed so many year-around creeks. So the remnants of the old herd had come to the South Platte with its water from the Rockies. But this time they found the south bank of the river lined with hunters who permitted none of the frantic animals to drink. Tortured by thirst, the buffaloes returned again and again, always to flee from the boom of the big guns. But each time they left some behind, perhaps to kick a little half circle in the sandy river bottom. Not even the darkness shielded them now. Fires were kept burning all along the water's edge for over fifty miles, reflected in the wild little eyes, and the guns boomed as usual. In this way the whole herd was destroyed in four days and nights, four days and nights without water. The valley stank with what was estimated by some as fifty thousand carcasses in one stretch of river and the few mud-cracked water holes off on the uplands, all fallen to the scattering boom of the buffalo guns.

Even Spotted Tail, the cosmopolitan of the Sioux chiefs, the one who learned to face the hard fact of the white man during a time spent in irons at Ft. Leavenworth years ago—even he wept when he saw this last end of his great herd. A few hundred buffaloes escaped to the farthest breaks of the upper Republican, perhaps to hidden, unknown springs and spring pools. They were wild now, wild and wily as mustangs, but it was a little late.

Although the depression was easing some, and fewer people would die of starvation in New York the winter of 'Seventy-four and five, the Santa Fe was still stalled for funds at the Colorado line. Times in general were harder in the settlements along the buffalo country. The grasshoppers had reappeared in the summer, coming in great shimmering, silvery clouds, to drop on garden, field and pasture. They worked with a steady hum of jaws. When they moved they were hub-deep in some of the rutted roads and so thick on the railroad tracks the grease of their fat bodies stalled the trains. Settlers fought them with flapping sheets to send them into the air, and with rings of fire against their march, but nothing helped and the earth was left clean as a table.

If it hadn't been for the flying plague the grass of the Republican and the Arkansas country would have stood thick and tall as never since the buffalo first came to the region, and even before that, before his long-horned relative, *bison crassiocornis,* grew up out of the richness of the retreating ice sheets as they left the Great Plains.

The slaughter had moved south and it was estimated that in the years 1872-4, mostly in the Arkansas region, more buffalo meat was wasted than there were cattle in Holland and Belgium together, or three-fourths as many as in Ireland, half as many as Great Britain. The result was the same as if a fearful murrain had destroyed all the cattle to these proportions. Yet the winter of 1873-4 thousands of people had died of starvation in the United States, and perhaps millions were marked for all time by malnutrition.

But now there was the Texas herd, which ranged over practically all the two hundred miles from Griffin west across the Staked Plains to the upper Pecos and from the north line of Texas four hundred miles south to the head of Devil's canyon. Here was a great region almost unhunted, due to the distance to markets, the ferocity of the Kiowas and Comanches who claimed most of this area as their tribal hunting grounds, and the danger of the great waterless stretches. The herd had been increased, hunters said, by the wiser and wilier bunches from the Arkansas fleeing the boom and stink of the big guns, as the fragment of the Republican herd had withdrawn to the sparse regions beyond the upper river.

To be sure hunters had long worked around the south and eastern fringes of this range, like wolves slipping out of the oak shinnery to nip at the drags, but it was not enough to bring caution to the great plodding animals who had so long trusted to their size, their power and number. For most of the world the Black Hills of Custer might be the new Eldorado, but to the professional hide man of the middle 'Seventies this Texas herd was a more tangible and immediate bonanza.

Some of the best hunters from the Adobe Walls region had been scouting for Miles but as soon as word came of the general's success against the Indians, everybody with an outfit standing idle felt he must move. Men like the Mooars, Rath and Reynolds were ready to follow the buffaloes and set up new centers of operation farther south, perhaps on the Clear Fork of the Brazos, even as far down river as Ft.

Griffin, well below the Indian depredation region of the Canadian. Perhaps Fort Worth would be a more likely outlet than Dodge but that couldn't be helped.

The first extensive hide crew to start out of Griffin was rigged up by Joe McCombs. He had gone to Texas on a cow-hunting job in 1871, at seventeen, for fifteen dollars a month, and made one trip up the Chisholm Trail. But the next year there were no jobs around Griffin and the Comanches stole his horses. Surveying westward for the railroad, he saw more buffaloes than he believed could exist, surely fifty thousand in one herd near Kiowa Peak. He had his first real scare from buffaloes near Double Mountain. There was a rising cloud of dust, like the beginning of a black blizzard, and suddenly all the buffaloes started to run, heading into the wind, toward the surveying crew. The men jumped into the wagons but already the herd was thundering around them in growing stampede, tongues out, running blind and unswerving in the thick dust. The men whipped their teams into a gallop, clinging to the bouncing wagons, hoping to avoid cut banks and arroyos, but there was no stopping for anything, the dusty heads and humps like the choppy rise and fall of a dark and menacing sea against the wagons. It was a terrifying experience, and it was mostly accident that the surveyors escaped.

But such herds represented money, and with John Jacobs and John Poe, McCombs left Griffin on Christmas day, 1874, going until they hit buffaloes and then established a camp on Mocking Bird Creek. McCombs shot while Poe and Jacobs skinned and pegged out the winter hides. During the two months they saw not one man, Indian or white, and heard no boom of buffalo gun outside of their own. Then suddenly one morning there was only the empty prairie so recently spotted with the dark, browsing creatures who were not afraid of anything that was not straight upwind from their wet, flaring nostrils. The hunters had seven hundred hides.

Back at Griffin they heard of a camp attacked by Indians, with several hunters killed. But they felt so secure that McCombs and Poe left Jacobs to haul their hides in while they went on farther west. They rigged up a team of Indian ponies, tough and hardy enough for winter grazing. With these hitched to a light wagon they went up the Clear Fork of the Brazos and stayed to the first of May, while Jacobs followed them around with the hide wagon. They got thirteen hundred but one of the ponies slipped a shoulder on a hard pull. They had a few close calls, too. At one place McCombs killed several bulls close together. When Poe came over to skin them, one big bull sprang up not over fourteen feet away and charged. McCombs jumped behind Poe and shot past him. There was only time for the one bullet but it dropped the bull at their feet, his heavy body rocking the ground as it hit. They did no more hunting that day, the sway of the earth under that thunderous rocking stayed under their feet until the sun went down.

On windy days the kill was usually strung out a mile or more into the wind and the hunter had to pass the down buffaloes, perhaps only stunned or crippled. These times were not for old ammunition, sputtering or dead. On such a run one of Jacob's partners had to pass a big cow. Suddenly she was up and charging. He gave her one slug and with no time to reload, he drifted. It was a race. When she finally went down she was so close she snorted blood on him. He went straight to camp and meditated the rest of the day. Jacobs was sympathetic; he knew a buffalo could hook a pocket handkerchief to shreds on the ground.

At Griffin they got two dollars for the skins that passed for robes and one fifty for the hides—the first kill of any consequence ever marketed there. But Charlie Rath had anticipated a growing business and was already in partnership with Conrad, the post sutler. He built big yards, ready for a rush like the one he had seen at Dodge.

Another new hunter was young John Cook. He had

been driven from the settlements by hard times and
the Texas fever brought up the trail and the grasshoppers.
First he tried prospecting and then hunted with a Mexican
outfit a while. He got lost in the Adobe Walls region, so lost
that even his rifle was gone. Finally he ran into another reckless man, one who had all his family along, his wife, son, and
his wife's brother with his family, including small children.
The Woods were blithely crossing the Indian country southward from the Picket Wire (Purgatoire) River only a short
time after the hunters at the Walls had to be rescued by the
army. They welcomed Cook, even without a gun, paid him
thirty cents a head for skinning and pegging, and agreed to
let him use the old Enfield rifle sometime. Wood shot sixteen
buffaloes the first day with his Big Fifty, the carcasses strung
out neatly over half a mile, and young Johnny Cook was as excited as a dog under a coon tree to see them.

Then a big party of Indians took over the camp while
the men were all away. The white women and children were
terrified, but fortunately the Indians had been hunting with
a troop escort, who came tearing up. The officer pointed out
angrily that the country was full of hostiles on the loose—
Indians who would have left them dead on the ground.

"This is no place for women and children," he
snorted, and ordered five troopers to escort the Woods to his
camp on White Deer Creek. The next morning he started
them off on the Dodge City-Ft. Elliott trail. It passed the
only dwelling in all this region, the Springer ranch on the
Canadian—a blockhouse that faced the river, with a square
pit, six by six, and six feet deep, inside the building, joined
by a fifty foot covered trench leading out to another circular
pit with a roof above the ground and portholes all around.
Another trench ran from the blockhouse to the corral and
the stables. Evidently Springer expected unwelcome visitors,
red or white.

He took all the hides Wood and Cook had at two fifty
for the old bulls, three dollars for the choice cow robes and

one seventy-five for the others. They got provisions and ammunition, and Johnny Cook traded for two fair suits of underwear, socks, boots and other necessaries. Springer said there was no danger from Indians until March, but perhaps this was to sell them range supplies. He said the great mass of buffaloes was south of the Red and would be on the Canadian in May or June. Wood built a log cabin four miles southwest of the Springer ranch, the first pale-face family in that part of the Panhandle. Cook bought a Sharps .44 and a reloading outfit. He got the owner's interest in the buffalo ranges and the gun, almost new, for thirty-six dollars. The man had shot himself seriously with it, a hoodoo, he said, but it was an elegant weapon, with fine buckhorn sights. Wild turkeys were plentiful and on moonlit nights Cook shot them from the roosting trees against the moon. Bears were common in the persimmon grove, and there was small game everywhere. It was a fine place for a man to live.

When Johnny Cook finally got to Ft. Elliott toward Indian Territory he discovered that Charlie Rath and his partner Bob Wright had a large store under way at Sweet Water Creek, three miles below the post. They were busy hauling their unsold stock from Dodge and soon had acres of piled hides behind the place. Sweet Water was fast becoming a wild and wooly hide town with a large dance hall, two restaurants and three saloons. Hide outfits, large and small, from ten to fifteen a day, were in and out from the herd of buffaloes below the Red and moving south toward the Pease and the Brazos as the weather chilled.

At Sweet Water Cook met Charlie Hart, from north Kansas. He was a six-footer, supple and lean as a poplar. He had been through Andersonville prison and knew how to take hardship—a casual, easy-going man until his periodic sprees. Then his imagination ran free and fancy. Sober, no man knew more about the hide business. He had brought his experienced skinners along but the buffaloes were so plentiful and tame that he could use another man to keep his freighters busy. While the six-man outfit got ready Johnny Cook went around the surprised garrison at Elliott with a gunny sack begging newspapers and magazines to take along. They left Sweet Water with provisions for three months, including two hundred fifty pounds of St. Louis shot tower lead, three twenty-five pound cans of Dupont powder, with a little extra, and four thousand primers. Soon after New Year's 1875, the two light wagons started southward, leaving the oxen to plod their heavy freight wagons behind. For five days they picked up stragglers, mostly old bulls, and spread the hides at night, rolling them up on the wagons in the morning. The seventh day, from the Pease River divide, they saw the rear of a great dark herd. Hart made camp near five other outfits down from Sweet Water, including Hi Bickerdyke, son of Mother Bickerdyke, the famous Civil War nurse. Hart met him with so much enthusiasm and gratitude that he seemed drunk, drunk on Texas snakehead.

They met Carr and Causey here too, with their big bull train, said to be one of the most efficient outfits on the range, everything run like a factory, no lost motion, no guess work, beyond the vagaries native to animal and weather. They had followed the buffaloes all the way down, entirely too far from the Sweet Water trading post, but now that they were here they planned to stay for the final kill, which might be soon.

"Oh, hell, we plan to be huntin' all our lives," Jacobs and Poe protested once to one of the Causey brothers.

But the hunter only ran the ramrod down his gun once more, held it toward the sun, the glistening bore cut by the thin dark spiral of the rifling. By spring the Causeys had thirty-seven hundred hides, a high percentage of the robes carefully selected from the herds that were already growing a little wilder and pushing westward out on the Staked Plains a little farther than the buffalo chip signs of other years.

Hart and the others found ideal camp sites in the breaks of the Salt Fork of the Brazos, in a vast rough region of decomposed mica, isinglass, a little west of the 100 meridian, with Kiowa Peak to the east and Double Mountain south. There were antelope, deer and turkeys, even poults, although even these young were bitter and sickening from the chinaberries, the soap berry tree. They gathered by the thousands to the roosts just below camp. Deer were always around, also panthers, polecats, swifts and wolves. Sometimes when Johnny Cook looked around the camp with all the hides, all the game, he wondered what he would do if he were the son of an Indian and saw all his commissary, his whole living, killed like this. But it was a case of survival, and Johnny's qualms were forgotten when Charlie Hart got sixty-three buffaloes in two hours. On a February day he shot one hundred and seventy-one, and a little later two hundred and three in one day on less than ten acres of ground. From a little rise young Johnny looked over the scattered buffaloes, mostly cows, robes, worth two fifty each. It was like gold, while up in Kansas Johnny had seen only drouth and grasshoppers last year, and always the danger of tick fever. Swiftly he motioned the skinning wagon up, and drawing his Wilson knife, fell to his work.

The hides dried very slowly in the chill moist winter of the south, and had to be turned several times before they were cured. Then they were stacked eight feet high, sorted as piled, bulls in one, cows another, and the young stuff in the kip stack. Strings cut from green hides were tied to a peghole in each corner of the bottom hide and then up through the holes of the top hide and drawn tight.

Usually Charlie shot from eight to noon, with some good killing time in the evenings too. But these late carcasses had to lay all night and were more tedious to skin and more difficult to keep free of knife gashes. The big guns boomed in every direction until the last of February. Then

suddenly not a buffalo was to be seen. Hart had two thousand
and three hides drying and stacked. Johnny Cook had
skinned nine hundred two of these and earned two hundred
twenty-five dollars and fifty cents in forty-one days, averaging twenty-two a day.

While they were cleaning up camp, ready to move,
Johnny saw twelve bulls come along in single file about a
mile off, marching towards the camp on the trail of the
vanishing herd. Charlie Hart sent Johnny to try his eye on
them. With the .44 in his hand he went at a trot to a ravine
where the buffaloes would pass. He made it in time, dropped
to a sitting position and set up his rest sticks, trying to
settle his panting as he waited, excited that the wind and the
terrain were both good.

The bulls came in sight in single file, following the
narrow trail at an ordinary walk. At about sixty odd yards
Johnny got a good lung shot on the leader. The bull crowned
his back up high, made a jump forward, and stopped stock
still. The others jumped too, but sideways at the crack of the
gun, and scattered up the slope. The hunter reloaded, gave
the lead buffalo a quarter shot into the vitals. The remainder
whirled and started back up the draw, giving Johnny a good
sight at the new leader. Hit, the bull turned around and
started down the way they had been headed at first. The
next bullet struck with a loud crack, perhaps on a horn.
The buffalo whirled clear around a couple of times and ran
back and hooked at the one shot first, now down and struggling.

Johnny Cook took a slow breath to steady himself
and then fired again, this time at the bull that was farthest,
three hundred yards and escaping, although he knew his gun
was too light. By now the hooking one was bolting off down
the ravine and about to turn the bend, about a quarter of a
mile away, kicking up the dust as he galloped. Johnny shot
after him and glanced swiftly around. There were only three
of the twelve left in sight now, one dead, one kicking, and

the other down too, and weaving his great mop of head right and left, probably dying. Johnny grabbed his rest sticks and started up the draw but the weaving bull was on his feet again, back bowed, his tail straight up. With two more shots, fast, he fell. There was still another buffalo at the head of the draw, some two hundred yards from Johnny, standing there alone, head turned away, apparently wounded. Johnny drew a fine bead just to the top of the rump as Charlie Hart had showed him. As the heavy bullet hit, it seemed to lift the whole hind part clear off the ground. The bull gave a few awkward jumps, turned sideways, crouched on his hunkers and finally fell over on his left side, kicked a few times and died.

Triumphantly the hunter took the four tongues to camp. In his first shooting for the old-time hunter, he had got four bulls out of twelve with thirteen bullets from a .44. He felt worth the soft thick beard he had been growing this fall.

"You'll make a good hunter yet, Johnny," Charlie said to him. "But I need you worse with the skinning knife—"

They moved camp across the Brazos and over the divide to fair hunting until March that fat year of 1875. Then their stock of primers got short. Big guns were booming in every direction and one of the skinners was sent around the camps to borrow some. He found Carr and Causey with their thirty-seven hundred hides and out of flour. Hart traded them flour for primers and sent his freighter to Ft. Griffin. Seven weeks later the man wasn't back. By then the camp was out of both flour and coffee. After three days without bread Hart heard that Goff, with a camp off to the southeast, had nearly a thousand pounds on hand. He sent Johnny Cook with a light wagon to find Goff's camp, reminding him not to get lost this time.

Johnny started out ruefully and hadn't gone five miles, watching the sun and the terrain carefully, when he found himself up against a great herd of buffaloes turned into their northward swing, one dark mass east and south of him as far as he could see, the horses faunching, afraid. Either Johnny had to go through, turn back, or go around. The wind was brisk from the north and the buffaloes were heading into it at their quick step. The new hunter had heard of buffalo stampedes but he was afraid of ridicule if he turned back. By now the west and southwest were solid black too, so there was no going around. Surrounded by the swiftly moving herd, he stood up in the wagon to line up spots of barer ground as he whipped the horses against the movement of the buffaloes. He didn't know how they would act; perhaps attack the team, or try to walk right over them as he heard they did trains. But the buffaloes calmly separated off before him, turned to the right and then closed in behind, the others barely changing their course at all, streaming past him, grunting, their dew claws rattling. The stink of them, and the rolling motion of the flowing herd made him sick as from a dark and restless sea as he had heard others call it.

After a couple of hours Johnny got more used to the rolling motion of the great humps passing him, and began to enjoy himself a little. The horses plodded on quietly now and he was free to watch for breaks in the herd, for gullies and washouts, to plan. John Poe was right. The hunting would go on forever. It would take the whole standing army of the United States to exterminate just this one great herd.

When Johnny figured he should be about two miles from Goff's camp, he was in the very center of the herd and couldn't see how to get sidewise through the streaming animals. But he could hear the boom of the big guns off northwest, not over half a mile. Then suddenly the buffaloes shifted to their right and started running, jamming together, crowding like stock in a loading chute, crossing the route directly ahead of Johnny, going eastward very fast, so fast none could stop. Johnny had to go with them or be run down. Almost upsetting the wagon in the short turn, he whipped the team and went with the run. For a mile he tore along with his horses at a gallop, watching for arroyos by the dip and rise of the backs before him. The compact mass of buffaloes was a jam of fleeing, wild, frantic, ferocious-looking beasts, their hoofs sharp upon everything that fell before them. And on each side and ahead too, now, he could hear the same deep tones of the Big Fifties and wondered how soon he would be in line with some heavy bullet gone wild.

Then suddenly the buffaloes east of him wheeled right again and began to gallop southward. He looked behind him, expecting to be run down by the frantic, stampeding herd, but the buffaloes on the north kept on in that direction, heading towards the breaks of the Salt Fork of the Brazos, and left a spreading prairie clear. A horsebacker appeared from somewhere, one of the Quinn brothers, camped not far off. Next Johnny met Goff, out horseback too. He had left his shooting to investigate the strange team. Goff's hair was as long as the pictures of Wild Bill Hickok and Bill Cody, but Goff's was tangled and dirty—the man altogether the dirtiest, greasiest, smokiest mortal the greenhorn Johnny Cook had ever seen. But he was riding a fleet-looking horse, and his Sharps .44 grasped carelessly in his hand was shining and new.

With the old muskrat cap pushed back, his sharp, suspicious eyes considered this young man with a light wagon revealed by the sudden parting in the midst of the buffalo herd. Hide thieves had been reported up north a few days ago, and only the fact that his wagon was empty saved Johnny Cook from a danger worse than any buffalo stampede.

Goff turned out to be a reasonable man. "Yeh, I know Hart," he said, nodding his shaggy head, cooling a little. Yeh, he had some flour to spare, he guessed, and even volunteered to show Johnny a Hickey pricelist he had in his pocket. Hickey was Lobenstein's Irish agent down here at Ft. Griffin, he said, and was authorized to buy all the hides offered. "Pays for 'em right on the range and hauls 'em to Fort Worth—"

The next day Johnny was driving through the herd

a second time, a quieter herd, loitering to graze. He found
Hart's camp deserted, but Charlie's buffalo horse was there,
close-hobbled, and no sign of Indians around that Johnny
could recognize. Only a big pile of empty cartridges ready
for reloading. So he cleaned up around camp and toward sundown he ripped open one of the flour sacks and wet up a
batch of biscuits in the top of the sack as in a big mixing pan.
The biscuits were browned and hot for the men when they
came in, with fried young buffalo steak and red gravy. The
herd had hit the region yesterday, Charlie said. He got a
hundred ninety-seven that had to be skinned, with enough
new killings left to keep Johnny busy all tomorrow. They
turned in early, thankful that Hart had the foresight to put
the camp under a steep bluff which was now splitting the
moving herd that passed quietly on both sides. All night the
buffaloes went by, their grunting gentle, their hoofs silent
under the rattle of their dew claws.

Hart's camp got three thousand, three hundred and
sixty-three hides the ninety days here on the Salt Fork before the herd passed. There were a lot of old bulls down
here, old stub-horns that would have died in the fierce blizzards of the Republican country or farther north, where
snow laid on and the cold dropped to thirty below and lower.
The old hides were heavy, took a good close shot and mighty
hard to skin. The other hunters around did a lot of shooting
too. Hickey set up a base at Quinn's and gathered twelve
thousand hides before the freighters arrived. Rath and
Wright of Sweet Water had agreed to come for Hart's kill, at
top prices, no matter how far south he went, but Lobenstein's
Irish buyer was a genial man, quick and impulsive, and he
didn't like to see his competitors get one hide south of the
Red River. He had Lobenstein's European market to supply. All the accoutrements of the British army were made of
buffalo leather because it was more pliant, more elastic.
The hunters found Hickey an entertaining talker, emotional,

with a thick brogue. It hurt his soft Irish heart to see
one horn that could be cut into a lady's comb go to waste,
one buffalo bone lost. And the meat! It was a God's sin and
shame, the waste of it.

So Lobenstein's Irishman talked Charlie Hart's harvest away from Rath and Wright, with a check for two thousand dollars laid down on the spot, the balance payable
with the hides at Griffin. Then he went on to buy Hi Bickerdyke's pile too, seventeen hundred hides for Hi and his two
helpers. Still genial, Hickey threw in most of the plug tobacco and sourballs he had along.

Charlie Hart staked a trail from Quinn's with thin
box lids pegged out on the prairie marked "To Hart's Camp"
in soot and tallow, and then left. Johnny Cook stayed alone
to guard the hides until Hickey's long string of freight wagons came. By then the hunters were suddenly brought back
to cold reality. Johnny found a fresh Indian trail. Not certain
what he should do, he cached the powder and lead and hurried over to the old frontiersman, Arkansas John Great-
house. The four men were killing time playing draw poker
under an awning of buffalo hide against the hot spring sun.
They staked their interest in the piles of hides around
camp, anteing with the long cartridges instead of chips. At
Johnny's excited story the men ran for their horses and
spread the news round the other camps. Some were already
deserted, the outfits among the thirty camped under the pecan trees at Griffin, where Charlie Hart was having a nice
spree after a big winter.

Nothing was disturbed anywhere by the Indians, not
this time, but there was news of an outbreak by the Cheyennes in Indian Territory, and more news from up on the
Republican River. It was Indian news to set the hide men to
gnawing thoughtfully at their Lorillard plugs, perhaps not
talking at all until they had their cuds juicing.

CHAPTER X

TWO BIG KILLS

ROMERO, the scout and interpreter who worked around the army posts of Indian Territory, was suddenly back in the Mexican meat camp where Johnny Cook had worked a while when he first left Kansas. Johnny ran into him when he took Billy Dixon over there on an errand for the troops. Billy was in a light wagon with Amos Chapman along, Amos ready to get back into the saddle, as soon as the scar was well hardened over the amputation from the buffalo wallow fight with the Indians last year.

On the way back they camped with Cook's outfit a couple of nights to ask about the Indian sign reported. Some northern hunters down recently came over too, Hank Campbell, Sol Rees and a couple of others. At first the sunburnt, hairy men sat silent as the two scouts told the news of the military operations the last year. But after a while the newcomers began to talk, too, Campbell first, and it was just as well that the next day was one of scuddy wind and rain, for none of the hunters got to the bed robes before dawn.

It had been a night of big talk and big destruction, not of buffaloes but of Indians. Now it seemed the Indians were really whipped, gone, the buffalo ranges cleared, first by troops down here in the southwest, now up in the Republican region, and although they were not to speak of it, by army orders, the hunters had got in the good licks that cleaned out a nest of bloody Cheyennes, Hank Campbell said. He had been there but he was supposed to keep his blab shut.

Nobody had told Chapman, Billy Dixon and Romero to keep quiet about what they knew and as Johnny Cook listened he felt guilty for the doubt he had had last winter, when he wondered what he would do if he were the son of an Indian and saw his land taken away, his stock, the fine buffaloes, destroyed, left to rot. The men told Johnny the bloody story of the Germaines killed and the daughters captured, and of the rising number of buffalo hunters shot, many in the back, to fall into the ashes of their campfires.

The scouts had seen much of the campaign down here in the Panhandle, until Mackenzie struck the Indians in Palo Duro canyon, September 1874. Although he destroyed the camps, most of the Indians got away so he killed their horses to prevent recapture, killed over fourteen hundred it was said, over in Tule canyon near where some hunters were working now. That had put the Indians afoot in the snow, without shelter or beds. They had dragged into the agencies in Indian Territory, ragged, starving, the smaller children and the tired old people left behind as they died, although one Kiowa woman carried her dead baby two hundred miles on her back, and fought before she would give it up at the disarming.

Afterward the Indians were thrown into a guarded camp, their shelters mostly dugouts that they made with their knives, for there were no skins to replace the lodges lost. Then on April 6, a windy day, all the men of the Southern Cheyennes were lined up between the troops, and the two eldest of the rescued captive sisters brought over in a carriage. Mighty pretty young ladies they were in their new white woman fixin's, old Amos Chapman said, fixin's paid for by money to come out of the Cheyenne appropriations, and rightly so.

Yes, that was true, Romero said, in his broken English. He had been interpreter and counselor for the two girls and walked beside them down the line of Indians as they pointed out those who had killed their family and captured them. Most of the guilty were still out but they selected fifteen, including some old chiefs and one woman. General Neill had been ordered to take thirty-three prisoners from these Southern Cheyennes, and, maybe because he'd been hitting the bottle a little too strong, he filled out the number by cutting off the eighteen men at the end of the line, without any accusation by the girls or Romero.

"It still don't seem quite right—" Old Amos said slowly over his pipe, perhaps out of the affection he felt for his Cheyenne wife.

The southern buffalo men laughed, their wind-narrowed eyes crinkling above their bearded cheeks in the firelight as they passed the brown jug once more to those who drank the rotgut, and asked about the devilish Comanches.

Some Comanches were put in irons too, and Kiowas, enough to make seventy-five prisoners altogether, counting the Cheyennes. Their leg chains were fastened to rods bolted down the center of the wagons that hauled them away to the railroad for the Florida prison. But there had been a little trouble with the ironing, perhaps because the Cheyenne women were taunting their men for letting the whites put irons on their legs with no more fight than the foolish horses of the white men accept the hot shoes.

"Are there no men left fit to be the fathers of our children?" one of them had called out. She was a mighty handsome woman, Romero said, in recollection. It made one of the warriors break loose from the guard with the blacksmith and run towards the Indian prison camp. The troops fired after him, killing some women and children, and the whole camp fled for a sandhill near the river, leaving the dead and wounded like rag bundles on the ground. The man with the ring forged around his leg was wounded too, but helped to get away. The Indians had hidden some guns there before the disarming and, digging breastworks in the soft sand, they managed to stand off the charging troops even with a couple of Gatling guns to help, until the drizzling, rainy darkness. By morning a cannon had been fetched up; shells were lobbed into the breastworks but the Indians were gone, their tracks joining the small band of Medicine Arrow. The old chief had stayed out until he knew how those who surrendered were treated. Now they all headed up across the Arkansas River and north together.

Two weeks later troops sent to intercept these Southern Cheyennes fleeing to join the Sioux, heard reports that they were somewhere on the Middle Sappa in north Kansas. There were still a few hide men up there chasing the scattered buffaloes, including Hank Campbell sitting at the fire here in Texas now. They had had trouble during March with some of the hunting Sioux and the Utes come down from the mountains for meat. The second of April Sol Rees had seen a man shot down by Indians. The next day two more buffalo hunters were killed, one of them Dan Brown. So Dan's brother Joe and around twenty-three, twenty-four other hunters, including Hank Campbell's big outfit, joined the troops to help clean out the Indians, with Hank as leader.

By now Rees and Campbell were telling the story together, their promise not to speak of it forgotten. The scouts had located the Cheyenne camp in a little snake bend of Sappa Creek, and on the twenty-third of April, 1875, the troops and the hunters came riding out of the frosty mist of morning. Old Medicine Arrow hurried from his lodge without stopping to put his pants on, waving a towel as a white flag of peace and surrender. But the Big Fifties of the hide men roared out and he and the Indians who came with him went down. The troops held back on the shooting at first, and so some of the Indians got away into a hole that later cost the life of a hunter to clean out, Brown, whose brother had been killed by Indians three weeks ago. True, these were other Indians—but a redskin's a redskin.

"The women and kids were hid out in holes under the bank like they do," Hank Campbell said. "It took us over half a day to dig the last of them Cheyennes out and to burn up the little stuff they had—"

The hunters then whooped the Indian pony herd away from the smoldering camp, the smoke and stink of burning flesh following the snake bends of the creek. The lieutenant in command of the troops was the Austin Henely who had been stationed at Ft. Dodge a summer or two ago, when Warren was shot near Crooked Creek. Henely was a broguey big-talking Irishman not long from the old country but he didn't have much to say about this fight and asked the hunters to keep their mouths shut about it. They had made a clean sweep of the camp, with not more than an Indian or two escaping, he told the hunters, but Washington was cranky as an old woman about informal alliances between troops and civilians like the buffalo hunters. He would simply report a successful engagement with the Indians, nineteen warriors killed and two soldiers. He wouldn't mention the women and children. The eastern Indian lovers would howl that these should have been taken captive. Custer took no male captives over ten or around that; Lieutenant Henely and the buffalo hunters showed they could go him one better: they not only destroyed the lice, they got all the nits too.

A light general rain over the buffalo ranges of Texas kept the hunters in camp the next day. Mostly they slept, although those from up around Kansas got all the news they could out of Campbell. He said Cody had been out from his show to McPherson a while, with some of the actors along, visiting, one a woman that Mrs. Cody tried to run off. Texas Jack and Doc Carver took the Earl of Dunraven on a hunt. Nothing like for Duke Alexis. Where Custer and Cody had

put on the big royal hunt less than three years ago was all
settled up now. Sunflowers edged the buffalo trails and sod
corn cut through them.

Campbell heard Wild Bill had been up to the Black
Hills. Went with a party including a couple old Nebraska
trappers he had known for years. They panned gold on
Frenchman Creek but were driven out by Indians. To the
questions of the eager young hide men, Hank said there was
plenty of gold up there, all right, but if the Indians didn't
jump a man, the troops marched him overland to Laramie or
sent him running for Sioux City. News was that Hickok had
been seen at Cheyenne lately, not doing too well. But an Indian conference was called for September to buy the Black
Hills, probably by force if necessary. Then the country would
be wide open and a genuine gold rush on.

"I hear say you can make three dollars to ten dollars a
day with a gold pan and sluice, better if you find a nugget,
which ain't often," another hunter from up north said.

"Hell, that ain't so good's here," a young skinner objected, in surprise. It was true that all the hunters did better,
and many of the skinners and camp men.

Johnny Cook had tried to sleep through part of the
day, but although the gusty rain hit the hide of his tipi he
kept thinking about the story the scouts and the hunters from
the Sappa had told last night. It didn't seem right to talk
about killing people, even dirty Indians, like that, calling
them nits and lice. He had said this last night, with a tongue
unusually loose from the brown jug, and was told to keep
his goddamn mouth shut about the fight on the Sappa. He
would change his tune fast enough when he found a friend
or two face-down in the grass. Or maybe himself, one of these
times when he got lost and threw his gun away.

So Johnny had to make himself laugh a little at this
old joke. He didn't want trouble. He was a hunter by this
time, with a new wagon and an outfit of his own, working in
partnership with another Cook, Charlie Cook. Each had a

skinner, Charlie's the son of a neighbor up near his homestead in Kansas. A tall, sinewy, fine-looking plainsman, Charlie Cook had been driven off his homestead by the drouth
and hard times. Now he was caught, trapped by the lure of
the migrating herds as so many men were caught before him.
He had followed a scattering of buffaloes from north of the
Arkansas to the herd on the Clear Fork of the Brazos. He
sold three hundred hides at Dodge last summer, made four
hundred dollars in the Washita country in the fall, then three
hundred on the North Fork of the Red and four hundred and
seventeen on the Clear Fork—all in four long strides southward during nine months, and his only outlay was for ammunition, his meager supplies and twenty-five dollars a month
for the boy.

At Quinn's he had offered Johnny Cook his first
chance to shoot. Charlie had injured one of his eyes and
wanted a chief killer, somebody to keep his Big Fifty hot.
When Hart, for whom Johnny was skinning, heard of it, he
offered Johnny a partnership in the hunting, the first time
Charlie Hart made such an offer in his long hide career. But
Johnny was already committed to Charlie Cook.

On the way up to their hunting grounds on Commission Creek the Cooks camped one night in the gap of the
Wichita mountain near the western cattle trail. As they
looked off both ways over the hazy prairie they saw a herd of
three thousand Texas cattle coming north, headed for Ogallala and beyond, to the Wind River mountains of Wyoming,
while from the north a covered wagon, a buggy and thirty-
two cowponies were going down the trail as they heard later
for twenty-five hundred Texas cattle to stock a ranch on the
Cimarron in southwest Kansas. And nowhere was there an
Indian or a buffalo in sight.

As the Cooks neared Commission they heard the boom
of the Big Fifties and the sharp crack of the Forty-fours. They
camped one night with Wrong Wheel Jones. He and his three
employees had been there ten days and had six hundred

hides. The Cooks were pleased to meet him, to add a third to the hunters named Jones: Buffalo Jones, who was to build up a herd of buffaloes by roping the fine yellow calves, and Dirty Face Jones. Wrong Wheel admitted he got his name last summer. He broke down the right hind wheel of his wagon, and when Carr and Causey's freight train came by they told him they had seen an abandoned wagon like his in the sandhills about eight miles back. So Jones rigged up a pack outfit and went after the wheel. All were broken down except the left hind one. Disappointed he returned and told his hard luck at camp. His men roared at the joke and so he went out once more and got the wheel and simply turned it around. The name stuck, but he didn't mind so long as the hides piled up.

There were five other outfits besides Wrong Wheel here close to the military trail, which lowered the freight rates to Dodge. The Cooks pulled off westward, around Wolf Creek and found excellent hunting, with not another gun close for twenty days, and in that time they got five hundred hides. There were buffaloes in every direction here this summer of 'Seventy-five, but Johnny had started off with a poor showing the first day, until he discovered that the sight of his gun had slipped.

He made up for this lost day late in June. The air was hot and still, the buffaloes thirsty. Perhaps they had been shot at up north on the Beaver. Around a thousand came in a straggling dusty run to the creek, black tongues out, pushing and tromping each other at the water. Afterward they spread out over the second bottoms. All had shed their old hair and were smooth, fine animals. Half were down and chewing their cuds when the hunter got close, one large bull up and looking. At about eighty steps Johnny started to shoot into the mixed herd with the Fifty, taking first bead on the watching bull. He cringed a little when he was hit, but not half of the resting ones arose at the report, and Johnny got three dead shots before the closest began to move a little towards

the creek. He dropped the leader. When the rest just
stopped, excitement ran through the young hunter. He knew
he had a real stand going, his first. He recalled Charlie Hart's
advice: never push the shooting fast enough to heat the barrel, and always get the outside ones, those starting to walk
away. A heated barrel gave the bullet a wobble; one bad
shot might break a leg and start a bolt; a neglected wanderer
would start the whole herd following.

After about twenty-five buffaloes lay dead, the smoke
was so thick and so slow in spreading in the quiet air that
Johnny had to wipe his stinging eyes and find a new location
where he could see. He got even closer now, certain that many
of the buffaloes saw him move, yet they stood as quiet as ever,
grunting, now and then one belching up a cud to start chewing again. Then he heard a whistle and could have cursed
the greenhorn hunter who didn't know a stand was a man's
private property.

It was only Charlie, creeping up with more ammunition and a canteen with the extra gun. The buffaloes ignored
him too, seeming entirely without care or caution. While
Johnny took over with the fresh gun, Charlie cooled the
heated barrel of the Fifty with water and cleaned it with a
greasy ramrag, ready for another switch. But finally, in his
hurry, Johnny grabbed the wrong cartridge, just as a big bull
came walking towards the two men, his great horned head
high, the beard long and flowing, the nostrils wet to test the
wind. Hurrying, Johnny managed to fire, and hit. The buffalo went down and for a moment the young hunter squeezed
his left hand over the fingers cradling the rifle grip, straight-
ening his trigger finger to stop the trembling.

After a while he shot again and brought down five or
six that would stay down before he stopped to change guns
again and wonder at the stupidity of the herd, the thing the
old hunters liked to tell about, before the animals got wild.
Some of the buffaloes who did move came to stand beside the
dead ones, almost as if in silent mourning; some hooked at

them, while the rest stood, coughing new cuds up into their mouths and grunting, grunting all the time.

When the stand had been going a couple of hours Johnny was back to the Forty-four again, but the first shot went wild and struck a big bull above the knee, breaking the leg. He was at the outer edge of the herd, about ninety yards off, and began jumping around, almost as in play. He jammed against the others, his bleeding leg flopping. Finally he plunged into the herd and through it, the others beginning to fall in behind him from both sides as he went his awkward, hopping way. Johnny switched to Charlie's Big Fifty and started to move from one dead buffalo to the next, shooting from behind them as the herd went on, slowly following behind the poor crippled bull out of sight of the hunters, but going. Finally Johnny quit, even before the last were out of range. He already had eighty-eight scattered over the narrow little creek bottom and felt ashamed somehow, the glassy eyes staring as he passed, the arcs some made by their kicking a saddening thing to see.

A little sick, he fell to work at the skinning, principally bulls, more valuable as summer hides than cows but harder to skin. When they finally left the bottoms, the naked carcasses gleamed white in the darkness, he was still not hungry.

July 1875 was curiously still, windless, and the buffaloes, perhaps because of this, changed their usual pattern of movement. The Cooks profited from a weak wind that came out of the southwest for seven consecutive days and brought the buffaloes moving slowly back past their camp. On the eighth day the wind shifted to the east about midnight and little bunches started coming past from the west. The next night a thunderstorm in the south brought rain there and by daylight the buffaloes were moving fast again in one dark rolling mass.

The Cooks and some of the other hunters went back to their earlier camps to put South American Hide Poison into the dried stacks against insects, including beetles as big as filberts. The running season was at its height and the air was full of the muttering noise of the bulls night and day. The wroo-wroo-WROO of one didn't carry over half a mile alone but so many thousands together multiplied the sound until it could be heard twenty miles. The air was thick with gnats and the mosquitoes that could be smudged from the evening camps but were bad on the horses and sent them to hit the end of the picket rope on one side and then the other, the green head flies deviling them during the day. In the intense heat the buffalo carcasses hummed and boiled with maggots, and stank so it seemed impossible to eat, and yet it was good business.

Towards fall Charlie Cook took his cut of the summer's hunt and with his pockets heavy headed for Dodge City and his homestead and family. Johnny and his Mexican helper followed the buffaloes as they scattered quietly southward until they were very close to the danger ground, the region of Indian raids. One day as the two men were pegging hides on the baked earth, a silent shadow fell over Johnny. He glanced up, to a circle of mounted Indians. There were more than a dozen not twenty feet away, and Johnny's gun was at least as far. He jumped for it, but the head man held up his hand, grinning broadly. "No shoot; good Indian!" trying to speak the white man's tongue.

Finally Johnny let the man come close enough to hand over a grimy envelope he drew from his beaded pouch. Inside was a pass for this band of Cheyennes from Ft. Reno, up in the Territory. So they made a bucket of coffee for the Indians and broke out a little keg of molasses and some boxes of hard tack. The Indians went away apparently content, but it gave Johnny Cook some uneasy nights, remembering how they had managed to ride right up on him.

Long before the buffalo hunters arrived at Ft. Griffin on the Clear Fork of the Brazos, it was a place of bloodshed, a hell hole. There were many hideouts there, men who wished to put a lot of miles between themselves and the sheriff. Their swift anger and violence seemed less conspicuous here, less lawless among the southerners, where the best citizens prided themselves upon a filed-trigger temper and a proud-flesh sensitivity. In the spring the great trail herds of cattle going north camped nearby and the drivers had a few wild days in what they called "town." In the fall they returned, without the responsibility of a herd of stampeding longhorns. Sometimes there were two thousand cowboys around Griffin at a time, many hitting out for the Bee Hive, the main saloon and dance hall. Some of the women from there were well set-up, but most of their kind in Griffin had little shacks and hide huts down along the bank of the river, offering almost anything from Mexican and other Indian breed to cultured New England, including several foreigners. Some of the shacks were the refuges of every kind of cutthroat and murderer.

Although it was already a town with a newspaper by 1875, and troops and Indian scouts trailed down horse thieves, law and justice was still a matter of speed on the draw, and while there were murder trials there were no convictions because there were never any witnesses. Sometimes the lights had been shot out, more often the spectators had other, perhaps better, reasons for temporary blindness. There was much trouble between the whites and the Negro troops of the post, and several times only cool, quick action prevented the beginnings of race war. Inevitably a vigilance committee was formed with, some charged, the bloodiest murderers among the members.

Every now and then the pecan trees along the river bore a tilt-headed body or two swinging from the branches. A newspaper correspondent from Griffin wrote that the vigi-

lance committee was astonishing the authorities by the off-
hand way it did business. Already several suspicious characters have been ordered to leave town or fare worse. So long as
the committee strung up or cleaned out the right party or
parties, it would have the good wishes of every lover of tran-
quility.

But some said the whole idea was just the boisterous,
drunken southern buffalo hunters trying to run out the damn-
yankees, who often happened to be the more skillful and experienced hide men. Yet although the buffalo hunter north
or south brought trouble he also brought money to every
merchant and the seller of diversion too, whether it was cock
fights or bigger play.

By the fall of 1875 Joe McCombs organized his own
outfit with three skinners, a span of mules to the wagon, saddle horses, eight hundred pounds of lead, five kegs of powder
and a Sharps sporting rifle. They went to Phantom Hill and
on southwest to the Colorado River of Texas. By the first of
April they had a little over two thousand hides taken in a
world that seemed theirs alone, with not even the sound of
another gun. At Griffin McCombs hired a bull outfit, six wagons with their trailers, to haul in the hides, making two trips.
They came in over a prairie strung full of other trains of high
wagons, the slow wheels cutting deep into the sod. Who
needed to speak of gold strikes and the new Deadwood, or of
the Black Hills at all?

By November of 'Seventy-five the big hide outfits had
found Ft. Griffin too. After the confederates of the Mooars
sent back word that the fort was in the heart of the great
Texas buffalo ranges, the two brothers followed, fitted out
at Griffin, and joined in the hunt, bringing their careful and
profitable northern ways with them. During the winter at
Twin Lakes and Haskell Springs they killed, skinned and
cured the meat of two thousand buffaloes. The meat was sold
at Griffin, the hides at Denison, to be shipped to Lawrence,

Kansas. The one rare and perfect white skin they got went to
the Philadelphia Centennial Exposition.

Dodge City, the daughter of the hide men, was deserted by them now, for all the world to see. Still, as a dutiful
father might buy his daughter a bolt of calico now and then
until her new husband could keep her clothed, she got a little continuing buffalo trade through such men as Rath, Reynolds, and the Mooars. But as the new hide towns moved
deeper into Texas, Fort Worth became a nearer, handier
outlet. It was already a gathering place for buyers. As early
as 1873-4 there had been public auctions of hides there, perhaps as many as two hundred thousand sold to the highest
bidder in one or two days.

With the trickle of buffalo business Dodge managed
to survive the panic in the east. She survived the drouth too,
and the grasshoppers—a shabby little border town of weath-
ering false fronts, some with barrels of water on the roof to
tip over if a fire burned through, to put it out or at least slow
its spread through the tinder-dry streets.

The railroad had been stalled two years at the Colorado line, the rails rusting. Then, the spring of 1875, it began
building again, with Dodge the nearest frontier metropolis
on payday. There was still a large bone business, although
much of the picking was by settlers. A ragged drylander
might haul in a load of bones as he once filled his wagon
with butter, eggs and garden truck back east. Some traders
made a big business out of buffalo bones, buying them up at
two fifty a ton on the range, and getting eight to fourteen
dollars at the railroad, sometimes swelling the profit a little
by watering the sun-baked midsummer pick, as the beaver
traders once rubbed sand into the fur when the hides sold by
the pound. Many a farmer who lost his crop kept the family
alive on buffalo bones. Under the influence of former hunters
and freighters a kind of order came to the business. A bone

man selected a promising location, perhaps a flat of short mesquite grass dotted in white or a long grass bottom full of darker, taller fertilized spots showing where carcasses had rotted. He gathered his bones into great piles that were like reluctant snowdrifts left behind by a plains blizzard, each ton of bones representing approximately one hundred dead buffaloes, worth around eight dollars at the railroad. These piles were the picker's property solid as though he paid taxes on them, and were usually left strictly alone, although on the public domain. Later he hauled them in to the ricks growing along the railroad at all the jerk-water stations, some perhaps a mile long, to wait for an empty freight.

The big prairie wolves had also been an ace in the hole as the herds began to shrink. All a wolfer had to do was plant strychnine in the skinned carcasses, increasingly effective as the buffaloes got scarcer and the wolves got hungrier and less cautious about the smell of man and the bitter taste of the poison. Unfortunately strychnine killed all the dogs too, which caused trouble around army posts and along the settlements. But the wolvers discovered that dogs seldom eat snowbirds and that this bait is harder to expel by a revolting stomach than slick meat without bones, hide or feathers, so the number of pelts per hundred doses increased. A few cartridges loaded with fine shot fired into the feeding circles of snowbirds might get the hunter as high as fifty or more baits and kill almost as many wolves. With the poison inserted into the brain pan of the bird or under the flesh and feathers of the breast the canny wolf couldn't taste it, particularly when he bolted the little bird whole.

While wolfing was always more profitable around the upper Missouri where the winter pelts were almost white and very dense, the hunters did well for a year or so behind the shrinking herd of the Arkansas too. The poisoning, through the carcasses, killed thousands of the western raven, so many that sometimes the prairie looked speckled for miles, a worthless slaughter that left black feathers to blow over the grass and drift into washouts and rosebrush. As the settlers moved in with their crops, the place of the ravens was taken by the smaller, noisier and rustier crows. The raven, like the buffalo, was a creature of the wilderness and fell before the civilizing implements of man.

But a few thousand wolf hides and train loads of dead bones would not keep Dodge City alive. The town just about hit hard pan when the Santa Fe cut the wages of its employes twenty percent. When it seemed that a good fire in a high wind was all that could save the economic skins of a lot of people, the bawl of the Texas steer came up on the south wind. It wasn't the roar of the buffalo, but it rescued Dodge. With the Kiowas and the Comanches driven to the agencies and herded there more or less effectively, it seemed safe to move the cattle trail straight through to Dodge, away from the thickening settlements, where farmers watched with their guns, their ropes and whips, for the men whose tick-infested cattle brought Texas fever to their stock.

Now suddenly Dodge was the queen of the cowboys, the same cowboys who fought it out with the hide men on the dusty streets down in Griffin on the way north. At Dodge they fell into gun play, and found that a few of the pistoleers made in the buffalo days, men like Bat Masterson, Bill Tilghman and Wyatt Earp, shot well on the side of the law if it paid a good salary. Death could be swift and undiscriminating in Dodge. Even Tom Nixon, Assistant U. S. Marshal and the holder of one of the records for buffalo stands, was killed by Deputy Sheriff Mathers, called Mysterious Dave, and supposed to be a lineal descendant of Cotton Mather. It was a day of mourning for Dodge City, like the mourning for an old relative who had hung on long enough. Dodge was a big cowtown now and the old buffalo hunters of her youth were about as exhilarating as the white rick of bones down at the tracks.

But running blood still made the whisky flow, particularly south of the tracks where no one with money enough

to sleep under a roof went without a good gun and the in-
surance of a fast draw. There were some ornamental girls
from the dance halls over there. One, who it was said had
been an opera singer, kept hidden the whole week that Ed-
die Foy was in town with his troupe, but the rest of Dodge
gave him a fine reception. Two Negro freighters, up from
Texas, put on a game of lap-jacket in front of the harness shop
for him. Equipped with long bull whips, they toed the marks
in the dust and at the bark of the starting pistol, took alter-
nate cracks with the sharp leather lashes at each other, cracks
much louder than a pistol's and sharp enough to cut the hide
off the rump of a trail ox. People ran to see, high-heeled
boots kicking up the dust from every direction. Horsebackers pushed through the crowd as the clothing was cut from
the men, the dark skin bursting into wide red rifts, and the
blood ran from body and neck and face. But the town policeman came pushing in to stop the contest. It made the prize
fight held a few weeks later seem soft as the rabbit's tail in
Dora Hand's French powder box.

Prominent people stopped for a drink and to be seen
at Chalk Beeson's Long Branch saloon, where, instead of
dancing and girls, there were pictures of Chalk with Duke
Alexis the time he took the duke on a buffalo hunt in Colorado. But the Long Branch could never compete with Drum's
of Hays back when General Sheridan lolled his short legs in
the back room, and out in the bar were the Custers and Bill
Cody and Wild Bill Hickok. Such romance comes only once
to a frontier, like the swift short blooming of its spring.

But these activities were all part of the new business
with the cattle trail, and were a respite from the violence
and bloodshed that had raised a new law-and-order faction,
to be strenuously opposed by the wealthier merchants, even
men like Charlie Rath, and the saloon and dance hall men.
These all depended on the cattle trade, cattle going through
to the growing ranches up north, or to feed the hungry Sioux.
A large percentage were shipped east from Dodge, shipments

that had become regular by 1875. The longhorn had taken
the place of the buffalo.

The hide men were sad to give up their Dodge City,
looking back to the early town as to a golden age. But they
went and they took their equipment, most of them all their
goods, to The Flats, the growing settlement under the hill
that was crowned by a little Texas frontier post called Ft.
Griffin.

Even the officers' ladies had reason to welcome the
great bull trains from the north. They had been dependent
on the post sutler too long, and on the occasional calico and
tinware peddler. The ladies had always swarmed thick as
flies around his wagon, and since he seldom planned to return, he charged all he could get for pans that rusted through
before the week was out, and calico that ran red as Comanche blood in the first wash water.

Not all the movers from Dodge went as far as Griffin.
Many stopped at Sweet Water, near Ft. Elliott, with a stage
or buckboard running to Dodge City with fair regularity now
and a telegraph line out from the post. Here Charlie Rath's
long string of wagons had already set up their Hunters Supply Town with dugouts and pole-and-hide shacks, some so
low that Charlie had to duck his shaggy cap to clear the doorway, which was usually closed by a flapping hide until the
time for blue northers came. It was a hundred and ninety
miles to Dodge, the nearest trading point north, and farther
than that to Griffin, south in the rich buffalo ranges. Great
hide yards grew up at Sweet Water, and gambling and dance
halls followed.

Soon the quiet, reserved Emanuel Dubbs came hide
hunting here too, with his side line of farming and dairying.
He bought the squatter's rights of an old buffalo man to good
bottom land, and although he knew there was Indian danger
and had to plow with his Big Fifty strapped between the
plow handles, his cartridge belt always around his waist, he

soon had his wife there, with her flying skirts to cheer him as
she worked about the house or walked the flowered prairie.
It was as well that he carried the Fifty, for although most of
the Comanches were in around Ft. Sill, deep in the Territory, Shafter on his three-pronged march through the buffalo
country found much Indian sign. His men were in several en-
gagements, destroyed a large camp and pursued the scattering Indians, but there was still danger.

Yet, for most of the southern hunters the deepening
winter of 1875-6 brought very prosperous times. Many small
fortunes were made, and the stories of big kills grew and
grew. There was the stand of Tom Nixon, before Mather
killed him—one hundred twenty buffaloes in forty minutes,
and two thousand, one hundred and seventy-three from the fifteenth of September to the twentieth of October. Brick Bond,
too, had had a good day of two hundred fifty killed, some said
three hundred with five thousand, eight hundred fifty-five for
the fall, averaging around ninety-seven a day and keeping five
skinners and a lot of hide handlers busy. But old hunters
shook their heads at such shooting. Nixon's forty minute
record had ruined his Sharps. They preferred a steady, day-
after-day killing, never too far ahead of their skinners.

As the word of the new killings spread there were
more protests about the destruction of the buffalo. The *London Field* in 1876 predicted that the extermination of the
buffalo would "be a scandal to civilization, and a subject for
undying shame and remorse to the children of men who did
nothing to stay the hand of the destroyer." This brought re-
plies, pointing out that English sportsmen had been particularly ruthless slaughterers of the American bison, the buffalo,
and that there were many from the British Isles making their
fortunes in the Texas herd.

These continued protests made the hunters uneasy.
They still feared legislation, and some were considering or
taking up side lines, outlawry perhaps, or looking up prospec-
tive farm land. Some considered saloonkeeping, or eating the

dust of the summer trail herds. Many thought of ranching, now that Goodnight was stringing a herd of cattle in, going the wrong way, southward, against the general pointing. Dubbs saw him pass the hide and meat camp for a look at the Palo Duro canyon country.

But not all hunters looked ahead with gloom; Poe and Jacobs were still making plans for a lifetime of buffalo hunting.

CHAPTER XI

DEAD MEN AND COMANCHE YELLS

THEN the news came of Custer's defeat June 25, 1876, up on the Little Big Horn in Montana. The hide men looked out beyond the coals of their fires into the darkness, out to where the Comanches might be waiting, and spoke in anger.

There were those, however, who recalled the fights between the hunters and the troopers of the Seventh Cavalry around Hays and at Wallace and on the buffalo ranges, and soon a few fights started among the hunters themselves over Custer. Some saw him as the vain, reckless, over-ambitious fool who could leave Major Elliott and eighteen men to the Indians at the Washita. The general's adherents recalled the Washita too, but for his glorious defeat of the blood-thirsty Cheyennes, and the long string of captive women and children he led through the hundred miles of winter to Camp Supply. Some thought of him only as the dashing figure at the head of his troops, from the newspapers and his books, and some remembered his ineffectual campaign against the Indians of the Republican country in 1867, and the hunters who died for this stirring up that ended in the desertion of his post and the year of suspension. For the gold-hungry he was the daring man who sent out the news of it from the Black Hills, his expedition the spear into the vital heart of the bloody Sioux, while others pointed out that he had no legal right there and that the Indians had paid him out for it now. A few, like Amos Chapman, recalled Custer's meeting with the Cheyenne chief Medicine Arrow in the Sweetwater country here seven years ago, in the peace ceremony of the sacred arrows that promised death to the man who broke his word. Immediately afterward Custer had set a trap for the chief and while the Arrow escaped, four of his emissaries did not, and these were killed or crippled. Now Medicine Arrow was dead, shot by the buffalo hunters on the Sappa under his white flag of surrender, but Custer was dead too, with his officers all around him. If the Indians always got their vengeance so completely then some of the hunters here were in for a hot time themselves, some day.

The vengeance of the Little Big Horn already included one of the early hunters. Those who knew the neat and cautious Lonesome Charley Reynolds recalled that he got more buffaloes, more meat per hundred cartridges than any other hide man, and that the Indians were always skulking at his heels. Now they finally got him, but not until he started throwing in with Custer and the mismanaged Seventh Cavalry. Even so there were stories that old Lonesome left the ground covered with empty shells before he died.

"I bet the Indians knowed somebody'd been shootin' at 'em!" one of the Kansas hunters said.

"Yeh, but he'd a done better without the troopers holding him down," another replied.

Plainly Bill Cody, Broadway's Scout of the Plains, had to get into the story of this momentous summer in the west. He came to attach himself to troops going north, wearing a black velvet suit part of the time, or fringed buckskin. He talked the words and stories of New Buntline, and drank like the high-life characters he had seen in New York, people not very different from those who once hung around Drum's, down in Hays City, except that these crawled into their claw-hammers every night, the hangings were velvet, and every-thing cost a lot more. It was his great regret, Bill said, that he wasn't at the Custer battle to lead his friend, the general, to victory. But he did what he could to make a Buntline story. He decided to join a scouting group of civilians from around the Black Hills and the robbers roosts along the gold trails, who called themselves the Montana Volunteers. Bill came up from the Platte to the troops of Colonels Merritt and Carr on the way to reinforce General Crook in the Big Horn country for a concerted pursuit and punishment of the arrogant Sioux. They had dared to annihilate Custer when he came to their camp not far from the surveyed right-of-way the Northern Pacific intended to use up the Yellowstone as soon as the Indians were gone.

Cody didn't make it to the interception of some Cheyennes leaving the agency near Ft. Robinson, in north-west Nebraska, for their summer hunt. One young warrior, Yellow Hand, was killed in a volley from the troops. Cody had been in no shape to ride in the heat of that July day but he grabbed the scalp from the soldier who brought it in, and paid him five dollars for it. He and the gathered Montana Volunteers joined General Crook on the Tongue River. Bourke, Crook's aide, said that most of these ruffians must have belonged in one jail or another, for everybody had to sit on his saddle to keep it after the Volunteers came, and to watch anything else he might value.

With Cody was Buffalo Chips, the man who drove Bill's whisky wagon on former expeditions. Now he tried to stuff the newspapermen with big stories about Cody, but most of them looked on Bill's associates as a bunch of horse thieves. When it was plain there would be no Indian herds to plunder, most of the Volunteers left Crook at the Yellowstone. Cody left too, boarded a boat for the Missouri and another season in show business, with a new incident for Buntline—a knife duel to the death between the Intrepid Scout of the Plains, Buffalo Bill Cody, and a most unIndian actor who was called Yellowhand. But it ended right, with Cody gripping a red-stained knife in one hand and a hank of black hair in the other and crying out, "The first scalp for Custer!" to the thunderous patriotic applause.

In spite of Cody and his Indian scalp, the summer of 1876 seemed a season of hard reckoning for the men of 1867. Only a little while after the news of the Custer fight, the Texas hunters heard of the death of Wild Bill Hickok. All fall more bits of the story came in, followed by news that California Joe had been shot and killed too, up on one of the Sioux agencies.

But it was Wild Bill that interested the young hunters, particularly those who came to what seemed a duller west. Bill had kept out of the buffalo ranges most of the time since he killed Whistler four years ago. Perhaps he had needed the nourishment of the plains under his feet, under his belly as he crawled up on the herds, for life had lost its sheen, as the curls that still fell over his shoulders had lost their brightness. When he had trouble seeing the spoor of otter and mink up in the Yellowstone country, he had slipped secretly to the army surgeon at Camp Carlin near Cheyenne. The doctor had looked very grave. It was advanced glaucoma, incurable, and in a few months he would be in total darkness.

Sworn to secrecy—"There's a hundred as would brace me on any street if it gets out how little I can see,"—the doctor promised to do what he could, but it would be little.

Bill, however, could still see well enough to find his name, pointed out to him, on a dodger tacked up in Cheyenne, warning him and other lawless men to get out of town. He cut the paper to ribbons with his ripping knife and hung around the saloons making it his business to stuff new-comers and tenderfeet on the way to the Black Hills with his windy stories of his prowess and of his wonderful discoveries of diamond caves up north with California Joe. He drew them into card games but mostly he was interested in getting up parties to guide to the north, or southwestward, down near the Colorado border, where diamonds were scattered around among the gravel common as grey flintrocks.

But somehow none of this worked out, not even the gambling. Luck had just about dumped him in the cactus. Even his last copy of *Harper's*, with the Nichols' story of Wild Bill Hickok, the Prince of Pistoleers, was gone. He had been convicted of riot and assault on the sheriff at Evanston, Wyoming, and fined fifty dollars. Here in Cheyenne he was ordered to leave, get out of town.

Then Mrs. Lake came to Cheyenne to visit a friend. He met her again, married her, and went to Cincinnati with her. But in two weeks he was back and hitting out for the Black Hills. He went up with Charlie Utter, an old friend from back in Wichita and Denver, and a party, including Calamity Jane Canary and another woman of the frontier posts. Wild Bill and Charlie lived in a tent and avoided Calamity, not an easy thing in the narrow gulch of Deadwood when she was in what she called her howling drunks. Bill made a little gambling, but that was no business for a man who could only see the spots through the hazy blur when the light fell square on them. Now he was dead, shot down in cold blood. It happened to the man whose gun had once been like a striking rattler.

But when those from the north were asked about Jack McCall, the murderer, they turned evasive. One or two knew him back around Riley and Hays, and the hunters from the Republican River had seen him up around Ft. McPherson on the Platte. He traveled under several names, as did many right here in the buffalo camps. Sometimes he passed as Billy Sutherland, so the newspapers first said: "Wild Bill Murdered by Billy Sutherland." A lot of times he called himself Billy Barnes, the name that Wild Bill and Bill's brother both used in Kansas.

"They was some talk around Hays a while that Jack was a brother of the Hickoks," an old freighter said. "I guess ain't no tellin' now."

But many things were remembered of Wild Bill, his quiet reserve, his dandyism, his swift and fatal anger, his excellent marksmanship. In Nebraska some recalled only the killing of McCanles or of Chief Whistler, but as happens, many recalled too that they had heard of only one man who equaled Bill with a gun—Spottswood of the Overland Stage on the Platte, although some thought that Buffalo Bill Comstock would have out-shot both on the range and at least half a dozen were better at still targets than Hickok. No one could say now if that would have been true eight, nine years ago, when Bill's eyes were still sharp, before the light went out of one, and the other was beginning to look like a boy's smoky marble.

There was a kind of sadness about the death of James Butler Hickok, about his passing, as though the romantic times were gone. Perhaps he had been the essence of the frontier, of the men who moved out upon the early buffalo plains, flashy, flamboyant, with no sense of obligation, no respect for any law beyond the whim, no respect for any power beyond that of his buffalo gun and his marksmanship, whether against beast or man. It was unthinkable that such men should live beyond the romance of their own creation.

Custer, Hickok and California Joe, all longhairs of that beginning year of 1867, dead within a space of five months, and the sober-appearing Lonesome Charley too. Only Bill Cody had survived this year. Any way it was sized up, the year was a saddening one for those who remembered the hunters of the Republican herd back in 1867, and gone now as the herd was gone.

There was fair to good hunting in the Texas Panhandle the rest of the summer, but few buffaloes went north of the Cimarron now, and by October the herd was back in the breaks of the Red and going south, carrying their winter hides closer and closer to Griffin.

For four years, to 'Seventy-six, Griffin was only a huddle of makeshift dugouts and hide huts, with a few sod shacks along the bottoms of the Clear Fork of the Brazos, the fort on the hill above, out of the mosquitos. But by the spring of that year the merchants decided it might be worth building permanent houses. Meyer and Frankel were rivals, each boasting his was the best saloon west of Fort Worth. Meyer had a big cellar dug back into the low bluff and filled it with river ice, enough to last most of the summer—the only ice west of the railhead. So Frankel put in fresh seafood as his attraction, but without Meyer's ice it was a failure, a total loss.

Business had boomed most of the winter. In one day back in January Conrad, going into partnership with Charlie Rath, sold four thousand dollars in goods out of a shack not worth more than a nickel for fire wood, twenty-five hundred of it guns and ammunition, no fancy stuff. Most of the hunters still ate around the skillet in camp, dipped their dutch oven bread into the gravy and speared the meat with their ripping knives, usually cleaning them by a couple quick swipes on the grass. When bread failed it was buffalo straight, and only the tenderfoot newcomer had never been pushed to this, maybe without salt too and had to make a sprinkling of gunpowder do for savor.

There were some fine freighting outfits into the town. Garrison ran one between Griffin and Waco. He traveled with the trains much of the time, but in a buggy with a top against the sun, wind and rain, and once in the early days of Griffin, when a stampeding herd of buffaloes cut across his trail, upsetting several of his wagons, he got his buggy through unharmed by turning into a little clear space and holding it by whipping his team into a run, going with the rise and fall of the buffaloes on both sides, close up against the wheels.

"In a stampede you have to go along," he said laconically.

Although far from a railroad Griffin was a good rival for Dodge City. The fort had protected the cattle trail before the hide men came, but the buffalo business pushed up like a puff ball after a rain, between suns. As at Wichita, Abilene and Dodge there was trouble between the two outfits from the start, with no law but the gun recognized. Once two cowboys full of redeye and the devil decided to run the town. They fired a few shots up the crowded street between the low, sprawled buildings, several down it, and as the dust cleared of man and beast, they pushed into Donnelly and Carroll's saloon to break up a social dance. A deputy came on the run, and the county attorney. Shooting started, the bystanders fought to get out, crowding the door and the walls, some hitting the floor. Several were killed and the deputy slightly wounded as the cowboys backed their spurs towards the door, letting out a puff of stinking blue smoke around them as they kicked the door open and were gone into the night.

Now the town must be cleaned up. The vigilance committee was conspicuous for a while, a few more dark figures hung heavy from the arms of the pecan trees at the river. Then matters settled back to private killing privately avenged.

There were the gamblers, always the same, except for their linen, perhaps. More women came too, particularly to the shacks at the river, the row called Hunters Heaven. Those who catered to the men who lived, and more cleanly, off the hunters, were around the dance halls and the gambling dens. In appearance even the top were a cut or two below Dodge on the railroad, and several cuts below those who could hope to do well in the new gold rush camp of Deadwood in the Black Hills.

At the river there were some with unflattering monickers, like Big Ollie or Wall-Eye. Big Ollie was over six feet tall and the admiration and perhaps the identifica-

tion of the scabby little hide men, but when she cut the throat
of one with his own knife, the others got a little more
cautious. Fortunately she was naturally clumsy and cut more
beard than throat; the post surgeon, just up the hill, made
very good time getting down. The girl called Wall-Eye was
prettier than most in the dance halls but she had the white-
ringed eye of an outlaw mustang and the killer instinct that
all but the hunters feared. They were inured to danger and
alert to it, the skinners and peggers too, and not squeamish
about the carrion stink that followed her and some of the
others of Hunters Heaven. The worst one of the lot was an
Indian breed, a spy, in with all the small hold-up men and
the hide thieves that might rob a man's camp while she held
him in her arms. Often the thieves worked in paint and moccasins to throw the blame on the Comanches.

Griffin, too, had her gunmen, men drifting down from
Kansas and other, more settled regions where law was moving in. One of these was Doc John H. Holliday, from
Georgia. He had finished a dental course after the Civil War
but contracted consumption and was sent west. He opened
an office in Dallas and worked up quite a reputation as a
killer, even for Texas, but his cough kept patients away, so
he took up gambling. He was lucky and bold and reckless,
and when he saw that he would need real sixgun skill, he got
it. He also learned to drink whisky all day without staggering.
He gambled in the northern gold camps until winter neared
and then he showed up at Griffin. He met Kate Fisher, the
dance hall girl called Big-nose Kate. He lived with her spo-
radically, and after she saved his life Doc called her Mrs.
Holliday when he thought of it.

John Holliday was ash-blond, long and gaunted to a
skeleton by the consumption, the deadliest man with a sixgun
—a gentleman turned border badman by disease, a philoso-
pher of the smoking Persuader. When he killed Ed Bailey
over a poker game Kate met the emergency. While the Ft.
Griffin marshal was holding Doc prisoner in a hotel room

Bailey's friends were at the bar gathering liquid fortification for a lynching down at the pecan trees. Kate threw their stuff into a gripsack, hid two saddle horses out handy and then slipped around and set fire to the back of the hotel. Buffalo hunters, freighters, gamblers and women of the town, everybody, ran to fight the flames in the high wind, all except the single guard left to watch Doc. He wouldn't leave his post and so, pistol drawn, Big-nose Kate pushed into the room and ordered the deputy to throw up his hands. She took his guns and ammunition, and rearmed Doc with his own Colt. When the fire was out and the posse had a last round to wet their gullets, the two were gone, nothing left but the deep fresh tracks of two horses running hard.

It was a good story and the hunters enjoyed the joke on the Griffinites, whatever the truth was. They had heard Doc's drunken tongue blister poor Kate until she got howling drunk too, and ended up in a bawling jag. A hunter just back from a little gold panning up at Deadwood claimed, with a touch of local pride, that Kate could out-howl Calamity Jane any day come hallelujah.

The fall of 'Seventy-six couriers and small detachments of troops had been sent to warn all the Texas buffalo ranges that the Indians were suddenly very aggressive. The success of the Sioux against Crook and Custer had made sudden irreconcilables of many coffee-cooling agency loafers down there too. Hank Campbell, who had led the hunters against the Cheyenne camp on the Sappa put off his visit back home. The buffaloes would be in soon, and besides he felt a little safer far away from the Sappa country now, with relatives of those killed there probably slipping away for a little avenging. Perhaps none of the Southern Cheyennes knew him by sight, but even so Hank kept off the Indian trails and worked with a small crew, two men instead of the eight, nine he ran up on the Republican. Had greater mobility this way, he thought.

Johnny Cook was out with a new partner, Crawford.
They found good hunting and got sixteen hundred hides by
the end of November. As the herd left they moved westward
with Campbell until a blinding storm struck them December fifteenth, with seven inches of snow in one night, an
unusually deep and silent fall so far south. The next morning
Johnny pushed out to look after the horses and suddenly
found himself staring at the fresh trail of around a hundred
seventy Indians within two hundred feet of the camp, barely
missing Cook's team. Before the sky cleared troops came
riding hard on the trail, shouting to the hunters that they
were following Nigger Horse and his Comanche band who
had jumped the agency. The troops trotted smartly past but
they didn't stay on the trail as Miles, Custer or Crook would
have. By the next morning they were dragging back, the
chase abandoned because of the storm.

With so many Comanches loose among them, the
hunters moved their camps even closer together, although
this made hunting difficult and brought clashes and a smoking
gun or two. Nobody knew just where the Indians were and
so Campbell and Rees, also from the Sappa fight, went
scouting. They took along an old Texan who had lost his
gun eye to the rotgut of Griffin but still retained his feel for
the lay of the land. In three days they were back. Nigger Horse
and his band were hidden off somewhere in the Thompson canyon region, a good twelve miles beyond Billy Devins',
the hunter nearest the Indian camp, with Marshall Sewall
almost as close. Maybe Nigger Horse was tired of agency
starvation and just wanted to make a little meat.

But soon rumors got around that hunters had seen
lone Indians here and there, slipping off into some canyon
or over a ridge. The buffaloes were drifting southward, and
Johnny Cook moved his camp along. The evening he settled
again he took the horses to a broad grassy ravine about a
quarter of a mile from camp and hobbled them. Another
hunter, stopping for the night, went to a hill to take the

customary evening look around the country. Just as Johnny finished with the last horse and was picking up his gun, a bullet whistled past him, with the sharp crack of a carbine, followed almost immediately by the heavy boom of the hunter's gun from the hill, and the man shouting, "Injun shooting at you, Cook!"

The Indian fled afoot, leaving his horse behind, but like with rattlesnakes, where there's one Indian there are sure to be more, so Johnny and the others gathered in all their stock and tied them to the wagons. While they took turns standing guard night and day, they tried to decide what should be done. Then another hide man brought word that Charlie Rath was on his way from Dodge with a small supply train—lumber, nails and tools to build a supply store, a new hide town near Double Mountain Fork of the Brazos. Russell's big train of fifty wagons, six yoke of bulls to the wagon, was following with Rath's supplies.

It was good news and the uneasy hunters started over that way, but they ran into buffaloes. After barely making expenses the last month, Cook and the rest suddenly found themselves in the depths of the winter herd and so they decided to take chances and hunt a little. They camped close together for protection, not more than half a mile to a mile apart, southwest of Double Mountain, on good water. Johnny's camp was the farthest out. The evening they arrived he went out and got seventeen buffaloes. As he was coming in toward dusk his horse kept looking off west, ears up, feet dancing a little. A horsebacker was coming, and Johnny was easier when he could see the man didn't ride Indian. It turned out to be Pat Garrett,* with a camp about eight miles northwest near Salt Fork. He was coming to warn the hunters against taking these chances with the Indians out. Billy Kress of Kress and Rees' outfit nearby agreed; he thought it was very dangerous. The hunters would fool around just a little too long and then those left would have to get together and

* In 1881 Sheriff Pat Garrett shot the killer, Billy the Kid.

clean up on the bloodthirsty Comanches. Both he and Rees learned about Indians as hide men up in Kansas. After wiping out the Cheyennes on the Sappa they had given up hunting as too dangerous there and went to the Philadelphia World's Fair last summer. After their money was spent they had to go back into hides again. To be sure Indian trouble generally didn't start until April up north, but grass came earlier here.

The twentieth of February, 1877, a runner, the Cherokee breed Louis Keyes, came to Cook to warn them. Billy Devins' camp, nearest to the Comanches in Thompson canyon, had been destroyed by the Indians, the horses swept away, the men barely escaping with their skins. At the camp of two Englishmen over that way the wagons had been run up between their two great stacks of hides and with wood and brush thrown on top, the whole pile was set afire, several big cakes of tallow thrown on for a hotter blaze. Their ammunition was all stolen, the harness cut to pieces, and there was no sign of the men anywhere.

Now the hunters began to stream off the range toward Rath's new place at the base of Double Mountain. Campbell rode out to spread the alarm to the camps off south while his outfit prepared to pull away for Rath's too. The runner, Louis Keyes, had come on a slow work horse, so he stayed to help Crawford load Cook's wagons for flight, leaving all the hides behind. In the meantime Johnny whipped out to warn Kress and Rees, then on to Pat Garrett's. But Pat's dugout was already deserted, a card tacked up: "Gone to Rath's store."

On Stinking Creek Johnny overtook his wagon. With eight other outfits, twenty-three men altogether, they set out at dark, scouts riding all around. After a few miles of zigzag course, they corralled the wagons and hobbled all the horses except the saddlers, which were kept under leather. Because Carr and Causey had seen sixty painted warriors on the route between here and Double Mountain that day they didn't dare risk a fire for a little hot coffee although the night was cold even for February.

Before dawn the hunters moved out and struck the trail marked with piles of buffalo skulls, each pile holding a stake in the center saying "Rath's Store" and pointing the way along the ruts left by Russell's heavy wagons. They traveled twelve miles of mesquite, chaparral and live oak so thick a whole tribe of Indians could have hidden within two hundred feet of the trail and not a feather show. There was no water for stock or man, but hunters willing to leave all their winter hides behind were desperate enough to push on without seeking out either creek or pond.

They reached Rath's by evening, both men and animals thirsting even though it was winter. They found almost three hundred men driven together by the scare, including many old acquaintances. Rath's agent, George West, knew every northern hunter from Colorado and Nebraska down to the Red, but new outfits were always pushing into the range from the Texas settlements, and West was gathering all the new names and camp sites that he could and asking too about the missing ones, men like Hi Bickerdyke and the Deacon, Marshall Sewall, Smoky Hill Thompson, and dozens more. Sewall and his two men were out near Billy Devins' destroyed camp, on very dangerous ground and should be warned first.

A party was organized and early in the morning Billy led the mounted hunters out, followed by a pack mule of supplies and ammunition. They made a good forty-five mile ride with barely a halt to Devins' camp. There Johnny Cook and another man were sent as lookouts while supper was hustled together. From far off they saw a man coming, a white man, afoot. He dropped to the fire half dead, bringing news of his boss Marshall Sewall. Two days ago he and the other skinner had started with the hide wagon to follow Sewall's kill. They heard shooting that turned out to be Indians, fifty mounted Indians circling around a wallow out on the prairie, narrowing in closer every round against the thunder of Sewall's big gun from the wallow, the powder smoke rising like a grey puffball into the clear air. Finally the Indians were together in a tight little knot, the gun still. The skinners turned their wagon and whipped back toward camp, the Indians hot after them now. Seeing they couldn't make it, they headed their team for a deep ravine, clinging to the wagon as it bounced into the air on the buffalo trails. At the bank they ran the horses over the edge and took to the brush afoot.

The Indians barely hesitated. Dividing, they rode along both edges of the deep cut with their chilling Comanche yells. Some exposed themselves daringly to draw the betraying blue smoke from the hunters while the other Indians cut the team loose and stripped the wagon of the ammunition. But the two skinners kept hidden until dark. There was more shooting off north later but they risked going out on the prairie to bury Sewall with their skinning knives. Then one of them headed for the camp of the Englishman, without knowing that their camp had been burned out. The other struck the fresh trail of the hunters here, and turned to follow it.

The hunters decided this was an emergency. Johnny Cook was sent back to Rath's to get enough men to clean out the nest of Comanches for good. Perhaps West would give them a wagon load of supplies. The rest of the hunters were to stay here together as observers. Johnny started on the back trail, still so fresh that even he should be able to follow it. He was careful to keep off the high ground until dark, slipping along cuts and draws, his mind as uneasy as his weary body, with little rest or sleep for three days and nights. Sewall had been an educated man, courteous and polite, one who never drank nor used tobacco, but carried small leather volumes of poetry in his pocket. Evenings he read aloud from them once to Johnny Cook and the two Englishmen, something about a man called Don Juan. He had glanced over the book now and then, gauging his listeners as he would watch all the herd while he shot. The Englishmen had listened very closely, their wind-watered eyes almost running over. One of them started saying some of it by heart and didn't stop for a long time, what must have been pages and pages. Then he apologized for what seemed a rude interruption, a showing-off. "The old boy seems so extremely alive, out here—" he added lamely.

Yes, it was an honor to know a man like Marshall Sewall, and the blood-thirsty Indians better look out now. Yet Johnny Cook couldn't help but remember something else, something that he had seen once—a map of Texas with a great patch colored pink as a prairie rose all over this region here and marked in black letters: KIOWA AND COMANCHE HUNTING GROUNDS.

It was after sunup when Johnny Cook reached Rath's. The frost-rimmed bottom around the huddle of earth and hide and pole shacks was so thick with hunting outfits it looked like the nighting place of a herd of buffaloes. Charlie Hart was there, three sheets to the wind, but he recognized his former helper and drew him away to one of the saloons. There were about twenty men in the dark interior, some that Johnny had met before. They gathered close to hear the news but when Charlie asked how many were ready to help hunt down the treacherous Comanches, there were only four, including Limpy Jim Smith, the bartender who was an ex-railroad agent from Montana. He had two thousand hides taken since November and piled in a safe place, but he would go anyway. Most of the others made one excuse or another, some saying they had lost no Indians, and laughing aloud, their open mouths red in the bearded faces. But tall Hank Campbell was going, and old Smoky Hill Thompson, the white-haired veteran of the frontier who had hunted, trapped and fought Indians from the Missouri to the Rockies. He cautioned that a strong party of hunters should remain here to protect all their stock and their great accumulation of hides that the Indians hated so much. Campbell was picked to stay, to command the forces here against any general attack such as the one up at Adobe Walls.

They left with a lot of noise and shooting, and an exuberance that distance from Rath's whisky house would chill. Everybody was out to watch them go, but nobody seemed to hear the two grim old hunters leaning against a hide pile out of the wind, "Might be headin' out for a clobberin' like old Custer got, up north there—"

"They ain't as many Indians out here like they was there."

"No, but they wasn't them howlin' Comanches. Me, I ain't lost me no Comanches."

The party headed straight for Devins' camp, but at Godey's there were men standing around the great hide piles. They turned out to be the two Englishmen and Sewall's other skinner, all their horses lost except those they were riding, in a fight with the Indians that forenoon. One man was badly wounded and only the long range of their buffalo guns had held the Comanches off.

That quieted the party, that and the long fast ride. At Devins' camp, Billy and the rest admitted that with the few men Johnny Cook brought they couldn't risk taking up a chase that the troops had quit, so they stood close guard that night and started back to Rath's early in the morning.

Two days later forty-five men, well-armed and equipped, rode against the Indians, the women and children to be destroyed as they were at the Sappa. "Get the nits with the lice!"

Johnny Cook was uneasy. Perhaps the Indians believed the hunting grounds were still theirs. And even with murderers one didn't fall upon their families. Yet if anybody else saw a difference in this he kept his damn wind-burnt mouth shut too. The Comanches had been raiding the Texas settlements, and in this white women and children died. Any way that a man looked at it the Indians had to go.

Johnny Cook had the Creedmoor Forty-five Sharps he had bought at Ft. Elliott, the caliber that most of the old hunters were using now for its longer range as the buffaloes grew wilder. Fully a hundred twenty-five men had been driven off the buffalo grounds, and around eighty-five pledged themselves to go along as a buffalo militia the night before, particularly after some ranchers who had lost stock rode in and offered saddle horses to any hunter who needed one, and bills of sale for all horses bearing their brands that the hunters might capture. Yet at mounting time only forty-five men were actually there and ready: Hank Campbell, Sol Rees, Limpy Smith, Hi Bickerdyke, Jim Harvey, Johnny Cook, old Billy Benson, the two Jacksons and some other good men—including veterans of both sides, and the two Englishmen. They took three wagon loads of ammunition, horsefeed and provisions along, including a case of bandages and pharmaceuticals in charge of Shorty Woodson, a former druggist called Shorty because he was the tallest, slimmest man working the ranges.

At Rath's all the resting wagons were drawn up to the buildings, parallel and as close together as insect eggs, to offer protection for the buffalo guns of the camp, with old Smoky Hill Thompson in command and West as his assistant. There were nearly a hundred men around, many Texans and many so new to the frontier that there was no telling how soon they would stampede for Griffin if some likkered up yahoo thought he caught the flash of a looking glass signal or mistook a weed for the feather of a skulking Indian.

The forty-five hunters took the field under the command of Hank Campbell from the Sappa, with Limpy Jim Smith and Joe Freed as lieutenants. Thirty of the men were mounted and fifteen rode protection in the wagons, each carrying a hundred to two hundred fifty rounds of ammunition, in addition to the bar lead and powder in the wagons—

enough hot lead to singe the breechclouts off all the Comanche braves in Texas.

The party struck for Sewall's camp, guided by José, one of General Mackenzie's scouts on his march through this region in 1874. José picked up the tracks of the Indians out on the Yarner, the Staked Plains, not far from the old Comanche war trail to Mexico. The Indians scattered, and so the hunters followed an old travois trail to a deserted camp ground in a canyon, to the remnants of a scalp dance, probably over Sewall's—the red devils.

From there the trail led out on the Plains and scattered once more, but the Mexican José was certain the Indians had returned to the protection of the canyon for the cold night. While the horses and men rested he led Johnny Cook and Keyes, the Cherokee breed, out in a night scout. Creeping carefully through the breaks and the canyon, they located the Indian pack herd in the darkness, but slipped away before they were detected and the village aroused. The three men followed the canyon to Double Mountain Ford, seeking the influx of a little cold water creek that José knew flowed out of an almost perpendicular bluff. They ran into one of the Comanche outlooks, and for one moment it seemed he would get away. But they managed to kill him before he could give the alarm, or at least they hoped so.

There was a lot of hunting now in the long and torturous Thompson canyon for the exact pocket in which the Indians were camped. José examined the trail with matches lighted under a blanket, and then moved on, so silently that not a pebble rolled or a frosted stick crackled.

When they finally returned to their party, waiting impatiently in the chilling darkness, Hank Campbell accused José of deceit. He was trying to delay them, help the Indians, Hank insisted, and so preserve the buffaloes for the Mexican meat hunters. Cook and some of the Texans defended José. "Hell, you're goin' soft, Hank—" Rees accused.

Although Campbell wasn't convinced, the party decided to follow the guide and Johnny Cook. At daylight on the eighteenth of March they moved toward the Comanche camp, probably about three miles off. The two scouts were a little over a mile ahead of the rest when, through Johnny's field glasses, they saw two Indians going out towards a large horse herd. The Comanches walked along easily and openly towards the higher ground beyond the camp site, clearly located now by the blue twists of smoke rising into the thin air of morning about a mile ahead. The scouts could see the tops of several tipis too, so José motioned Cook back to fetch up the rest. Johnny let his big chestnut out, and brought the force at a gallop up the canyon.

On the bottom at a big water hole, Hank Campbell stopped the mounted men, got them into line, and divided them, fourteen to go with him to the right, the rest with Limpy Smith to the left. They dismounted, adjusted cinches while their horses drank, tied their hats behind the saddles and looked to their guns in the boots, the pistols at their belts. Johnny Cook and Bickerdyke were in Campbell's platoon that went up the right slope for the tableland, Smith taking a similar course on the left. On top they were nearly two hundred yards apart. Freed and the men from the wagons were down in the canyon between, moving afoot in an open skirmish line but ordered not to enter the camp under any circumstances. No women or children were to be killed if it could be helped. Hank Campbell had already seen enough of that for all his life.

But there, ahead, were the Indians who destroyed their business, and at the order to advance Louis Keyes started an old Cherokee war chant and got far ahead in his excitement. Squirrel Eye gave a Rebel yell and spurred up too, so that Hank's line was ragged as a buffalo advance in spite of his orders. By now they could see the warriors pouring from the lodges and the brush wickiups. The hunters started to shoot, but they couldn't keep the Indians from taking the rise between them and the camp, falling to their

bellies and firing into the charging hunters at two hundred
yards. Campbell saw the danger. Plainly this was not to be
like the Sappa, with surrender offered under a white flag.
He spurred his fast horse ahead of his men and waved them
back to the draw, his mouth working open, the words lost
in the thunder of the fighting and the running hoofs on
rock and gravel. But before half could turn, Joe Jackson was
shot out of the saddle, and Lee Grimes' horse was hit in the
forehead, going down like a rock, throwing his rider too,
breaking his wrist. Billy Devins dismounted, Cook too, both
foolishly letting their horses go as they ran to Jackson, to
drag him back. Then Billy got a bullet in the arm.

"For God's sakes, boys, drop flat or they'll get you
both!" Jackson yelled the best he could as he was jerked
along on the ground.

They dropped beside him, glad to get their heads
down as the bullets cut the scattering of brushy weeds around
them. Lee Grimes came crawling over, keeping low as a
snake through the whistling bullets. They couldn't see one
Indian now, or guess what these Comanches were up to, or
what was happening down in the draw where the big guns of
Freed's men were booming through the sharp hail of smaller
Indian arms.

Cook and the others, who were trying to ease Jackson's
ugly groin shot and get away before a Comanche charge rode
them down, noticed about a hundred Indians creeping to the
crest of a little hill on the north side of the draw, out of
sight of all the other hunters. Then Smith and his men, dismounted now, began firing at them, while more warriors
were creeping up the other side on Smith. Cook raised his
head to shoot at these, to hold them down, and to warn
Smith and his men.

In the meantime the rest of Campbell's platoon was
coming along the flat, creeping in to rescue the wounded
men. Gradually the firing over them stopped and they managed to get Jackson and the others to a little side draw. As

Campbell pulled his men back to the head of this draw too, twenty mounted Indians broke into sight above the hunters, coming at a dead run, strung out, clinging to the far side of their horses as they passed, shooting over the necks down upon the men in the pocket. Another party of warriors did the same thing from the opposite side but closer, the paths of the whooping files crossing. For the next three hours the hunters clung together to the head of the draw in the dust and smoke and gunfire, cut off from their supply wagons, not knowing what might be happening to their ammunition, and with no word or shot from Freed and his buffalo infantry, no telling where he was, or if still alive. No one spoke of Custer but everybody must have thought of him, even Campbell and the others who had had such an easy time of it with old Medicine Arrow's tired and worn little band who had believed in the power of the white flag up on the Sappa.

Once five of the hunters, including Cook and Hi Bickerdyke, ran through the smoke and dust to a little side cut near the crest and flattened down there. Limpy Smith took five, six men up about seventy-five yards to where another side draw led to the main ravine. As the warriors came by in their regular charge down and across the draw from the north, Limpy's men fired fast. One Indian fell in the surprise, another's horse went down. Then they were within two hundred yards of Cook's party and they brought down two horses. The Indians lit running through the dust, the hunters spurting up earth and rock all around them, but they got away. Now the five were fired on from the front and so they had to crawl back to the wounded in the draw. The firing of Limpy's men slacked too, until suddenly they were all back together, driven up the side draw, with Indians all around them.

There had been a little firing from heavy buffalo guns down towards the camp, so Freed's men were still in action, but Indians swarmed between them and the men shut into the little pocket, and without reserve ammunition it looked pretty bad. They better get out if they could, Campbell said, but first they had to give Freed a chance to retreat. So Smith took the horses and the wounded down farther, ready to slip away with such men as could be spared to protect them, while Hank's force crawled to the crest to fire one good volley down into the Comanche camp. Perhaps this would draw the warriors back to protect their families, and cover Freed's foot retreat.

The eighteen men crawled up together through the ragged grass and weeds of the eroded slope. They looked down upon the smoke-filled Comanche village four hundred yards below, a red flag blowing on a pole, a large herd of horses behind the village, with fifty or sixty under packs or being loaded, the women and children working fast. Up on the clear table land an Indian was signaling to the warriors along the breaks and down in the draws with a looking glass, sending flashes dancing in the sun. A strong wind blew from the camp to the hunters, carrying the smoke back upon them as they shot and that of the return fire too, the bullets in it throwing dirt into the faces of the hunters. Campbell ordered some fast volleys at a crest this side of the camp where the smoke was cut by rifle flashes. Three hundred rounds went fast, but under its protection Freed and his men managed to get away. They came slipping up a side draw, luckily all still together, mostly because they had made it to a little pocket where the Indians couldn't get a down-hill shot into their position. José, with them, had a shoulder wound. He had been exposed getting the lay of the village. He said there were three hundred Indians down there and at least two hundred more Staked Plains Apaches camped just around the bend.

Campbell laughed sourly, the inside of his curled-down lip bright red in his bearded, powder-sooted face. "We sure bit off more'n we can chew today," he said. He was worried about the men left with the wagons and their horse holders. But he no longer tried to command. Cornett and Squirrel Eye had both been hit too now. There was a better position they could have taken up except that the thickening smoke rolling toward them was from a fire the Indians had set in the scattered grass, the low blaze swept along in the high wind, jumping from clump to clump and shrub to shrub over the broken ground. The Indian charges were wilder now, bolder, as though they had the hunters whipped already. They rode openly across the high ground upon the draws where the men were hidden, whooping, waving their shields, coming in a great rolling cloud of dust with the red flashes of their guns shooting from it upon the hunters in the grassy draws, and the prairie fire leaping towards them.

Then Silent Ben, the other Jackson along, made his first remark of the fight. "Keep your eyes on the camp," he warned. "The charge up there is a diversion."

He was right, for a solid force of warriors was pouring over the crest of the side draw that the hunters had just deserted. But the smoke was not quite thick enough to hide them and some were killed there, although the fighting was hot. The ammunition of the hunters was running low, their wounded begging for water, particularly Joe Jackson with his groin shot, and not a canteen or a cup in the whole force. Johnny Cook slipped off his new boots and three of the men started to crawl the hundred yards down to the bottom of the canyon for water. They managed to get the boots full and Shorty did what he could for the wounded, bending his great lanky length over them as gentle as a woman. Then he gave each a drink of fourth-proof brandy from a bottle in Bill Kress' saddle pockets. They were here nearly an hour but now they had to get out, and as soon as possible. Divided into two squads the hunters started to crawl down to the main canyon while a few went back to cover them with a little more skirmishing. It was time, for a large party of warriors was already skulking along the draw. Campbell ordered the men to try to get back to the wagons. They needed no second invitation, moving as fast as they could, bent and running for the main canyon and down it. While Smith covered the retreat some made stretchers for Joe Jackson, Squirrel Eye and George Cornett. Hi Bickerdyke and Cook managed to slip back for Grimes' saddle and made it to the supply camp an hour before sundown.

There was no exuberance now. Silently they loaded the wounded and got under way. Joe Jackson had to be hauled all the hundred and fifty miles to Griffin. The post surgeon extracted the bullet from the groin. It was a bad wound and although he was up a little once, he had a relapse and died two months after the fight. Even so, some thought Jackson got off easier than those who had to take the slurs around Rath's and Griffin, the loud-mouth bull-whipping.

"Here's another a them buffalo militiaers! Got them Comanches cleaned out yet?"

There had been more snorting when, about the first of April, Captain Lee of the Tenth Cavalry and seventy-two colored troopers took the field against the Indians. "Niggers to fight them bloody Comanches!" the southerners said.

Although the hunters had returned to Rath's the twenty-second of March, May came in hot, and still there was no hunting. Scarcely anyone dared to ride out to see about the big hide piles the hunters had left when the Comanches struck—not with five hundred bloodthirsty savages on the loose. All this time the returning hunters talked a good fight, but it was plain from the first that the Comanches weren't cleaned out, only stirred up. It was further humiliation to find that most of the Texas hunters had deserted Rath's soon after the expedition started, and gone home, predicting that the hunters would fail. An old Seventh Cavalry man talked with hearty cheeriness. "It takes army discipline to go against Indians," he said.

"Well, by God, at least we got back. Not like some a them blue-coats we hear about up north!" the hunters roared.

So there was a little gun play, the bullets going

through the hide and canvas roof to make leaks if it ever rained.

Finally some of the northern hunters moved out in small parties, anxious about their winter kill of hides, in danger from the beetles as well as Indians. Rees, Kress, Crawford, Cook and several others went in a body. Charlie Rath sent well-armed freight trains to haul the hides in. It took nearly two weeks. By then buffaloes were moving north in thick little herds and some of the impatient hide men risked going out ten, even twenty miles, gradually careless again. Once more the Indians swept over the range, this time to within five miles of Rath's, killing three hunters and destroying several camps, the stock run off. Two days later Tom Lumpkin made some remarks about the buffalo militia foray against the Comanches back in March. A man who was having his hair cut by Crawford in the saloon objected, and Lumpkin shot him through the shoulder. Crawford called Lumpkin on this but Limpy Jim Smith, tending bar, jerked Crawford aside, fired and missed. Now it was for blood, as Lumpkin backed towards the door, shooting as he went, holding Smith back, but only a little, the bartender following out into the street, limping but relentless, bullets flying both ways, men ducking everywhere for cover. Finally one of Smith's bullets hit and Lumpkin fell, within ten feet of Cook and Godey, who were sacking up dried buffalo tongues in a wagon.

The bartender had had trouble with Lumpkin over the failure of the expedition several times before. Now he stood the funeral expenses and then went to Griffin to be tried. The verdict was swift and easy: justifiable homicide.

By now news had come that Captain Lee and his black troopers did capture the Comanches and were bringing them past Rath's. That would make the southerners who scoffed at the Negro troops eat dirt. But that was underestimating the Texans, who calmly said their opinion of black troops wasn't any better, only their opinion of Comanches worse. There was also word that the Indians had lost some good warriors in the fight with the hunters, and that many were wounded in the firing into the lodges, some women and children killed. In Captain Lee's attack Nigger Horse and his wife died together, riding on one pony trying hard to get away.

And up north Crazy Horse, who had cut off the retreat of Custer on the ridge above the Little Big Horn last summer, had finally surrendered to the troops with all his Sioux followers this spring of 1877. Now only Sitting Bull was left and safely out of the way across the border in Canada. The Indian resistance was broken everywhere, and once more the big guns boomed, and the buffaloes fell to the green spring grass.

BOOK III

RETREAT TO THE STAKED
PLAINS

CHAPTER XII

THE EDEN OF THE ANIMALS

I N JUNE 1877, the year of drouth, a waterspout moved over west Texas and dropped its load on a broad hardpan table, where a few mudholes had been cracked and drying. Then the empty gray funnel lifted and all the rolling darkness of cloud moved on, leaving a lake to reflect the untroubled blue of the sky.

The buffaloes, fleeing westward from the boom of the big guns pushing up the rivers and from the smell of their dead on the wind, had withdrawn to the fringes of the Staked Plains, up to the farthest headwaters of the streams. But beyond this they could not go, and as the early heat of spring dried the few wallows and the little sandy runs, the buffaloes were pushed slowly back eastward, back down the drying stream beds, no matter in which direction the wind blew, the wind that had once guided them so well.

Then one day a light little breeze from the west brought not only the hot dusty smell of the Staked Plains, but a hint too of water somewhere under its passing. Slowly a cow at the edge of a little herd lifted her head, swung the clumsy bulk of it this way and that, her nostrils flaring. Slowly, deliberately she turned and began to move, her head down in determined march. One after another the rest fell in behind her, then other little bunches, more and more. In a long string they wound up around the breaks as the land rose to the high table. And there, beyond all water, they marched into the wind once more as the great herds had been doing since the beginning of their time.

They marched like this all night, joined by more and more buffaloes hurrying up from behind and the sides, moving into the burning heat of the next day, the young calves lagging, the mothers turning back impatiently to urge them on, stopping a moment to their hot searching noses and then walking again. The rest of the herd were as thirsty, as wild for water as the calves, and yet they kept moving behind the young cow who had first smelled the moisture on the wind. Unlike the eye in the desert, the nose did not mislead them; a dozen times shimmering lakes appeared and then were gone, seen no more by the near-sighted buffaloes than the real one that finally rose on the western horizon.

But now the growing smell of water drew the clumsy animals into a hurried walk, and then a run, the great mass spreading a little as they came, grunting, their tongues hanging out long, the thousands of hoofs shaking the earth, the herd moving in a rising fan of dust that climbed in a high plume behind them, while ahead lay the blue lake like a looking glass framed in the burnt June prairie.

But the buffaloes were not the first to find this surprising water. Snipes, curlews, gulls, ducks and pelicans, cranes, shitepokes and loons had flown in as though they had followed this water from where the whirling funnel drew it up and carried it over the land. Dragonflies poised on the new grass just starting in delicate transparent green along the margins, and butterflies, white and yellow, drifted on the light, hot wind.

Then everything, even the smooth surface of the water was suddenly agitated, for the dust cloud of the buffaloes was approaching, the thunder and roar of the herd that pushed and trampled those ahead into the water, spread in a dark wall both ways along the banks and kneaded them into the mud.

But finally the thirsty animals were satisfied and began to drift back from the lake, scattering over the hot dry plain to rest and ruminate. Slowly all the smaller creatures startled away came back, flying in from the prairie, or creeping cautiously near. The rabbits were soon there, and the wolves and coyotes. Out on the prairie a herd of mustangs that had smelled the water far off too, were hesitating. The lead mare tossed her head, testing the wind for any danger beyond the defense of her swift hoofs and the slash of her teeth. Gradually they drew near, coming up obliquely, shaking their long, dark manes, then finally they nuzzled the surface clear and drank, long and slowly. Afterward they went to rest and switch lazy tails at the flies, here where only a few days ago none would have found a creature upon which to feed, nothing except the well-armored lizards, horned toads and rattlesnakes.

Before long men came too, soldiers first, Negro and white, with breed and Mexican guides. None of the buffaloes and mustangs, not even the wolves or the curlew, did more than move aside as the men ran in naked surprise into the water, splashing, swimming out where it was deeper, and then finally settled on the sunburnt, shadeless banks to rest until the smell of coffee boiling crept along the wind.

But the new waterspout lake was not the only place where the animals, driven by the noise and stink of the hide men, sought refuge. Back in the winter the two Johns, Poe and Jacobs, had found the fleeing buffaloes gathered at Sulphur Springs at the foot of the Great Plains, far from a good supply of water. The hunters reached there at night and because an immense herd had also just arrived and was watering, they had difficulty getting to the springs at all. The water came out of the bank of a draw, flowed a half to three-quarters of a mile before it all sank into the earth. This whole region, from the springs to the end, was worked into a loblolly of mud, with thirsty herds of buffaloes driven here to drink at every hour of the day and night. That first night the men stood at the head of the springs and chunked the buffaloes off with stones so they could get a taste for themselves and their horses. It was a sight that overawed them, old buffalo hunters that they were. Afterward, fearing a fatal stampede, they rode out five miles from the springs to spread their blankets for the night. Next morning when they went back, a circle three-quarters of a mile in every direction from the spring was covered solid with buffaloes. The wildest dreams of any hunter fell short of Sulphur Springs. Wolves and antelopes stood around for a chance to crowd in to the water. And all the animals seemed to regard the men as just another of their kind come to drink, and were tame and unafraid before them. Jacobs and Poe threw stones at the wolves, who ran after them as they rolled, and patted at them with their paws like puppies.

The two hunters made sixty-two hundred hides that winter and spring, and while they only brought a dollar apiece with the market so flooded, the sale was for the hides picked up at their camp, with no freight expenses—still very good pay even for expert hunters. Joe McCombs, their former partner, worked a little south of them. He got forty-nine hundred buffaloes, doing all the shooting alone. A little farther out were several more hunting camps, and still the buffaloes came, undiminished. The hunters looked over the moving prairie and were once more certain they had found lifelong careers.

But in other places the buffaloes were dying by the thousands and more, without the firing of a gun. Driven to seek water in the unaccustomed marshy lagoons of the Staked Plains, they mired down in the churned up mud. Others were driven into the quicksands of the upper Red River forks by the thirst-wild hordes crowding up behind, or in the upper

Pease River and the headwaters of the Brazos. One after another, the better and more familiar watering places had been shut off by the hunters, and the herds were kept moving in their panic until so crazed that when they did find water, they came crowding, stampeding in everywhere, trampling the weak and those ahead in their frantic need to drink.

The true phenomenon of the buffalo ranges of Texas was the hide town, established far from any settlement or post, made from the materials at hand, with sometimes a million dollars changing hands in a few weeks over the buffalo hide counters. There had been Adobe Walls, Dubbs' camp, and Rath's up on the Sweetwater. But the most ambitious was the town that Rath and Reynolds established last year at Double Mountain Fork of the Brazos, far out from Griffin, in the true heart of the Texas herd. This metropolis of the hunters carried the stamp of the builders, particularly the large, expansive, well-living Charlie Rath. No one else could equal the number of hides and robes he handled, the trainloads of buffalo meat, dried and frozen, besides carloads of tongues. Few killed more buffaloes on the range than Charlie, and from his Indian trading days he was an excellent sign-talker and had acquired many Indian habits. One of the most useful was anticipating attack every moment of the day. Another was knowing how to live off the country. Charlie knew a man could keep sharp-witted as a wolf or an Indian on meat alone if he ate the softer parts and the internal organs as well as steak and roast hump. He was the man to build a hide town, grow it out of the earth as naturally as a willow clump or a nest of prickly pear.

Although Rath City was over a hundred miles from civilization, almost a million hides had been hauled down the one dusty street on the way to Fort Worth. The store that outfitted the hunters was thirty by a hundred feet, and included a cookhouse and sleeping rooms, all of sod and hides, with a canvas roof. The inside was never free of a rancid, tallowy odor on hot days, and of the stink of hides outside, but no one except the newcomer noticed this. A small shack near the store housed the Chinese laundryman that Rath's supply train had brought from their Sweet Water hide town. Across the street was the big saloon and dance hall, thirty by eighty feet, mostly hide stretched between studding of cottonwood poles too. Just west were the expanding corrals with a bunkhouse for the guards. Around this center, small sod and hide shacks were going up, and farther out the great hide drying acreages spread each way, with the camps of the hunters scattered along the creek—in one week, out the next—each with his assigned space.

Rath City provided everything the hunter could need, even an occasional nice, lady-like young girl who stayed behind the restaurant counter and left the bolder business to the professionals. But it was difficult to keep either the young lady waitresses or the dance hall girls here—at least any that were presentable enough to please Charlie Rath. They were always running off, generally to be married at Ft. Griffin, or by the wandering sky pilots that both Rath and Reynolds encouraged to come through so long as they kept sober enough to see the difference between sin and good business.

If anybody at Rath's recalled the attack on Adobe Walls and wondered how soon it would come here, in deep Comanche country, nothing was said about it beyond a little codding that was not without some irritation, like the thorn of a cactus in a wool sock.

"Guess we're safe so long's Charlie Rath's hangin' around," a hunter down from Dodge said at the bar after the buffalo militia returned. "When Charlie hits out for civilization we better be tromping hard on his heels."

"Oh, come off!" Rath laughed good-naturedly. "You think I would leave my help to get hurt, maybe killed?"

"I seem to recall you was off to Dodge before the Adobe Walls fight got goin'," the hunter replied. But he didn't push the matter, for the town owner would make two

of him and enough left over for the magpies. Besides there
were a lot of the buffalo militia boys around, and all still a
little tender.

Yet it was true that Charlie Rath knew Indians almost as well as Amos Chapman did He wouldn't risk this big
investment, and money rolling in. Besides, the Comanches
were licked, with nothing left for th. buffalo militia to do
but hunt.

Late in April Captain Lee had brought most of the
women and children of the Nigger Horse band of Comanches
past Rath's. He camped them out on the bottoms, the Indians
crouching in dark little knots, like dropped bundles of dirty
rags, worn out by their long fast march over the cactus plains.
Johnny Cook, Limpy Smith, and some others who were in
the attack on their camp in Thompson canyon, went out to
see them. Lee had killed five warriors in addition to Nigger
Horse and his wife in the eight miles of running fight to the
Blue sandhills. Some had got away there, but the troops
captured and destroyed what must have been all their ammunition and their dried meat. Johnny recalled what Rees
and Campbell had said about the fighting on the Sappa, and
wondered how many women and children had died in the
eight miles of pursuit. Lee mentioned none, but he made
himself popular with the hunters by saying their attack
had killed thirty-one Indians, four more dying the next day.
No one believed it, not even those who were there, unless it
might be a couple of the loud-mouths who had claimed at
least a hundred Indians killed, just to save their faces when
they came back without a warbonnet or a scalp. But the
fights around Rath's over this had died out since Lumpkin
was killed.

Unfortunately the Comanches who eluded Lee were
not cowed. Before long Cornett came whipping in to Rath's,
shouting that John Sharp had been wounded by Indians, and
not any seventy-five or a hundred miles away but very near

here, right around the foot of the Double Mountain that loomed over Rath's camp, with the eagles circling its crest. The Indians plundered Sharp's hide camp and ran off all his stock. Keyes, Cornett, Squirrel Eye, Hi Bickerdyke, Freed, Cook and some others, enough to stand off attack—all men who had been at the fight with the Comanches—took Rath's buggy and team out for the wounded man, with a good horseback escort. Returning towards dawn the next morning they heard firing as they neared the hide town. From a high point Squirrel Eye saw a flying cloud of dust moving west from Rath's, about seventy-five Indians driving away over a hundred head of stock. They cleaned out the place, including Cook's horses, as he discovered.

The crowd around Rath's looked mighty cheap, caught flat-footed like that, and there were no smart-alecky remarks about the buffalo militia that morning. The herders didn't know anything was happening until the horses were stampeding before the blanket-waving, whooping Comanches. There had been only two men on guard at the hide town, and at daylight, with no alarm at all, suddenly about fifty Indians charged shooting and yelling straight through the town, between the store and the saloon, and on after the horses being swept away by the other Indians. The hunters driven off the ranges were spread out over forty acres of bottoms, many sleeping in their wagons. They would have made easy picking, like buffaloes in a stand, for a general massacree.

A glum, horseless crowd sat around Rath's that day, organizing what was later called the Forlorn Hope. Thirty-eight men here had lost all their stock, including Sam Carr, who, besides a valuable team of mules, mourned for his Prince, a fine dappled grey gelding of Kentucky blood that he had raised and trained to do show tricks, to come to him even over burning buffalo grass, and never to leave him. A couple of tears slid down the round, sun-burnt cheeks of the fleshy man for whom Prince had done all the walking, practically, outside of the saloon and the hide sheds.

No one dared hunt now, and so a large party decided to go on a summer long Indian chase, an expedition to set the Comanches afoot as they had set the hunters in the cactus. But this late spring of 'Seventy-seven there was no big talk of killing the nits and the lice. Jim Harvey, a former infantryman around Ft. Dodge, was commander, Dick Wilkinson chief packer, Sol Rees in charge of medical supplies and Johnny Cook as interpreter for the Cherokee-Mexican English of the guide José. Carr and two others were sent to the cattle ranches around Griffin to buy horses and pack animals, going in the wagon of Powderface Hudson, who came in from Quinn's camp, where there still were horses. The ranchers, acknowledging that the hunters were the buffer between them and the Comanche raiders, mounted the whole expedition, with stock for packs too and gave them bills of sale for all their branded stock they took from the Indians. Cook got the big chestnut-sorrel he borrowed for the pursuit of Nigger Horse last March, and was proud of the ownership.

The twenty-four hunters started with ten pack animals, set up a base out near the Yarner, the Staked Plains, and arrogantly ordered the Mexican meat hunters away, to clear the region for their pursuit of the Indians. They found the tableland around the battlefield of Thompson canyon so full of blooming flowers that Burns, the poet of the two Englishmen and Johnny Cook were in constant awe. The whole air, which should have stunk from the old buffalo carcasses out on the plains, was fragrant instead, fragrant as it would be all the next few weeks, alive with the sweetness and the brilliance of flowers in arid lands. In places the whole sweep of prairie was a golden rug, then perhaps blue as the reflected noontime sky, or purple with evening.

The hunters scouted in wide circles, to Casa Amarillas, the Yellow Houses, and to Silver Lake, near where Lee had captured the Comanches. Once they struck an Indian trail that headed towards the waterspout lake and then led them all over hell 'n' gone. Plainly the Indians knew they were being pursued and drew the hunters away from their supplies and from water. They saw small bunches of buffaloes and antelope out that way, but all Indian sign was lost now, and they went on past Double Lakes to the Colorado River of Texas and then skirted the edge of the Staked Plains back northward, to where Sewall was killed, and west, out on the uncharted Yarner again, from water to water. Three times they found Indian sign, always apparently just gone, and each time the hunters found a trail that ended, a flying jackrabbit trail.

Back at the headwaters of the Colorado, Harvey sent out three scouting parties. Waite and Cook went together. With their fieldglasses they picked out something that proved to be horses, not wild, but some that had been stolen from Rath's, one of them surely Carr's grey Prince. The horses seemed loose, no Indians around, and were easy to round up, with Prince coming to the call of his name, worn but unharmed. When they rode him into camp Carr was almost in tears again. He identified two of the mules as belonging to the man who had saved Johnny Cook's life from an Indian before the fight against Nigger Horse in March.

Carr worked all the next day with Prince, rubbing him down, picking out burrs from his mane and tail. The gaunted horse was still imposing with Carr in the saddle, the hunter holding his flesh very well, even with all the joking about his mammoth appetite. He and Cook went to look for an Indian trail where the horses were picked up, but there was no track except of a herd of mustangs, and those led them to water at some sulphur springs. The wild horses fled to the breaks at the approach of the men, wilder than the wolves or the coyotes and ravens gathered around the pools, a great eagle soaring overhead. There was still no Indian sign here and with their canteens filled, and the six-pound powder cans each carried, the men rode out to make coffee and rest a while, sitting together, Carr facing east, Cook west. But the wild horses out on a far slope were quiet; no Indians around.

Back at camp near Bull Creek, they found that Harvey had been joined by a scout called Spotted Jack and a couple of other men who had been holding a herd of longhorns at the head of North Concho and lost some horses to the Comanches. Next to come past were some buffalo soldiers, as the Indians called the Negro soldiers, with their tight bush of curls at the forehead. Capt. Nicholas Nolan had sixty troopers of the Tenth Colored Cavalry and four six-mule team wagons, also an eastern boy who happened to be visiting at Ft. Concho when they left. With Lt. Charles L. Cooper and this force, Nolan was to establish a base camp up in the Colorado country somewhere, make a two months' scout in all directions, and render protection to the hunters and settlers. He recognized Harvey, from the campaigns in the Indian war of 1868. The gathering of hunters including native Texans like Squirrel Eye and some veteran Johnny Rebs, sized up the aging captain and his colored troops while Nolan looked the hunters over with a tinge of the soldier's contempt for civilian Indian fighters. From the moment of that meeting to the end of their joint venture, there were two versions of what was done and said during the next few weeks. Three, perhaps; nobody asked for the version of the colored troopers.

Most of the hunters were glad to see the soldiers out, although some were still a little sore over Lee's easy victory against the Comanches, and with colored troops too. In the meantime Nolan was saying importantly that he wanted to help any hunters he found on his scout, and wished to form a junction with them here if they were agreeable. It seemed that the governor of Texas had wanted to send a frontier battalion of Rangers to disperse the hunters as an illegal body of armed men, but was dissuaded. Three years back Nolan had trouble with some green troops, couldn't get

them to go against Satanta and his Kiowas. Colonel Shafter
had Nolan stand courtmartial for it and only the captain's
good record in the Rebellion had saved him. Now he wanted
to show he could catch Indians and would welcome the hunters and their guide José if they would agree to get him to
water once every twenty-four hours, and to help him find
the Comanches.

Harvey described their weeks of scouting, the watering places they had located and that José believed the Indian
headquarters were in the Blue sandhills about fifty miles
west of Double Lakes. They would get Nolan to water every
twenty-four hours if it didn't work against finding the Indians and recovering their stock.

With this clearly understood by both sides, the captain took the leaders from his mule teams for the packs,
sent the empty wagons back to Concho for more rations and
forage, and left a sergeant and nineteen men to guard his
supply camp on Bull Creek. Then, with Lieutenant Cooper,
forty troopers and most of the buffalo hunters, he set out
towards Cedar Lake. Some of the hide men had been against
this, in such a dry summer, but Nolan asked them to follow
him this once, and if he was wrong he would then follow
their advice. Cook and several others had been over this
region when the rising slopes were still bright and fragrant
in bloom. Now they were sere in drouth, the heat far
above one hundred degrees. The command made a fifty mile
march the second night and reached the lake. But instead of
the usual shallow water holes there was little more than mud
and dry bottoms. The troopers dipped up water with their
tin cups and watered their horses and pack mules in the camp
kettles. The hunters did the best they could, keeping off
to themselves, plainly disgusted with Nolan's refusal to take
their advice. Next day José and some others, including Harvey and Johnny Cook, went to scout south to Five Wells in
search of Indian sign. They were out thirty hours without
finding water. The few buffalo wallows were blown full of

sand, and the white bars of the dry runs bottomless to the tromping of the hunters. Buffaloes wild for water and smelling it under the sandbars often milled around on the dry stream beds until water welled up around their hoofs. But here there was only dust in the sand, for the whole length of the spade that the hunters carried.

Early the next morning José and Powderface Hudson, sent scouting farther on the day before, came in. They had found a trail leading in the direction of the chain of surface lakes that ran northwest between Double Lakes and the bluffs called Yellow Houses. The waterspout in late June had left a good lake up there. The hunters had seen it early in July, greatly shrunken, but it still had about ten acres of water in the deepest part.

With this news of an Indian trail out on the Staked Plains, the hunters returned to Nolan, all except Spotted Jack and the men with him. They wouldn't risk following the captain out on the Yarner this year of drouth, and if the rest had good sense they wouldn't either. All the buffaloes and antelope had quit the country.

Nolan made a dry camp twenty-five miles out the first night. There was very little sign of any buffaloes around for all the last year, and at Double Lakes the water was very low too, the thin worn grass of the bottoms dead as the hair of an old buckskin horsehide. There was no Indian sign but they laid over to rest the stock and then took a fresher trail to the June waterspout lake, still covering around five acres and fairly deep in the center, with miles of drying mud. Here there were horses, mules, a few old buffalo bulls, some antelope and coyotes, wolves, sandhill cranes, Negro soldiers, white men, the Cherokee-Mexican José—all around the lake together in the early sun, the men bathing and then sleeping back away from the flies and mosquitoes. They had arrived around midnight and hid their camp in a gully at the north end of the lake. In the morning they saw a smoke signal at the south end of the old June lake bottom, perhaps six miles

off. Then another signal twisted up into the pale sky back
toward Double Lakes. Earlier in the summer the hunters
had been deceived by spiral whirlwind dust carried into the
air but there was no mistake now. These were smoke signals
from Indians on both sides of them. Looked like they would
get a big fight, and no canyons to protect them here.

José, off scouting, saw about thirty Comanches riding
out of a draw three miles away and heading towards the
upper Colorado. At José's signal the fight-brittle Negro bugler gave one good blast and ran for his horse, blaring all the
while. Harvey sent Carr and Cook with their good horses to
keep sight of the Indians. They were two miles out when the
troops got the pack train into motion. The Indians turned
southward when the two trailers were within a mile, and
veered off again, running, the two hunters spurring hard to
keep them in sight. Then they were signaled back by Nolan,
who believed this flight was a ruse. Wiping his scorched
neck the captain looked around his troopers, all stretched
out in the poor shade of their horses, inert as though sunstruck; he argued that the Indians were trying to get back to
Ft. Sill. They were tired of the hounding from the troops
and the hunters. Harvey and the others were dubious, wondering who had done the hounding, and José still insisted
that the main camp must be in the Blue sandhills.

The next morning the guards reported five, six Indians coming in under a white flag. It was Quannie, Quanah
of the Comanches, who had been at the Adobe Walls fight.
He had two old couples along, and a paper from General
Mackenzie ordering him to hunt up the Indians that were
out and bring them back to Ft. Sill. Nolan was furious and
profane but he had to let Quanah go, all the expedition
watching with angry faces as the Indians rode off, particularly
the Johnny Rebs among the hunters, those who despised the
bluecoat Nolan and his black troopers.

At noon the expedition saddled under the burning
sun and went back to Double Lakes, arriving around mid-

night. From there Nolan sent José, Johnny Cook and several other hunters to look for water up toward Dry or Salt Lake, seventeen miles to the west. In the forenoon, July twenty-sixth, Cook and another hunter hurried back to report that José saw forty Indians traveling and hunting leisurely toward the Yellow Houses as if there were no hunters and troopers anywhere. The captain got his men moving by one o'clock. In spite of the protests of the hunters, he let some of the troopers get away without filling their canteens, and many thought how smart Spotted Jack had been not to follow this man out on the Yarner. Every hunter had a full canteen or a six pound powder can of water covered with blanketing and hung from a sling. José had stayed out to keep the Indians within good field glass sight and Cook was sent ahead on his strong chestnut to overtake him, with orders to wait for the troops. He found José three miles northwest of Laguna Rica. The command came to them by a cutoff and so had missed the lake and made a dry camp. The heat was furious, the men falling out. The troops had exhausted their water and demanded that the hunters share their supply. Nolan, in the region for years, didn't protest, although the water could have been doled out over twice the time.

By mid-afternoon, more Indians had joined the trail ahead, but darkness shut it out and Nolan made a second dry camp. At break of day they were on the trail again. By nine it went west, at noon northwest, at three west, all dry-trailing, obviously planned to finish the troops, the hunters and their stock by thirst. The horses were gaunted and giving out, two sunstruck troopers were left behind with stronger men detailed to care for them. The hunters were complaining now too, some in angry profanity, some wanting to return to Double Lakes that night, others to push on, arguing that the Indians would lead them to water. Judiciously old Bill Benson, long a hunter in dry regions, suggested that the troops head for water without stopping while they were still able to travel, and then return to the trail. Impatiently

Nolan said the hunters were free to go, but he was responsible for his men and his stock. He would lead them into no night ambush or take chances on getting them lost.

The next dawn there was the trail plain to follow, but no water, a big pack train of grub and nobody able to eat. For a while it seemed they were gaining on the Indians, the horse droppings getting fresher even in the fierce heat that welled up like a prairie fire from the baked earth. They were all dazed now, confused and lost, it seemed, the biggest mouth among the hunters no longer suggesting they strike out across the desert that was the enemy of everything but the rattlesnakes and the Comanches.

Then, almost before the hunters realized it, the Indians had scattered like blue quail, the wide, distinct trail fraying out, thinned to nothing at the edge of the great sands. The troopers were dropping from their horses in fatigue, and the visitor along too, the boy, so Nolan gave up the chase temporarily. While the command rested José circled out wide and picked up the trail again, where the Indians had converged. Once more Nolan's men pushed wearily on, farther and farther west—fifteen miles deeper into sand. Now even the dark faces of the Negroes were burnt and raw, three of them tumbled from horses in sunstroke together, others were straggling, and a detachment was laboring to goad them on, keep them from death by thirst or skulking Comanches. The country was gently rolling now, dry, reddish, the sparse scattering of grass short and burnt, with stunted mesquite and scrub oak about a foot high. The men needed water but not more than the horses needed it.

Cook was ahead on the trail with José, both in physical torture. Their systems rejected tobacco, their saliva was dried up, their jaws falling open. Those who tried to eat had to dig the dry food from their mouths with their fingers. The column halted and a messenger came to stop the trailers. Some of the troops were getting ugly. Finally the command came in, totally demoralized. But the Blue sandhills were in plain sight, their outlines sharp in their blue haze, with the scattered brush a dark sweep along the slopes. The hunters were revived by the sight; even the horses knew there was water ahead.

But the panic of thirst and heat was working its unreason on Nolan. He demanded if José could find Silver Lake, and told him to take ten of the strongest men with canteens and bring back water by midnight. The command would follow on his trail the best it could. José was against this. He could find plenty of water in the Blue sandhills not over eight miles away, sweet water, not salt and alkali as some they had seen. Harvey backed him up; José had never failed them. They might have to fight Indians for the water but it was there.

The Irish stubbornness in Nolan came out very strong with his fatigue and confusion. He had twenty-five men prostrated, he roared as loud as his swollen tongue would permit, and the civilians were suffering too. They would all be maniacs soon. When the captain saw that the hunters were still against him, dark and unmoved, sentimental tears began to run down his gaunted old face. He was nearly sixty-five, he pleaded, almost ready for retirement. He had been a sergeant crossing the plains to Utah with Johnston's column in 1857. Here he had no guide except the hunters and their man José. Surely they would not desert him now.

So out of pity Harvey and the others consented to his plan, although it seemed like cutting their own throats; worse than that, for a jugular vein flows fast. The suffering of this might be a long, long ordeal.

Suddenly energetic now that he had his way, Nolan gave one of his private horses to José and sent him to guide the mulatto sergeant with his squad of water seekers, the men carrying the canteens of the expedition strung around them like the dry, empty hulls of some fruit. He also sent the boy who had wanted to come along for the adventure. José struck off towards Silver Lake and the Yellow Houses region, the desperate command following the best it could, those who were able to move. Slowly the hunters turned their faces from the Blue sandhills standing cool against the burning sky of evening and kicking their gaunt, worn horses into a shambling walk.

Now Johnny Cook discovered that Carr was missing, fallen out a mile back, he was told. Waite had stayed with him but the sun was sinking fast and so Johnny hurried back to help get the heavy man back on Prince. But Carr said he couldn't go on. His flesh was soft, not wiry like Waite's and Cook's, both lean as greyhounds. It took an hour to get Carr back on his horse and up to the command, almost the last of the stragglers to come in.

They found Nolan in a panic. It was everybody for himself now, and the captain too weak for the measures necessary to stop the mutiny, even if it meant the pistol. The command had scattered all over the plain, not even a guard set. The hunters, too, dropped before their worn-out horses were properly picketed, some lying across the rope end like Johnny Cook, but few horses were as reluctant to jerk against the rope as the big chestnut. Johnny saw several pack mules pass, and called to a soldier, but the men were snoring fitfully, or talking low, mumbling, and no one moved. Once two of the troopers who were bringing in one of the stricken soldiers came past, but they disregarded Nolan's shouts and went right on in the night. Later Cook awoke to a lot of shooting in the pitch dark, the muzzles pointed upward into the clouded sky. There was nothing he could see, no Indians, certainly not the men back with the filled canteens. Few slept much after that, and towards dawn Johnny roused himself and realized that neither he nor Harvey or even Benson had secured their horses against wandering off for water as soon as the animals had rested and cooled a little. Of these, few except his chestnut had stayed. As he stumbled out over the camp ground, he found scarcely a one of the hunters' horses in sight. Wilkinson was gone too, wandered off.

As the sun came up Nolan and Lieutenant Cooper scanned the empty landscape for a sign of José and the men with the canteens. But there was nothing in sight. Now once more the captain insisted on changing the course, vacillating as the inexperienced or the emotional do in trouble. He was sure the guide was lost and ordered that they reverse their course and head back to Double Lakes. The hunters argued that they were perhaps seventy-five miles from there or farther, and some here could never make it, while they could surely reach Silver Lake even on their dying horses within a few hours. Johnny Cook looked around the command and saw the last of it break up right there before Nolan's new and suicidal course, fly to pieces like a flock of hens at the shadow of a hawk.

Nolan's best packer was one of the three men who deserted in the night by simply walking by in the darkness, and so the captain helped load the mules. During this time most of the disgusted hunters left him, some trying to track their horses over the iron-hard earth, a few horseback, leading their two pack mules, others heading straight for water afoot, their rifles across their arms, the sun-heated metal burning through their clothing.

But as the hunters moved together into a ragged line, old Bill Benson, the most experienced man among them, stopped. He had to try to talk to Nolan once more, he said, and if necessary, stay with the troops. So he reined his horse around and kicked him into a sort of reluctant half-trot, the horse hound-bellied, head hanging down, tongue out. The others turned a moment to watch him go, then pulled their hats down and plodded on.

Gradually the sun was greyed by high, wind-blown mares tail clouds, the air still and hot. At the first rest the men on foot begged the few with horses to hurry on and return with water. Foolishly they had given up their containers to the water detail, and pint and quart cups were all they had left to bring the water back but even the news of it ahead would strengthen them. Cook pushed his lumbering chestnut out but he looked back several times to the troops getting smaller out on the flat plain, and saw Benson reach them.

The sun came out in terrible heat upon the hunters, the strongest sunken-eyed now, their lips black and breaking, their tongues swollen. Here and there one fell, men who had made it through frontier heat and blizzard and Indian attack for years. But each time there was one still able to go back and by feeble effort, by thick-mouthed abuse and profanity, to get the faltering man to his feet once more. At a halt Rees lifted himself to look around the men, like corpses, dropped any way. He got the medical kit from the packs and hauled out the two bottles of high proof brandy. With a piece of rag torn from his shirtsleeve soaked in brandy he moistened each man's lips, letting him inhale the fumes. It was magic for a short time, enabling them to hurry on. When the effect was gone Rees repeated it from the bottle he carried. The other one he had left behind with ramrods stuck up to mark it for those afoot. On this desert plain there was not one whitened buffalo skull that usually served as the bulletin board of the plains, so he scribbled the instructions on a piece of blanket, adding "For God's sake, boys, don't drink it."

When his bottle of brandy was exhausted around noon, Rees sent Johnny Cook and Waite ahead to signal news of water, to keep the falling men encouraged somehow. The two struck ahead, spreading apart a little, their sunken, bloodshot eyes watching the pale horizon with its fool lakes around the west, the shores lapped by shimmering waves of cool water that were only heat mirages. But by mid-afternoon Johnny saw what looked like the breaks of the Yellow Houses. He looked back. Behind on the hazy plain the men seemed to be scattering, separating, wandering, one group moving off towards the wider wastes. So he fired the signal shots, taking the chance of raising false hopes.

Slowly the men stopped and turned to look, then gradually began to draw together again, heading in his direction once more, at least for a while. But one man dropped as Johnny was watching, one more of the many strung out far back. It had to be now or never, and so Johnny, the Johnny who used to get lost, managed to whip his exhausted horse into a sort of stumbling walk, each forward lurch apparently the chestnut's last, hoping he was not lost this time.

Suddenly the horse lifted his dragging clubhead, whinnied, and started into a floundering loose-legged run. Cook was too weak to hold the chestnut now, although he was like a wasp, so thin in the gut that it seemed he must fall dead at every lunge. With a final lurch he went down over a bank into a water hole and had to be hit over the head with the bridle bit to keep from killing himself right there. The water that splashed into Johnny's face as he fought the horse was the most grateful thing of all his life and recalled him to his own need. He held a palmful to his burnt lips, managing to draw in a little, then more, but moderately. Then he bathed his face and hands and crawled out to the safer bank as he became dizzy and retching.

Before he could gather the strength to go back for those behind, a Negro trooper came peering out of a draw, with canteens of water hung all about him, his teeth white in his dark face when he saw it was a white man, one of the expedition. He had been with the squad that had started for Silver Lake but he got lost from the others in the dark and his horse brought him to an upper water hole here. He said two white men had come in too, and from his description Cook knew they must be Waite and Wilkinson.

So Johnny took the soldier's big, rested army horse and the seventeen canteens and started back on the trail. He could scarcely have held himself awake now, except that the

horse, a big, hard-gaited animal, would have jolted a deer
fly loose. Johnny met Rees who said that Keyes, Cornett
and Squirrel Eye Emery had given up and might be dead in
an hour or so. He spurred up his horse, clinging to the horn
in his lurching weakness. About a mile and a half out he
found John Mathias afoot. The gaunt, sturdy man refused
water. He would make it now; those behind needed it worse.
Carr was gone, he said, wandered off, but Keyes, Cornett
and Emery had to be reached right away. Cook hurried
along the back trail, dropping a canteen here and there to
the plodding hunters. When he found the three men they
were lying in a little row, side by side, their faces covered
with handkerchiefs, like corpses laid out. Two of their horses
were melancholy wrecks, Emery's dead, killed and the blood
drunk.

Johnny Cook saturated a handkerchief, wet the lips
and tongues of the men, and rubbed their faces, working
fast. They were all so motionless, as wooden as dead men,
with no pulse that he could find. But finally Emery
responded a little, the dried wound that was his mouth seeming to twitch, and then Cornett drew in a gasp of air.
Slowly, very slowly, all three revived. They had given up,
even the breed Keyes; with their names written on their
saddles they had composed themselves for death. It had been
quite easy.

Rees and Waite came back to help them now, and
Johnny Cook went to find Carr. He zigzagged over the prairie
toward the water holes, even the upper dry ones, looking for
Prince, trusting to the ears of his army mount to let him
know if they were near. Finally he found the horse, and
Carr on the ground beside the big grey who, only a rack
of bones now, was still waiting on his master despite his terrible need for water, with the smell of it coming to his
charred nostrils on the air, the horse making pitiful little
noises for it, deep down. He nickered a little as Johnny
neared, and Carr recognized the man's voice although his

eyes were blinded by the exposure. He managed to swallow a little water and finally got into the saddle with Johnny's help—perhaps the most shockingly changed of all the hunters, his flesh melted away like snow gone from within a ragged, dirty sack.

The horses led them to the upper water hole where the runaway pack animals had gathered, with Wilkinson following from the time they left that last camp with Nolan. He had shot an antelope, skinned the hide off with the hoofs left on to make a water bag and was tying it up, ready to fill and start back for Harvey and the others afoot. Cook headed back too, but by then a tremendous desert thunderstorm had come up with the night. Once Johnny fired his gun and got a reply, a shorter, sharper flash than ball lightning, half a mile away. It was Rees and the three revived men, moving under the sheets of heat lightning that lit all the sky.

As Cook returned to the water holes with them, Mathias called out. "Friend or foe?" he shouted. Nature had given him a direful expression and the long ordeal had not improved it, but he was still the most humorous, the most cheerful man of the outfit. Now, with his face ominous in the firelight he shouted that he had set the Negro trooper to work as cook. The antelope was roasting over the coals, with bread and hot coffee ready.

"We trust you have let nothing spoil your appetites for our simple little supper," he said severely.

But some of the men couldn't eat, only keep drinking water, and then more water when their stomachs refused it. But finally all except two felt strong enough to go back out on the Yarner to bring in the rest of those afoot. There was still a great crashing of thunder, the heavens brilliant with rose and lilac, or split by blinding bolts of lightning that fell upon the stunned earth. Yet there was not one drop of rain. Once for a while they heard a tremendous continued roaring and later they discovered a new water lake about six miles out, belly deep to the horses, where only dust and a few dead and worn roots had lain on the baked ground.

In the morning Waite and Wilkinson brought in the last of the foot plodders. The brandy bottle left behind had saved them; they could not have made it otherwise—that and holding lead bullets in their mouths to keep the saliva alive as long as there was a drop of sap left in them. Hudson was delirious and the rest very weak, but all were safe now, all except José and old Billy Benson. José would be all right but Benson was out with that damn fool Nolan, and no telling how many men would die before they reached his Double Lakes, or whatever place the vacillating fancy of the captain settled upon.

Then the next day, the last day of July, José with a trooper and the boy from Concho, came pushing along the hunters trail to Yellow Houses. They had found Silver Lake with the canteens, but the mulatto sergeant refused to go back on the Yarner to relieve his captain and his comrades, and he refused to let his squad return. Instead they struck out straight for Ft. Concho. One man disobeyed the sergeant and followed José with the boy and the forty-four canteens to where the troops and the hunters had been when he left, the place where Nolan started back to Double Lakes. José trailed the troops until he was confident they would find the lakes or the waterspout lagoon; surely they couldn't miss both, not if anybody had sense enough to let his horse take the bit. Then he cut across for the hunters trail and Yellow Houses to his own party.

When everybody was able to travel the hunters started back to Rath's by way of the old fighting ground in Thompson canyon. There they found the Mooars out looking for their horses that the Indians might have dropped this summer. Joyously the hunters saw that Benson was with them, suddenly white-bearded, sick and strange but alive. He had finally become disgusted with Nolan and left the outfit. The night of the twenty-ninth his horse was lost. So he walked, without water for ninety-six hours, his tongue out of his mouth when he reached a scummy pool, knowing nothing the last day except to follow his stumbling feet, but still with the long sense to take the water slowly. Yet even after they had all come up to him, one by one, to let him see them, hear each one speak, he still tried to slip away, particularly at night, crying, "I must go find the boys!" when he was caught and fetched back. As he gained strength his mind began to clear but it took over three weeks. By then they had even found the missing pack mules, so all the Forlorn Hope was safe, safe but greatly sobered.

Jim Harvey took the weaker men on to Rath's while the rest circled out to gather up a lot more stock on the way, stock dropped as the Comanches hurried to Ft. Sill and safety, perhaps to the call of Quanah's white paper. Johnny Cook and Burns, the Englishman, talked seriously about it one evening up on a windy knoll away from the mosquitoes. It seemed the Indians still had a treaty right to hunt here, where a million buffaloes grazed last year, and now almost none remained, their carcasses down in the tall uneaten grass. For this the horses that were stolen and the hunters killed somehow seemed very little revenge.

Cook went with those who rode over to the Blue sandhills, to the deserted Indian camp seven miles across the country from the spot where Nolan had decided to turn away and try for Silver Lake, and then Double Lakes. By now the hunters knew he had made it out finally, but with incalculable suffering and misery for all his force. It hadn't been long until Nolan and everybody with him was lost, and so once more men were sent out to look for water, and these too, did not return, for there was no one with the power to command them now. By the second day Nolan's men were killing and drinking the blood of the horses, the men fighting over it like the famishing animals they had become, sucking the heart and other viscera for the moisture. They became sick and vomited, and were struck by the same blind staggers as the horses. The twenty-ninth, with the temperature at a hundred and twenty, they still had not reached the lakes. The horses were all playing out. Nolan caught the thick dark urine of one and tried to drink it, and then the men tried to drink their own, sweetened with sugar, and were as sickened as those who tried that of the horses.

By now the crazed survivors left those who fell behind, each one trying to hurry on, fighting to be near a horse as it went down and its throat was cut. But the blood was thickened and their gullets adhered so that some could not swallow any more. Lieutenant Cooper tried to hold himself erect long enough to harangue those left around him, saying they must push on in the night, drive the horses they had left as far as possible, then divide the blood fairly. Hand on pistol butt he told the men there was no longer any room for fancy illusions. They must act like men if any at all were to survive, to get through. The gathering rain clouds might bring a shower, or they might reach one of the streams to the eastward, or be picked up by a relief party from Ft. Concho. Surely some of the buffalo hunters got out.

No one replied, only the sunburnt, bloodshot eyes moving in the yellow evening sun. No relief came; no rain, no men, and no streams or water holes appeared. So they dropped their last rations that none could eat now; they dropped everything but their pistols and carbines, which they must have against the Indians and in the hope of a buffalo, his paunch full of the acid water that had saved many a man, Indian and white, from death by thirst.

When they left camp the twenty-ninth only two horses lived. Because Nolan and Cooper must try to lead their men out, they mounted the two pack mules, stolider, hardier than the horses. They marched to the first tinge of dawn, and by now none could sleep in the frequent halts they had to take, the men falling, grey-skinned and as motionless as long dead skeletons under the matches the lieutenant lit, the dimmed eyes staring into darkness.

Then at three in the morning they struck an old trail. Cooper was afoot, resting his failing mule. He stumbled over the ruts and barely noticed them, so unsteady were his feet as he held his course by the fading north star. But there were more stumbles and then he realized that this was an old trail, and turning down it, suddenly he knew where he was, and shouting like a madman to the few troopers still within hearing, his voice only a hoarse croak, "I know this trail— We're not far! Near Double Lakes!"

By five in the morning, the thirtieth of July, a few of the stronger men fell on their bellies at the edge of the water. Cooper still had the strength to drive them back, as several other troopers, stronger men than those with Nolan now, came running up—six of those sent out ahead. The captain started them back on the trail with their horses and such containers as could be managed for water to bring in the men who had dropped along the route. But they returned saying they could find no one, not the troops or the buffalo hunter supposedly left behind somewhere. Other searchers were sent out and brought back the same story, although two of the stragglers finally found their own way in. That left five men dead out there. Twenty-two horses killed for their blood and five men dead out of the forty Nolan started with, out of the twenty-six left after the desertions of the water detail and the packer, out of the twenty after he sent the second group for water and they did not return.

"Damn smart Niggers," some of the hunters said when they heard about the desertions, speaking a little ruefully, pleased that an army man was low-rated by his troops, sorry that it was Negroes who had carried it off. But there was one figure to stand beside the picture of the unfaltering Lieutenant Cooper lining out the wild and thirsting men, bull-ragging them to act like human beings, even though he had to do it with his hand on his pistol. This figure was the big, raw-boned coal black Negro who remained a tough, staunch, cheerful and courageous trooper through it all, his correct courtesy failing only once, when he told the whining, panicked Captain Nolan he should shame himself before his men, to set such an example.

The day after Nolan reached Double Lakes Captain Lee and some Tonkawa Indian scouts arrived from Ft. Griffin. As the man who had captured most of Nigger Horse's Comanches he had been sent to strike the favorite haunts of the Indians, in the hope of intercepting any band that might be fleeing before Nolan. While on the way up Yellow House fork, Spotted Jack had discovered Lee's trail and brought him news of Nolan's probable plight, unwilling as the stubborn Irishman was to take the advice of José or the hunters. He might be in serious trouble unless he happened to strike the waterspout lake and stayed there until rescued, the place where there would be water and every kind of meat—one of the places that the Mexicans called the Eden of the animals.

CHAPTER XIII

THE TIME OF THE FLIGHTS

THE Comanches had broken up the spring and summer
hide business of 'Seventy-seven but the hunters of the
Forlorn Hope had aroused the army enough to send Nolan
out and the very futility of his Lost Nigger Expedition
brought national attention to the Indian raiders. To be sure
Quanah managed to by-pass all his pursuers and got the Comanches safely to the reservation, where, it was hoped, they
would be guarded more carefully now. Neither Nolan nor
the hunters had much taste for Indian hunting on the Yarner
right away.

Word had been sent around to the owners of the stock
picked up to come and get it. In the meantime Rath let the
hunters ride the grubline at his restaurant until September,
until they could get their equipment in shape and line up
hunting ranges for the fall. It wasn't all generosity; Charlie
was keeping them in the region until the buffaloes came
there. He ended up the time of waiting with a big blowout—
a regular buffalo town shindig, including horse-racing, shooting matches, a couple of imported gamblers for those who
were interested, although the better hunters were never
much on liquor or cards, and a big buffalo barbecue. For

313

the night there was a hoedig, with a couple of additional fiddlers from Griffin and some extra girls, to dance to the song of the buffalo skinners:

> Our meat it is the buffalo hump,
> Our staff the sore-thumb bread,
> And all we have to sleep upon
> Is the buffalo's hide for a bed.

the rougher men singing it "His goddamn hide for a bed!" and stomping the dust out of the packed earth with their boots as they swung the girls around. A long poem about the summer's Forlorn Hope was read by Harry Burns, the Englishman: "To the Hunters after the Ninety Day Scout." Burns, who signed himself *Vox Buffalorem*,* was introduced as a possible descendant of Bobbie Burns, to which there were loud hoots and much laughing that the poetic gift had become pretty adulterated, like the sand in Charlie Rath's sugar. But of course that was only for the Indians. The verses brought roars of applause when they were done, most of the men mentioned in them were sitting there, men "called by the names they are traveling under," as Harry explained.

Afterward many talked over the thirsting time out on the Yarner, and drank deeper of the cups here at Rath's. They talked of the time in varying ways, some conspicuously silent, for only scoundrels and fools speak easily of courage.

After the big blowout the hunters scattered all the way from the Pease down to the South Concho, secure and safe from the Indians. None would ever be permitted out again unless they had a good soldier escort, and there was much pressure, national and local, to keep them sitting around the agencies permanently now.

Johnny Cook and several others left late in September for the head of the North Concho and hunted along the edge of the Staked Plains, looking off northwest now and

* Later published in the *Dodge City Times*, Sept. 29, 1877.

then and remembering Nolan's expedition, particularly after Johnny heard that another one of the Negro soldiers had been found, nothing left but the wooly hair and the buttons of his scattered clothing to identify him as not just another hide man killed by the Comanches. The hunting went well this fall, but there was something on the mind of Johnny Cook, something that threatened to draw him away.

Last winter small fortunes had been made by hunters trading their hides at Rath City, Griffin, Buffalo Gap and Concho. After such news, with the romantic stories of the Nolan expedition and the report that the bloodthirsty Comanches were safely rounded up, at least five thousand hunters spread over the narrowing buffalo ranges the fall of 1877. The year saw the greatest pursuit of the Texas herd but it was, as always, the experienced men who found the hunt profitable. They followed the retreating buffaloes into the vast reaches of the Staked Plains, somehow much less frightening to the hunters since last summer, as well as to the buffaloes who had smelled the wind from the waterspout and left their sign. Carr and Causey's camp was clear out at the limerock formations of Yellow Houses. Perhaps none of the Texas hunters killed more buffaloes than Causey in his quiet, efficient way. Dalk and Decker's crew was out too, down at Big Spring, taking hides and putting up meat until Christmas, with Bob Parrack along. Bob had been hunting in West Texas since 'Seventy-two, mostly as skinner for such outfits as Causey and now the two D's. He used a straight knife and at twenty or twenty-five cents a hide had made more steady money than many hunters. When something happened to the shooter he could take up a gun, preferring the new Remington to the Sharps, and regretting that the new gun came out a little late. The first one he ever saw he got in a poker game.

Emanuel Dubbs was still up at Oakes Creek not too far from his farm, still saving the best of the meat to cure, and speaking regretfully of his venture into the summer hide business with the other Adobe Wallers. In January 1878 the little town of Mobeetie was established at Ft. Elliott, near Rath's old Sweet Water hide town, and there the quiet, religious man became Judge Dubbs, his neat beard setting off his narrow, intelligent face, with the high forehead balding a little. Billy Dixon too, moved there when he wasn't scouting for the army. At least two of the buffalo hunters wouldn't die from the bullets of an Indian, from some hot pistol in a hide town, or dancing at the end of a rope under a cottonwood or pecan tree. Mobeetie was a cattle town, one of the first to start up hard on the heels of the buffalo bone men. Everybody was going into cattle, it seemed, even Buffalo Bill Cody, up north of the Platte. He seemed to have a good partnership with Major North who had commanded the Pawnee Indian scouts before the tribe was brought from the Platte to Indian Territory, and dying there of hunger and malaria, Amos Chapman said.

Buffalo Jones had his roping outfit camped along the Beaver up in the narrow No Man's Land. He drove the calves he caught back to his growing ranch west of Dodge City, where he was crossbreeding, as Goodnight did too in Palo Duro canyon, hoping to get the tractability and heavier hindquarters of the domestic cattle, with the wiry hardiness of the buffalo. Unfortunately the cattalo turned out a singularly unsightly beast, without the majesty of the buffalo, the swift balance of the longhorn, nor the smooth compactness of beef stock. But Jones planned to improve the strain and the cattalo certainly looked hardy. There was, however, little hunting left around No Man's Land, even for the rope, and when another prairie fire swept a path fifty miles wide from the Canadian to the Arkansas River scarcely a buffalo hoof was sent running.

The heavy hide wagons were still coming in to Rath's but from far out now, mostly southwest for this hide town, in the heart of the buffalo country a little over a year ago, was now in virgin grass. Although a million dollars worth of hides had been hauled down the furry dust of the street, only two good gun booms away another kind of settlement was already started—Swedona, a colony of Swede homesteaders, nesters, hoemen, the women and children working in the fields. Hide men turned their faces away and hurried off into the southwest; the cowboys curled their windburnt lips as they loped past the patches of breaking that would toll other settlers into the grass lands barely freed of the buffalo herds and the Indians.

A few hunters, like Burns, mourned a little at Paint Rock down along the Concho as they passed, wondering about the long-gone Indians who had left their red, white and black pictographs on the cliffs, telling one could only fancy what story. In the movement southwest the trade was going mostly to the older posts in the region, although up at Griffin the screw-drive hide baler was still turned day after day by the patient old mares. There were always large piles of baled hides ready for shipment and still four, five acres covered with drying skins. The winter of 1877-8, a boom year, brought hide prices down some, to a low of fifty cents for many taken in the summer, winter ones going at one dollar and one sixty.

One of the hunters who made the winter a boom one was Joe McCombs. September first he had gone out to Big Spring, then to Mossy Rock Spring and here he made the biggest killing of his hunting career, forty-nine hundred hides through September on to May, 1878. Near Mossy Rock he killed twenty-two hundred so close together he could stand at one spot and see most of the carcasses. It was almost as though the remnants of the great herd had lost the will to run away. The buffaloes had disappeared along one river after another, from the Platte to the Clear Fork of the Brazos. Now on the western reaches of the Colorado of Texas it seemed that they had been fleeing too long, and suddenly were weary and would run no more. Or perhaps the Indians were right. Perhaps the buffaloes did come out of the earth in Texas, full-blown herds marching out of a cavern into the blinding sunlight. Perhaps this was near Mossy Rock and what McCombs shot were the newly emerged, the innocents. But these stories only entertained men like Burns and Johnny Cook, and only a few hunters believed now that the buffalo would last forever.

There were new hide stations like the second Sweetwater, this one off south of Rath's, just a trader store dug into the bank of the creek for hunters and government surveyors, but most of the trading of the new region went to Ft. Concho's San Angelo. There had been an early California stage station three miles from the post, and early buffalo shooting that was for meat and for hides to make walls and roofing in a region where lumber was scarce. Although the hide trade boomed, Veck and Frarey remained the principal buyers and no foreign dealers came in. Concho and its town was a wild place with bad feeling between the Texans and the Negro troops from the start, the attacks sometimes as swift as those of the vinegar-smelling whip scorpion or the javalina, the peccary. As the hunters increased, the killings grew to three, four a week. The sergeant who refused to return to Nolan with the filled canteens from Silver Lake with José was tried and sent to Leavenworth prison, for twenty years, it was said. So now the feeling in the little town of the post was no better.

As the hunters moved into the Concho region, McMillan's colorful freight outfit took to the prairie, each of the twelve big Murphy wagons with seven-foot wheels drawn by seven yolk of longhorns. The bulls were sleek and well groomed, their horns painted bright red, the yokes and bows blue as a field of Texas bluebonnets.

But by January 1878 thousands of buffalo hunters were already turning into other lines, cattle, or homesteading, perhaps, and a few joining the Texas Rangers. But many showed up in the growing gangs of horse thieves, all the way from the Concho north to Montana, and among the hold-ups and roadagents. There was even meat thievery now, particularly from Dalk and Decker, who dug great hide-lined pits to salt the meat that was then hung in smokehouses of buffalo hide, the smoke from slow fires of buffalo chips with sweet bark and grasses to bring out the flavor, their fancy customers bragged. Certainly it was an excellent cure, as a sliver shaved off with a hunting knife proved.

There were hide rustlers at work too, some at Griffin, slipping out of the river bottom shacks in the night, but much bolder at Ft. Concho. There they broke into the big hide yards and made great hauls—one that the thieves managed to sell at the front gates straight off their wagons, before the owner detected that the hides were his own.

There was more general violence around Concho than ever at Hays or Dodge. It was not just a few bad men, or likkered up troopers and tenderfeet, or even the usual conflict between the individualistic frontiersman and any soldiers that represented the only law outside of the gun and the knife. Here there was the color line too, and in addition, the periodic rise in the use of narcotics, present since 1871 at least. That year the post surgeon reported serious inroads of a drug among the troops, with the general belief that some of the Mexicans and breeds "were in possession of some poison that will permanently affect the reason and that Empress Carlotta is a case in illustration."

Although there seemed plenty of work for the Rangers in all this lawlessness, they didn't do their gunning on that line around Concho. Last fall Capt. John S. Sparks had come to camp his Rangers near the fort and, as the hunters heard it later, the night of their arrival, Sparks' rough and ready outfit took over a saloon and dance hall at San Angelo. They swanked around, jingling their spurs and dancing with the Mexican girls until some of the former hunters pointed

out that in the dim lights six or seven Negroes were swinging
the girls too. The Rangers pulled their guns; there was some
wild shooting, the girls screeching in excitement. The Negro
troopers were pistol-whipped, some of the noses flattened
down like a sway-backed old mare. Unarmed, they could
only reply with slurs at the bravery of some of the buffalo
hunters with the Rangers for deserting Nolan's outfit last
summer. Next day the colonel of the post called on Sparks
for an apology. Sparks called this a deliberate insult from
the federal authorities and said he and his little company
could whip the colonel's whole colored garrison. The bluff
wasn't called and the next night the Rangers camped off a
few miles below the post but some of the Negroes managed
to slip out to the saloon with guns. Thinking there were
Rangers on the floor, they opened fire on the dancers and
killed a hunter just in from the prairie.

After this Captain Sparks was replaced, but by a more
violent man. In February a carousing party of buffalo hunters
and cowboys, usually not friendly, stripped the chevrons and
the stripes from a sergeant's clothing, and after the general
fight, ran the Negroes out of the saloon. Some of the troopers
sneaked their guns out of the post and returned by a
side door. The bullets flew two ways now, with the Negroes
armed too. One buffalo hunter and a soldier were killed and
several men wounded. In protest the new Ranger captain
marched his men across the parade ground of Ft. Concho in
search of the man who let the troopers get to their guns. The
colonel ran out to challenge the Rangers trespassing on federal domain. Finally nine of the Negroes were indicted, one
of them given the death penalty. The shooting went on but
it gradually shifted back to the cowboys because the hunters
were fewer and fewer.

The year 1878 became known as the dire year. There
were a dozen twisters, tornadoes, over the fringes of the
Texas settlements, and as early as April great hailstorms

stripped the leaves from the pecan trees and the mesquite along the Concho. In one storm the stones were like goose eggs and beat out more than a thousand panes of glass around the post and San Angelo; five soldiers were injured, many horses stampeded, many injured, one killed, with much loss of sheep and cattle, particularly young stock. Game was scattered dead all over the prairie, deer and antelope, birds too, ravens and cardinals and mockingbirds. The hail lay a foot deep on the table, and was swept into great dirty drifts in the canyons and arroyos. It was also the year of floods on the Concho, with cloudbursts far up, and water in many holes out on the Yarner that Nolan and his men had found only baked adobe a year ago.

It was also the year of typhoid and other diseases from contaminated water. Even some of the older hunters were sickened, the lucky ones close to the post hospitals at Concho and Griffin, but mostly out alone in isolated hide tipis, while everywhere men shook with the ague, and ate the bitter quinine.

The year brought sickness to Indian Territory too. In 1876 the Southern Cheyennes had made sixty-five thousand dollars from the tanned robes of their own kill and those the women dressed for the Texas traders at five dollars a hide. But the fall of 1877, after the slaughter by the hide men, they had less luck. With the Northern Cheyennes that were brought down from the Powder and Yellowstone country, they got only a few buffaloes altogether—not enough meat to feed them until they reached their hungry agencies, mostly afoot, for horse thieves in the Panhandle had swept their herds away and sold them to Kansas homesteaders.

With death from starvation and disease in every lodge, the newcomers, the Northern Cheyennes, demanded permission to return to their own healthier country, where there were still buffaloes. They claimed they had been promised this before they agreed to come south at all, and when permission to return wasn't granted, Little Wolf and Dull Knife and their bands left, saying they would go peacefully, but if they were shot at they would fight. They started in the night, early in September, 1878, leaving their lodges standing to fool the troops with their watching cannon aimed down upon the moon-lit village. Most of the Indians went afoot, sick and hungry, too, because there had been no issue of rations for a long time and they were not allowed to hunt. They must have horses to get north before the blizzards, but even more urgently they must have meat, through a region where barely a hoof had trampled the grass of the buffalo trails or the rows of browning sunflowers that showed their direction far ahead.

The troops followed and there were skirmishes, with some killed on both sides—not many, but enough to start real shooting. The Indians managed to get a little meat too, a few buffaloes that had hidden in the breaks of the Cimarron.

Soon there was great excitement all over the frontier as far away as Washington state, with half a dozen other tribes jumping their reservations too this hungry summer. But always the Cheyennes were given the lead stories. There was news and rumors of their many depredations and atrocities through south Kansas, some at least two hundred miles east of their path, a hundred men killed, whole herds swept away, even an entire trail herd from Texas. Dodge City was in the path of the raiding savages and although there were only two hundred eighty-seven Cheyennes, with fewer than seventy-five warriors between the ages of thirteen and eighty, the talk in saloons, dance halls and the dusty streets turned to fire and massacree. Like dozens of other Kansas communities, they wired the governor for arms. It seemed that the wild Queen of the Cowboys might have the guns and the gunmen to stand off a handful of poorly armed, sick and starving Indians, but the governor was sending two hundred stands immediately.

The cattlemen who stood to lose stock to the raiders tried to intercept the Indians with the help of such Dodge loafers as they could round up. They were certainly better

Indian fighters than the troops who repeatedly let the wily Little Wolf slip his people through their guard as easily as he had jumped the reservation. They made a fine dash, by train, to a burning house on an island up the Arkansas River, but without an Indian sign. They rode out in a bold excited expedition but they came back without scalps, saying the troops had let the Indians get away again, the troops complaining that the civilians had run like rabbits before a prairie fire. The Cheyennes did surround a few buffalo hunters with eight or nine cows dead, ready to skin. The experienced plainsmen laid their big guns and their ammunition down on the ground and the Cheyennes took the meat and the arms, apologizing that they had no presents to make in return.

The troops hurried out by train to intercept the Indians at the Arkansas crossing but the Cheyennes were gone. By then most of the men reported killed by the Indians began to come in, and the trail herd too, which had taken the longer route, as was usual so late in the season.

There was still much big talk around Dodge, but mostly against the troops now, evidently not much better than Nolan's Nigger Expedition. Angry, Colonel Lewis, commanding Ft. Dodge, said he would catch the Indians or die in the attempt. No cowboys or hunters volunteered to help him, and by the time he died from bullets by the Indians that he encircled on Punished Woman Creek, the raiders were well past any cattle herds of Dodge. But Sol Rees, who had hunted in Texas and been with Nolan, was back home. He had hunted the Republican the spring of 1875, and was in the Sappa fight when so many Cheyenne women and children were killed. Now he hired out as guide for the troops eager to avenge the death of Colonel Lewis.

Amos Chapman was along too, guiding the troops following the Indians from Indian Territory. He rode the hard trail as stoutly as any, even with the crutch on the saddle since the buffalo wallow fight with Billy Dixon in 1874. As the Cheyennes neared the ground of the Sappa camp, and as more and more of their relatives were killed or died from the hard pace, the young warriors along grew angrier. They had lost their old-time chief, Medicine Arrow under the white flag in the attack there only three years ago, and now they went against the advice of Little Wolf and began to avenge themselves on the settlers along the Sappa and Beaver Creeks until they had killed a white man for each Cheyenne man who died in the fight of April 23, 1875. They killed no women and children, for there is no way to avenge the death of the helpless ones. For two bloody days they raided and then with the troops close on them, some of the warriors slipped back south. The rest rejoined their fleeing band and started north into Nebraska, their raiding over, for no white men, no troops or buffalo hunters, had harmed the Cheyennes there.

Rees understood why the innocent settlers of north Kansas had died, Rees and Hank Campbell, in command of the buffalo hunters who came shooting out of the fog that morning on the Sappa. But Lieutenant Henely, who had been in command of the troops there, was dead, drowned last July. The Cheyennes said it was because he made war on the sacred arrows in the keeping of Medicine Arrow when peace was offered. He died violently, as Custer had died, Custer who broke the word of peace he gave to the same Medicine Arrow in the lodge of the sacred arrows. Even Amos Chapman was not certain that the Indians were merely superstitious. He lost a leg with the buffalo hunters and he was willing to guide the troops against Indians, but he would break no word given to them. That was too bad luck.

In the newspapers and the magazines of the country the story of the great buffalo hunt of Texas took up considerable space while in actuality it had become a final pursuit. Many of the hunters were equipped with telescope sights and fast horses. The slow stupid buffaloes of even a year ago were suddenly very alert, getting the scent of their enemy a mile off and farther if the wind was right. With tails up they fled at a hard gallop, as wily and cunning as any longhorn of the brush country.

The two Johns, Poe and Jacobs, had settled at the foot of Signal Peak, around east from the camp of their former partner, Joe McCombs. The two were still optimistic, bringing out around fifteen hundred dollars worth of ammunition and provisions, including lead in twenty-five pound blocks, and powder in twenty-five pound kegs.

They scouted out a good little herd but they had to move with it, keeping other hunters away by the prior right of discovery—squatters' rights—so formalized were the rules of these last hunts. But the water had been scarce after Christmas and in spite of their vigilance the buffaloes were suddenly gone. Poe and Jacobs traced them and moved to the head of Sulphur draw, in advance of the drifting herd. That one day it was like old times. The buffaloes moving southwestward paid no more attention to them than a bunch of cattle would. The herd parted for the wagon and rejoined at the tailboard. These seemed tame buffaloes, tame as though they were actually new and fresh from the earth, so new they had never heard a hunter's gun. Now once more Poe and Jacobs thought they had a profession for life. Then suddenly all the buffaloes that were left were dead, naked, bloated and fly-blown. The hunters hung on a little longer, until some hungry Indians, probably Comanches, ran off all their horses and stopped to butcher one, with a fire to roast the meat.

Joe McCombs, it was said, got more buffaloes for his cartridges than any other man in Texas and for a while he had kept seven skinners busy, with an eighth man for extra good times. But that was in the past, now he went out September first to Mustang Pond. From September to mid-March he got only eight hundred hides, against last season's forty-nine hundred to May first. The buffaloes were very scarce and wild. They left early in their migration but they never made it up to the summer range. Hunters finished them off and left only a few stragglers, mostly calves and worth nothing for hides.

The last big bunch of buffaloes Johnny Cook ever saw
was about ten miles south of Mustang Spring, going southwest. They never came north again. The main part of the
little herd that was not killed crossed the Rio Grande and
took to the hills of Chihuahua. After that early spring day
Johnny and the others around him saw no more than isolated little bunches; fifty was surprisingly big. By May the
hunters were leaving, some to the San Juan mines, some to
the Black Hills, some back to the states, or to settle on homesteads, go into ranching, or into other, slyer business.

Horses were stolen everywhere now, with slick-hoofed
tracks and perhaps an Indian tobacco pouch or whip dropped
conspicuously. "Lot a them buffalo hunters took to rawhide
and paint and feathers, looks like," an old hunter-turned-
rancher said sourly when his horses were suddenly gone, and
then showed up pulling breaking plows in south Kansas.

But some were going after horses legitimately—trapping the fine wild mustang herds of frontier Texas, Kansas
and Colorado. Not every man could creep up on a rise down
wind and pick off the sluggish, half-blind buffaloes with a
Big Fifty when the herds were their ripest; even fewer could
outwit the wily mustang that had survived only by outsmart-
ing the wolf or the mountain lion, with his compelling fondness for horseflesh. Without shell, fang or horn, the mustang
had learned to depend upon fleetness of foot, sharpness of
eye, ear and nostril, the keenness of his brain and the trapped
lightning in his striking, iron-hard hoofs. These herds were
not to be crept upon as the buffaloes, or overtaken in the
chase as the Indian once got his meat, and certainly not held
in a milling, circling surround by a lot of whooping and waving of blankets. Given a space anything over six inches wide,
the wily nose of the lead mare would try to worm her way
out, lead her herd to freedom; given any wall that a stubborn
nose could clear and the whole herd was gone.

Even before the buffaloes were finished in the Palo
Duro region Charles Goodnight had brought in a herd of

two thousand cattle. The panic of 1873 had about cleaned him out but here he aimed for a new stake in a new enterprise and by 1880 the Panhandle was feeding more than two hundred twenty-five thousand cattle. This was nothing compared to the great wild herd that so recently grazed there, but the change had eliminated one factor, the Indian, who had to surrender because his women and children were starving.

There were some who regretted the precipitous slaughter of the buffalo for economic reasons, and wished some smaller herds, say fifty or a hundred thousand head, might have been preserved for the rougher, more rigorous regions, at least until cattle increased. But the migratory urge would have made that impossible. Nothing could hold the buffaloes starting to move into the wind. The new invention, the barbed wire fence, which helped the settlers kill off the free-range cattle business almost before it got under way would not hold buffaloes.

By the summer of 1878 ranching had already grown into such prominence behind the shrinking Texas herd that the Northwest Cattle Raisers held a convention at Ft. Griffin. The old hide men heard weeks ahead that they were to be cleaned out of town by the invasion of the cow outfits. There was a great deal of shooting-off at the mouth on both sides, with much show of guns and blue powder smoke along the hot, dusty street, but it all fizzled out, sputtering like over-age Dupont in a Big Fifty, partly because there had been so few hunters left.

Hungry nesters were pushing in on every trail much as hide men had once swarmed over the region, and they and the cowhands chased down the last few buffaloes. In May 1886, Charlie Norris, a ranch hand, saw a small herd about three miles off the trail between Coldwater, Texas and Buffalo Springs. He had no gun along but the next day he saw them come to water, a hundred eighty-six head. They drank heavily and then played like calves. Some jumped off a bank

four, five feet high into the water, climbed out a low place
and jumped again, almost as free and unafraid as the herd
that had been drawn to the waterspout lake back nine years
ago. The cowboy fired into them and they scattered. That
fall and winter hunting parties got the last herd left in the
southwest, fifty-two head. It was a long pursuit, but finally
they all lay dead. Ten were skinned entirely, and the heads of
all the little bunch were preserved for mounting. They
brought up to a hundred fifteen dollars for the robe of the
full-grown bull, with head on. Two years later a few more
were killed a hundred miles north of Tascosa, the wild cowtown on the upper Canadian. The hide and head of the
grown bull brought a hundred and fifty dollars; just the head
of one sold for fifty dollars.

The old hunters and traders like Mooar, Wright, Rath
and the rest shook their heads to this, thinking of the millions
sold for almost nothing. The hunters now punching cows,
settled on homesteads, mining, hiding out somewhere from
the law or perhaps in some penitentiary, looked glum too,
when they heard of such prices. Nine years ago, at the height
of the slaughter of the Texas herd, the hides had fallen below a dollar.

So the great hunt of Texas didn't even have a decent
climax but ended in a sad pursuit of the fleeing, a hunting
down of a few stragglers like criminals are hunted, but alert
now and wild, running at half a mile, a mile at the sight of a
man. Long before this many hunters had moved north across
the Yellowstone. Johnny Cook was among those who went
north too, to Kansas in 1879 and then to the Ft. Berthold
reservation far up the Missouri, into the Indian service—a
move that had been coming upon him all the years of his
hunting in the buffalo and Indian country of Texas.

The escape of the Cheyennes from the hungry south,
with other tribes trying it too, and the flight of the last few
buffaloes to the breaks, or across the Rio Grande, these were
symbols of an era's passing, and the hunters of it vanished

like the shadows of the great herds. In all the country from the Platte to South Texas a whole economy, a whole way of life was done, the Indians on the reservations. The final elements of its destruction, the few who would go on being hide men, were fleeing too, going to the northern herd across the Yellowstone. Here many southern hunters saw their first real winter robes, dense and heavy and beautiful, primed by weather that dropped to forty below and endangered every man who was a greenhorn to the country.

BOOK IV

THE NORTHERN HERD

CHAPTER XIV

ALONG THE WINTER
YELLOWSTONE

WHILE a few scattered buffaloes were galloping for the remote breaks of the Yarner, or marching in slow and final dignity across the Rio Grande, there was still a herd estimated at over a million in the north, ranging from the lower tributaries of the Yellowstone up into Canada. So Texas hunters put their Sharps into the saddle boot, and with a pack horse or two, struck out northward, standing their stirrups much of the time of the long ride, day after day, as the sun fanned their long shadows over the prairie. Now and then they stopped to wet the dust out of their throats at some saloon or hog ranch, to get a little news on any gold strike, but asking continuously about buffaloes. Some dropped off to join old acquaintances in more questionable ventures, perhaps running horses in the underground up across the Arkansas, the Platte, and on into the Wyoming ranch country, cleaning out the pony herds of the Sioux agencies around the White River, or holding up the gold coaches out of the Black Hills. Some wondered about the freezing winters they had heard tell about up in Montana. Others just rode northward, drawn as relentlessly as the buffaloes moving into the wind.

But the forty-below weather produced a fine thick pelage, one valued by traders the world over for a long time, back when the Texas herd drew no more than the natural encroachments of the Indians and the occasional Mexican meat hunters. As early as 1820 professional hunters were cutting into the Montana herd. By then hide-taking was already an organized business with the Red River breeds of Canada. It is estimated that they came south with an average of six hundred ten squeaking carts a year, men, women, children and dogs, with banners, chaplains, hunting officials, and rules for the hunt and for war with any protesting Indians. First, it seems, they came on an annual hunt, from mid-June to September, for meat and hides, later on two hunts, one mid-June and the second in mid-October, for the thick robes that sold so well. They watched the weather very carefully, not to be caught by the killing blizzards out on the open prairie, their heavily loaded carts creaking their slow way back home into the icy wind. Sometimes they spent much of the winter snowed-in but comfortable as far south as the Yellowstone.

This invasion of the Montana and Dakota buffalo herds was larger, some say, than the army with which Cortez subdued a great empire. In the years 1820-25 around a hundred and forty-six thousand buffaloes were killed, at an estimated value of seven hundred thirty-one thousand, two hundred and fifty dollars for the hides and meat sold. The expeditions increased until the five year period of 1835-40 they averaged one thousand and ninety carts, the buffaloes taken two hundred twelve thousand, five hundred, at well over a million dollars; the estimated value for the twenty years over three and a quarter million dollars, in addition to all those that the breeds used for food, which was largely meat, and their own hides and robes. By 1871 the buffaloes were scarcer and a family with six carts got the meat of sixty buffaloes as their share of the hunt.

Paul Kane, the artist, who went past Ft. Garry in 1846 said that the hunts were conducted by the whole tribe. Twice a year notices called all the families to meet on a certain day about twenty miles westward of Garry. Here the tribe was divided into three bands, each given a separate route for its five hundred carts, drawn either by ox or horse.

The hunt was what they called a race, a chase, with say four hundred or more well-mounted and armed men taking part in the carefully planned hunt. Once under way it became a wild run over rocks and gullies, badger holes and prairie dog towns, with guns booming, buffaloes going down, horses vaulting them, or falling, or, fleet-footed, bending into the exciting chase of an escaping bull. Sometimes as many as twenty, twenty-five horses and riders might be down at a time, here a horse gored by a bull, there a long-haired breed leaping and running, dodging, twisting to escape the blindly stampeding buffaloes, and the hunters running and shooting as blindly. One might break a shoulderblade, another burst a gun and blow off part of his hand, perhaps receive a spent bullet or ball. But from one such hunt they brought in one thousand, three hundred seventy-five tongues, the meat all cut into strips for drying, Indian fashion, much of it for the Winnipeg market where it was a regular item, carried in the stores outfitting travelers and frontiersmen. A handful of pemmican was a meal, easily portable and sweet a long time even in summer if protected from moisture.

Perhaps the most successful hunter of the winter of 1874-5 was Abraham Salois. He killed six hundred, got thirty-seven of these in one run. It made the still hunt of the hide men seem pretty tame.

On their way home with their two wheel carts loaded high with robes and pemmican, the Red River breeds sang the song made for the return; something like this in one white-man version:

Hurrah for the buffalo hunters,
Hurrah for the cart brigade,

That creaks along on its winding way
While we dance and sing and play.
Hurrah, hurrah for the cart brigade.

Mon ami, mon ami, hurrah for our black-haired girls
That braved the Sioux and fought them too,
While on the Montana plains.
We'll hold them true, and love them too,
While on the trail of the Pembinah, hurrah,
Hurrah, hurrah for the cart brigade of Pembinah.

The men with their French-bearded Indian faces sang
lustily to the fiddler sitting on a high-piled cart. And at night
there were dances around the big open fires, dancing the
French country dances, the girls swift-footed, their skirts flying, their dark Indian eyes coquettish, so one who saw them
did not wonder at the high places some of their stock adorned
in both Canada and the United States.

Another kind of hunting used against the northern
herd, in addition to the regular planned surround of the
Plains Indians, was the pen or pound. This dated far back,
before the white man brought his horse, his powder and gun
to the continent. The Plains Crees, the Assiniboin, Blackfeet,
Gros Ventres and others of the north made such pens, generally circular with a single entrance, preferably at the edge
of a steep bank ten to twelve feet down, or at a very steep
washout. It was hard work to make a pen but it provided a
great deal of excitement for all, the women and children too,
and furnished meat and robes for many people without gun
or arrow.

A pen that the Plains Crees used as late as 1858 was
made of a wall of tree trunks laced together with green willows and propped at intervals from the back. It was in a little
valley between sandhills, the approaches two converging
wings of bushes leading four miles out on the prairie. Hunters maneuvered the gallop of the frightened buffaloes by

popping out of hiding in hollows or holes, waving robes and shouting and then hiding again while the whoopers came along behind in a typical Indian pony run. In this way the frightened and confused buffaloes were turned towards the arms of brush clumps and deadmen. When they tried to escape through the arms, more Indians showed themselves, to wave robes or blankets, keeping the animals running down the narrowing neck of the pen to the enclosure itself, where a strong tree trunk lay about a foot off the ground. The buffaloes leapt it, and were inside a hole, the bank too high and steep for easy climbing. Those inside galloped around and around but silent women and children held robes before every possible outlet until the whole little bunch was inside. Then they climbed upon the fence to laugh and whoop, to keep the buffaloes in constant motion so none had the chance to see a place of escape.

When the killers arrived the confusion and slaughter was dreadful. Young and weak animals were crushed and tossed, bulls roared and cows bellowed, while the yelling Indians speared and clubbed them all to death. The hunters took two hundred and forty in one drive into a little pen, counting everything down to the three-month-old calves. But another time an old bull charged through a weak place in the brush wall and took all the herd behind him.

There are still signs of these pounds along the Yellowstone above the mouth of the Big Horn River. Stories were still told in the author's childhood of the big catches in such traps, and of the great and valorous men lost in these hunts.

Most of the commerce of the upper Missouri country had always been in robes, the fine, thick winter robes of the buffalo cow, taken from November until early March. Then the ice of the winter-locked streams began to crack in the softening night, and the pelage faded and dulled, ready to fall in the ugly, ragged tufts characteristic of the American bison. Bull hides were never dressed except for a few special purposes, not for market. This helped account for the preponderance of bulls in all the great herds. For his own use the Indian killed few bulls past two years old, preferring the cow for meat and robes and lodge skins because the pelt was finer, easier to handle, and the meat juicier and fat-laced. Even in good years fewer than a third of the skins of the buffaloes killed were preserved. The big meat hunts were in the summer and the early fall, when the robes were thin, the hair short. Tanning robes was too heavy and tedious work to waste on poor hides. Few lodges could make more than twenty a year. Still, Picotte, partner of the American Fur Company, estimated that in 1850 one hundred thousand robes were sent to St. Louis. Gerard, the Cree interpreter for twenty-five years around the trading posts of the upper Missouri country, said that in 1857 Ft. Benton, twenty-five hundred miles up the Missouri from St. Louis, shipped thirty-six thousand robes south, the other four posts in the region enough more to bring the year's harvest to seventy-five thousand. By 1876 Benton alone was sending out eighty thousand buffalo robes. It is not known how many of these were untanned robes, perhaps very few.

But now the Northern Pacific railroad reached Bismarck and the demand that the Indians be driven off the northern ranges grew louder than ever. Legally no white man had the right to enter the whole Powder-Yellowstone region which still belonged in large part to the Sioux. Another conference for the sale of the Black Hills and the Sioux hunting grounds was called. Last year the Indians had stubbornly refused to sell but this year the railroad that was poised to push in needed the hide traffic desperately, and there was the dead Custer to get public opinion behind the use of force. So the Indians would be cleared out. Once more they refused to sell, saying there were too few men at the agencies to make a legal sale. Only a three-fourths majority of all the males could sell the lands that were theirs so long as grass shall grow and water flow. Too many men were out in the north country with Crazy Horse and Sitting Bull.

But legality had seldom stood in the way of expropriating Indian lands. At Red Cloud Agency, in northwest Nebraska, the headmen were locked in the stockade and told that their women and children outside would get no food until they signed the treaty for the sale, legal or illegal. One after another the tame chiefs and headmen walked up to touch the pen, the curl of their broad lips bitter from that day to their deaths, except for a few months some years later, when it seemed that they might get their buffaloes and their lands back once more.

Although chased for a long time, the northern herd had been too far from cheap transportation to attract the destructive still hunt of the professional hide man, and so it remained a substantial one into the 1880's. In 1874 surveyors of the Canadian boundary line were held up twice for several hours by passing buffaloes. Then in September Colonel French, on the way to Ft. Benton, passed an immense herd estimated at between seventy and eighty thousand. At the same time the secretary of the Boundary Commission discovered another herd, the number beyond estimation. Looking out from a point of about eighteen hundred feet elevation above the buffalo-darkened plains, he was unable to see the end of the herd in any direction. Half-breeds, Sioux, Assiniboin, Gros Ventres and Blackfeet all worked around the fringes of this herd but for all their wastefulness they made little impression. The secretary called it wastefulness; apparently he had never seen the professional hide men in action.

As the buffalo vanished, Indian wars became impossible. Not only were the herds their commissary but also their bank. They bought with robes as with money, they gambled with robes as white men gambled with gold pieces. The Crows once wagered a huge pile of tanned robes worth around twelve hundred dollars that Jim McNaney's fast saddle horse couldn't outrun the best Crow race horse. They lost and paid almost cheerfully.

But by keeping arms and ammunition from reaching the Sioux in any serious amount, and by driving them night and day over the frozen hills of Montana the winter after they defeated Custer, the Indians were finally starved in to the agencies, those that didn't slip away with Sitting Bull across the line. The embarrassed U. S. Government worked to get the Bull back. By 1878 they were ready to starve him and his followers into surrender. A line of men, breeds, Indians and soldiers, was set to turn the buffaloes back whenever they started to cross the border, and it was there, some said, shut in by this line of prairie fire and guns, that the greatest slaughter of the northern herd took place. It was pointed out that such a policy adopted by the Canadian government would have brought a roar from the Americans fit to drown out a million bulls on the summer rampage. It seemed unjust that because the Americans failed to handle their own Indians successfully, Canada's Indians were to face starvation, and the job of the Mounted Police made almost impossible. The Canadian Indians as well as Sitting Bull's band looked to the buffalo for their food.

All the rest of the Indians of the Montana region were at agencies far from the buffalo herd of the north. The railroad was coming with transportation cheap enough to make hide-hunting worth while, and the heavy freight outfits and the steamboats of the Yellowstone and the Missouri stood eager to go to meet it. Soon the boom of the Big Fifty and the sharper crack of the later, more improved rifles were carried, faint and far away, to the bones of Custer and the men of his Seventh Cavalry on the ridge of the Little Big Horn. It was almost like back in 1867, when he was shaking down his new regiment in his first pursuit of Indians during that luckless year in which he won no battle but lost his command. Now he was safe on the roll of heroes, and the Sioux and Cheyennes who humiliated him so in 1867 and once more in 1876, were gone, sitting on the little reservations that seemed as narrow as the buffalo pounds of the north country.

Of the men prominent around the Republican herd in 1867 Bill Cody was still alive, still the handsome, gaudy show-off. One of his meat men of that year, Zack Sutley, was around too, up in the north country. After he shot buffaloes in the crew that filled Cody's meat contract for the Kansas Pacific, Zack bought furs for Ullman around the Red River breed post in Canada, and then went with Custer into the Black Hills. The general asked him to join the expedition in 1876 too, but Zack Sutley did not go, and so escaped a probable place up on the Little Big Horn with those others of 1867. Instead he was in Deadwood when Wild Bill Hickok was shot, and saw him as the tawny color was drained from him by the bullet of Jack McCall. Some said that McCall had been working with Sutley at the time, freighting to the Hills from the Missouri, and that Sutley was with the murderer the day he was hung.

By 1880 one of the big hide outfits of the north was Maxwell's. Young Jim McNaney, not yet sixteen, was shooting for them by the month. But he got so many buffaloes that after two years he decided to go out for himself. At seventeen, with an elder brother as partner, he started. They bought their equipment in Miles City, named for General Miles who had chased the Indians down in Texas the winter after Adobe Walls, and up here pursued Crazy Horse and Sitting Bull relentlessly. The McNaneys bought a good outfit, much better than anything the southern hunters ever needed, including the shelter and clothing to withstand a winter with possible drops to forty-eight and fifty below. The McNaneys got two of almost everything: wagons, four-horse teams, saddle horses and wall tents, with but one cook stove. They got three Sharps breechloaders, a .40-90, a .45-70 and a .45-120, and laid in fifty pounds of powder, five hundred fifty pounds of lead, forty-five hundred primers, six hundred brass shells, four sheets of patch paper, sixty Wilson skinning knives, three butchers' steles, and a portable grindstone. Their provisions, in addition to the usual staples like flour, coffee and sugar, included a good lot of air-tights, canned vegetables and so on. The outfit came to fourteen hundred dollars.

With two hired men at fifty dollars a month each, the McNaneys left Miles town November tenth, very late. Robes primed earlier up here, and the hunters were usually headed out about October the first. The brothers shipped down-river by railroad and then cut across the country southeast about a hundred miles to the head of Beaver Creek, a tributary of the Little Missouri. They managed to find a good range without trespassing on the prior locations of the earlier hunters. For their camp they picked the bank of a creek, well out of sight from distance observation by a circle of hills and ridges. The two wall tents were set end to end with the stove in the middle. They cooked and ate at one end and slept in the other. First they took turns at pot wrasseling, but one of the hired men turned out so good at breadmaking that he was appointed boss of the frying pan for the season. The other three hunted, separately, and each skinned his own. In the heavy cold, the skin set too fast to wait on a skinner to find the kill.

The buffaloes had come in before the McNaneys reached Beaver Creek and, impatient, they began shooting at the first daylight. Their Sharps weighed sixteen to nineteen pounds, and each hunter carried between seventy-five to a hundred cartridges in two belts or in his pockets, with a hunter's companion at his side, a flat leather scabbard holding a lean-bladed ripping knife, a skinning knife and a butcher's stele—a total weight of thirty-six pounds or more. With ten thousand buffaloes on the range around, it took luck to find fifty or so off in a draw or hollow, and to make the kill without disturbing the rest. The hunter was usually afoot here, with the distances shorter and no need to flee from Indians, although there had been occasional threats from Sitting Bull's warriors until he surrendered in 1881. First the hunter scanned the surrounding country from the top of a ridge or butte and selected the best little herd in his territory, preferably some that were down or quiet in a sheltered spot rather than moving. If the buffaloes were in motion the hunter had to run perhaps a couple of miles to head the bunch and kill what he could before he had to run again.

"This ain't much like the killin' down to Double Mountain, er them dryin' lagunas out on the Yarner—" Harry Andrews up from Texas complained. He had been in the big slaughter down there from 1874 into 1877. But he had to admit that sleeping on Montana robes was like sleeping on a fine wild goose featherbed.

The fifty years of chase for the Red River robes and those for the Indian trade had made the Montana herd wilder than some in Texas, more like hunting on the Arkansas. Usually the hunter had to crawl a half mile or more on his belly, through cactus and sage brush, more often over ice and snow. Some Montana hunters drew gunny sacks over the upper part of the body, with holes for eyes and arms, to hide them as they crawled over the greyish dun prairie. On snow they used white canvas or a feed sack. If the hunter was lucky, he secured a position one hundred to two hundred and fifty yards from the game. Often the distance was much greater. He got a comfortable rest for the huge rifle, with himself hidden. Then he adjusted the telescope sights that most of the hunters used now. However, with a stand working, the northern buffaloes were as stupid as any. They clustered around the fallen in the same way, sniffing the warm blood, bawling, doing everything but run. The hunter had to hold himself, shooting quietly, deliberately, dropping every buffalo that tried to start off. One shot a minute was the moderate rate but under pressure two a minute could be fired with sufficient accuracy, using the long-range sights and the dead rest.

Because the robes brought from two to four, five dollars apiece, the skinning was done with more care than in the south. Afterward the hunter cut his initials into the thin sheath of subcutaneous muscle that clung to the hide, for with the hide men working so close there was much room for an honest mistake as well as dishonest ones.

In the north the hunter worked alone. He rolled the heavy buffalo up on his back, feet in the air, the head wrenched around to the side in close to the shoulder, the horn grounded, the head used as a chocking block to keep the body up instead of the pritch stick of the Texas skinner. Most of the hunting season the ground was frozen hard as iron, too hard for the pritch and for pegging out the drying hides. If the ground was bare of snow the skin was spread out warm, hair side down, and tamped tight to the buffalo grass to prevent some of the shrinkage. Sometimes stones were laid around the edge for a day or two.

Not until 1881 when the railroad had drawn up very close to the buffalo ranges did the summer hides, the hairless ones, become an important item of trade in the north, and that only near the tracks. That first year seventy-five thousand flint hides came down the river to the railroad at Bismarck. Those were the only figures the Northern Pacific kept for the year. There is no record of the robes shipped out by railroad. Meat still did not pay for the double handling and the long river and rail transportation. Perhaps that and the small number of flint hides taken help account for the few stands to equal the great ones of the south, usually made in the rutting season, the summer, when there was little more than some bellering curiosity over the down and dying.

This hunting the north herd was no business for amateurs. Over four thousand hunters came to the region in 1880 and 1881, but there was little room for those who could not harvest around a thousand good robes a year. It was even more important that they knew something of survival in the Montana blizzard winter. This was not west Texas or Kansas; a man caught out here must know how to stay alive or he could freeze in an hour or two and only be found by the buzzards in April or May.

Hunters and hide buyers estimated in 1881 that

there were about five hundred thousand buffaloes within a radius of a hundred and fifty miles of Miles City on the Yellowstone, and that the entire north herd was still a round million head. In 1882 an immense herd appeared on the high level plateau across the river from Miles and Ft. Keogh. A squad of soldiers was sent up on the bluff and in less than an hour killed enough buffaloes to load six four-mule teams with meat, and managed to start the herd moving to save the post and the town.

By the fall of 1881, what remained of the north herd was carefully watched, its probable path well mapped. The expert hunters knew just where to go. James McNaney was out on Beaver Creek, about a hundred miles south of Glendive, when the main body came in. The buffaloes had been stringing in since mid-October to about the first of December. Then all one moonlight evening the air had been full of a vague rumbling, and about ten at night the first of the herd appeared, coming in a wide dark mass that was like a moving shadow on the silver-hazed plain. The hunters had been sitting in their tents loading cartridges and cleaning their rifles when the earth began to shake, and the rumble increased to a roar.

"There! That's the big herd coming in. And right on us!"

Everybody ran out, yelling, shooting to turn the buffaloes from the tents. The horses were picketed near a grassy coulee that the lead animals fortunately didn't enter. They came at a jog trot, heads down, moving along the terrain on as level a path as was possible, avoiding hills and draws, moving fast—like the first dark tongue of a thundering storm cloud to sweep over the land. In the morning the whole country was black with fine, winter-furred buffaloes. McNaney and the rest estimated that there were ten thousand head in sight. One large detachment was down on a low, broad flat. They spread out there, resting and feeding for about ten days and then gradually broke up into small bunches that strolled off in various directions for grass. The hunters attacked quietly, methodically, and as the buffaloes moved slowly southward, they followed, causing no more alarm than the great-jawed prairie wolves, white and thick-furred for winter too.

Newspapermen and magazine writers were out this winter to observe this new bonanza. One of them was at Camp McIntosh on Beaver Creek when the major in command got up a hunt into some scattered bunches at the fringe of what was said to be a herd of two hundred thousand buffaloes. In the region of Cabin Creek badlands their shooting stampeded a bunch over a seventy-foot precipice, sixty-four buffaloes and several antelope and other game caught in the panicked flight, all ending in a writhing, dying mass six to ten feet deep at the foot of the cliff. Accidentally they had done what Indians often worked for days and weeks to accomplish, particularly back in the days before the horse.

Around Christmas the McNaneys still had their main camp on Beaver Creek, but the buffaloes had been gone for some days, not one left around anywhere—only the frozen, tallow-white carcasses with the unskinned heads that made them look so much like short, fat, dark-headed grubs scattered over the ground. Then at daybreak another section of the great herd came in, going south too, heading into the wind that was building up a storm in the northern regions. They came in long files, the leaders growing out of the northwest. They disappeared into a creek valley and showed up again along a rise a few hundred yards from the McNaney camp, moving down a slope at full speed, their breath blowing back white. They were headed to pass not more than fifty yards from the tents, perhaps closer, or even directly over them, with no power on earth to turn them now.

The hunters ran for their guns and began to fire, one buffalo down, another crippled, swinging a foreleg until he fell too. By now the file had grown into an unbroken stream coming at a full gallop, in the long lope of the buffalo, four to ten abreast. The hunters had to run for safer ground, leaving the tents to luck, not shooting, unwilling to risk stampeding the herd from its course, over camps or men. There were short breaks in the herd, then tight little bunches again, as the column rushed by in its flight, the big spring calves running half in the flanks of their mothers, the young stock getting over the ground faster and easier than the old. For four hours, until past eleven in the forenoon, the column thundered past on a strip no wider than a city street, raising almost no dust from the frozen, iron-hard earth, their course still marked by a thinning frost of breath. Three miles south of the McNaney camp the bobbing column wound to the right and disappeared between two hills.

When it seemed nothing could turn the herd from its narrow path, or stampede it over anyone, the hunters had come in close again and fired into the running buffaloes, the big guns roaring, the blue smoke blowing back over the approaching herd that noticed the roar and the blue stink no more than their own vapor stream. Finally there were over fifty down almost at the door of the tents. Some had dropped dead, many ran in the herd until they could go no farther and then drew off to the side, and finally fell.

It was the winter of good stands in the north. Jim McNaney's best was ninety-one head and Doc Aughl killed eighty-five without shifting once, John Edwards seventy-five. But Vic Smith, considered the best hunter working the northern herd got one hundred seven buffaloes up on the Red Water, a hundred miles northeast of Miles City, in one hour without moving. He got about five thousand buffaloes that season, a good income in the heavier robes of the north, bringing him from two to over four dollars apiece.

Jim McNaney and the other hunters estimated the buffaloes in their portion of the range that winter of 1881-2 as around a hundred thousand. Old-timers in the north agreed that the forced marches the McNaneys saw were probably caused by snow-covered ranges and scarcity of food, or a swift storm coming. Usually the movement to the south was on an easier pace, with small straggling bunches moving out of the north gradually, and over a wide area.

The price paid for hides hadn't varied much at any given time or place, except for the very rare skin. It had fallen to sixty-five to ninety cents for a cow all over the Texas range in 1876, bulls around a dollar fifteen. But not long before that Wright of Dodge City was said to have paid Prairie Dog Dave a thousand dollars for the white buffalo he killed. Wright had the animal mounted in time for the Philadelphia Centennial Exposition and helped advertise the western buffalo ranges all over the world.

But in the north, where most of the hunting was for quality robes, robes of the cold winter season, there was a greater spread in the price paid. While in 1881-2 the ordinary untanned robes brought two fifty to four dollars, there were four special types that brought much more. The buckskin robe, from the so-called white buffalo, was really a sort of dirty cream. One of these was sold in Miles City in 1882 for two hundred dollars and was the only one from the northern ranges that entire winter. The Indians tell of taking pure white robes—the sacred white buffalo, and a few old-timers of the author's acquaintance had seen them, but the Indians usually decorated these robes and then left them on some hilltop as an offering to their Great Powers, so there were few eyewitnesses. The Wright buffalo is said to have been white, then cream and dirty cream but that may all have been true, beginning white and darkening. Even ermine and arctic fox yellow with time.

The second most valuable buffalo robe was the beaver, of very fine wavy fur the color of a beaver, with long coarse guard hairs that were plucked out in the manufacture. James McNaney took one of these in 1882, a cow robe, the only beaver in his twelve hundred robes of the season. He sold it for seventy-five dollars when ordinary robes brought him three fifty.

The blue or mouse-colored robe showed a bluish cast on the body, with long, fine fur. McNaney picked twelve of these out of his twelve hundred robes and received sixteen dollars apiece for them. The black and tan robe had the nose, flank and the inside of the forelegs black and tan, with the rest of the robe jet black. The price of these depended upon the fineness and the contrast in the color, but they always brought more than the going price for the usual robes.

By the spring of 1882 there were over five thousand hunters and skinners on the northern range. Thousands and thousands of buffaloes were killed around the far fringes of their migration, down in Wyoming, and westward into the foothills of the mountains. But mostly the hunters concentrated on the great central body of the herd. They blocked the buffaloes from the waterways in their annual spring march toward Canada. They set up a cordon of camps stretched from the big bend of the Missouri as far west as the Idaho line, completely blocking all passage north from the great pasturages of the Milk River, the Musselshell, Yellowstone and the Marias. Hunters from Nebraska, Wyoming, Colorado and farther south came shooting, driving the frantic buffaloes into the muzzles of thousands of repeating rifles cutting them off from escape to Canada, where the hunters could not follow. With the rifles and wide expanses of fire and new-burnt prairie, very few escaped.

As late as the spring of 1883 a herd estimated at seventy-five thousand crossed the Yellowstone a little above Miles City, with a few reservation Indians and white sportsmen after them, in addition to the ravenous hide men booming away rear and flank as the herd fled north. Not five thousand ever got to the border. But the period from October 1882 through February 1883 did just about finish the outlying sections of the northern herd still on their usual stomping grounds.

George W. Grinnell, the squaw man wolfer who had turned rancher decided to make some of the easy hunting money the next season. With a partner he outfitted at Ft. Buford, loading between eight and ten thousand dollars worth of goods, principally flour, sugar, tea, coffee and blankets and ammunition on eight heavy wagons. They crossed the Missouri at Ft. Peck and went up the Dry Fork. Grinnell got his camp located early in the region of the great slaughter last year, where half of his lifetime he had been seeing great dark herds spread browsing. Most of the hunters in the country were there too, ready for the migrating herd. But they were all a year too late. No buffaloes came.

The northern buffalo business had been well and tightly organized long before the large-scale invasion of the professional hunters. As early as 1876 I. G. Baker and Company of Ft. Benton, far up the Missouri, were sending out around seventy-five thousand buffalo robes a year, with a rapid falling off to twenty thousand in 1880, five thousand in 1883 and none at all in 1884. But this was not a true indication of the number of buffaloes taken. Most of the hide men who exterminated the heart of the northern herd worked out of the Yellowstone country, shipping by boat to meet the approaching Northern Pacific instead of down the Missouri. Besides, northern Montana and Dakota, with their nearness to the streams running to Hudson Bay, always sold a lot of robes to traders of the old Hudson's Bay Company.

The spring of 1881 it was estimated that the winter's haul out of the Yellowstone country would be a hundred thousand untanned buffalo robes, half of which were sold in advance to two firms, Boskowitz and Ullman. In 1876 Boskowitz of Chicago had bought thirty-one thousand, eight hundred thirty-eight robes for thirty-nine thousand, six hundred twenty dollars, increasing his purchase to one hundred seventy-six thousand, two hundred dollars for thirty-four thousand, nine hundred one robes in 1880, and declining to none at all in 1884. The firm had never dealt in hides before 1880. In 1881 they paid eighty-nine thousand, thirty dollars for twenty-six thousand, six hundred ten hides, but by 1884 there were only five hundred twenty-nine for one thousand, seven hundred twenty dollars.

The figures from Joseph Ullman of St. Paul and Chicago show a similar trend, the term *robes* here apparently reserved for the Indian tanned:

1881—14,000 hides at $3.50; 12,000 robes at $7.50.

1882—between 35-40,000 hides at $3.50; about 10,000 robes at $8.50.

1883—between 6-7,000 hides and about 1,500-2,000 robes at a slight increase in price over last year.

1884—less than 2,500 hides, thought to be hold-overs from the previous year for a better market. The few robes received were carry-overs too.

1885—little or no hides.

The robe shipment on the Northern Pacific in 1882, mostly from the winter before, was about two hundred thousand. It dropped to forty thousand for the whole year of 1883 and to one carload in 1884. The estimated number of buffaloes skinned in the three seasons of the northern herd was one million, five hundred thousand with a value of four million, five hundred thousand dollars.

Up to 1881 the buffalo skins were divided into two kinds: robes with a good growth of fur, and the heavy but short-furred bull hides formerly sold to robe tanners. Later the bull hides were sold to hide tanners in the United States and Canada at five and a half to eight and a half cents a pound. In 1882 Ullman established a tannery for good robes in Chicago and disposed of these as he did his Indian-tanned robes. In the last four years of the northern herd, Ullman and Boskowitz together paid out one million, two hundred thirty-three thousand seventy dollars for buffalo robes and hides, and there were half a dozen other big buyers working the north.

In the meantime there were curious rumors, rumors of buffalo herds, real or phantom, seen to the eastward, in a region where no buffalo had been for ten, fifteen years.

CHAPTER XV

THE END OF THE DREAM

THERE was a phase of the northern herd that those
farther south did not have. That was the sudden, the fren-
zied hope of the Indians that the buffaloes were actually
coming back, not to replenish the regions of the fierce and
ruthless hunt but back to the quieter prairies near the
Indians, particularly near the Sioux agencies of Dakota.

The buffalo had been vanishing east of the Missouri
River for a long time, and fifteen years ago most of the south
half of Dakota Territory was cleaned out by the hungry eastern Sioux from Minnesota and northern Iowa, pushed westward to hunt as their cornlands were preempted by settlers.
There were often equally hungry white men too, and other
hungry Indians from down towards the Platte, as well as the
robe hunters urged on by the Missouri traders. By 1882 the
agency Indians, who were to be fed in exchange for their re-
linquished lands, were starving, and yet no chief could get a
permit to take his people out on a hunt because plainly the
buffaloes were gone.

Many Indians and even some breeds and white men
who had lived close to the great herds a long time refused to
believe that these multitudes had been all killed off by hunt-

ers. "Man never could have exterminated them; they went
back into the earth from whence they came," an old Hudson's Bay Company employe said.

As early as 1880 rumors had reached the starving Indians, rumors that the buffalo was coming back. They were
even louder when Sitting Bull returned from Canada in
1881, not only because of the stories of the Bull's great
power in dreaming that helped his reputation as a medicine
man, but because some white men told of seeing buffaloes
in new places. In September 1882, an old plainsman saw a
herd on the Riviere du Lac, which joins the Mouse River
near the present Minot, North Dakota. This was well east of
the Missouri, and no buffaloes had been seen there in a long,
long time.

Sitting Bull and the other headmen listened to these
stories, which were not of a few old bulls hidden out in the
badlands but good little herds of young stock with silky pelage. The hungry widows of the Sioux wars heard the stories
too, and were reminded of the old holy men who foretold a
time when the whites would be driven from the Indian's
earth. Then the buffaloes would return, and now there was
this news that they were coming.

Scouts slipped out of Sitting Bull's camp in the night,
not to shoot but only to look, no matter how hungry, for
shooting might break the medicine, the holy spell. It was
true as they had heard—not just a few leaderless old bulls
that had wandered far from the regular path of migration or
fled into rough country from pursuit. This was a real herd,
with fat young cows and the darkening calves at their sides,
very many of them fat young animals. As proof of this they
brought back sacks of new buffalo chips, round as great brown
maggots, firm, from young stock and plainly not dropped over
five, six days ago.

The old men examined the chips carefully and peered
into the faces of their scouts to see what might cling there
from all that the men had seen, all their eyes had laid upon.

None of the scouts told what the old ones saw they were holding back—the number. And when the leader of them finally made the quick signs for thousands, the old faces broke into almost fearing smiles. At last it seemed good.

So there was a little of the old-time hunting medicine to make, and some dancing to lure the buffaloes, to welcome their coming as brothers are welcomed. Not with big ceremonials, which were forbidden by the white men, but small ones, and carried out in the remote reaches of the reservation, around fires upon which the medicine men threw bits of the buffalo chips and watched the old-time sacred smoke rise to the Powers who were bringing the dark herds back.

The news of around ten, twelve thousand buffaloes about halfway from Bismarck toward the Black Hills, between the Moreau and the Grand Rivers, brought out the whites too. Zack Sutley, a one-time meat man for Cody, Vic Smith and many other hunters and meat men gathered. With their improved rifles and the telescopic sights, they were set over the route the fleeing animals must surely take, to pick them off. Between eleven and twelve hundred escaped into the badland country. The rest fell.

Now the agent at Standing Rock, Sitting Bull's agency, got up a big hunt to help feed his hungry Indians. Some Sioux from the Cheyenne River Agency came along too, making around a thousand Indians, with an escort of troops, some publicity seekers and the white hunters that flocked in. Vic Smith was back, and Sutley with wagons along to haul the surplus meat to Deadwood. There was word that Bill Cody was coming too, looking for publicity, now that he planned to put a real Wild West show on the road.

By the time the party had made camp, the Indian scouts appeared on a ridge riding in the little circles that told of buffaloes seen, some buffaloes seen. It was sad for men like the Reverend Riggs, who had known his Sioux in better times to watch hope grow in the old Indians, and even sad for Sutley, who had seen the whole face of the Great

Plains and its life changed within less than sixteen years, the
flower of its fauna exterminated, the native expropriated.
Zack still shot true, but he found himself hanging back a little
with a few other hunters, keeping out of the way of this last
Indian buffalo chase, they called it. Because the Indians had
been disarmed not many years before, all but the headmen
had to borrow guns and Sutley and a few of the others
loaned theirs out a while. Some of the older Indians used
bows, a little shame-faced before their young men who talked
so big about the fine rifles of the hunters. But all this was forgotten in the surround, in the whoops and dust and thunder
of hoofs, the cracking of rifles, the crashing of bodies, including an occasional horse and rider.

And by evening over half of the herd was dead, the
rest guarded by the Indians who still knew the use of wind
and man smell to hold a wild herd from drifting. In the
morning they finished the rest, all except a few old bulls who
managed to slip away into the breaks and badlands. The Indians packed some of the meat across their horses for immediate use, the green robes laid on first, hair side down, the meat
on top and the ends of the hide lapped over each way and
tied securely with new-cut rawhide strings. But most of the
buffaloes were to be dried for winter.

And in this last camp Sitting Bull sat alone much of
the time, his pipe cold beside him, remembering the great
Indian and buffalo country he was born into. It was just over
on the Grand River there, the year before the fire boat, the
Yellowstone, came smoking up the Missouri. Now all of it
was gone, vanished like wind on the buffalo grass. True,
he had known glory, much glory, but his broad face was hard
as the walls of the upper Yellowstone when he thought
about it, for what is glory to a man who must see his people
as he saw them now.

It seemed he could no longer believe that the buffaloes would all return as had been foretold, and that the white

men around him here, the agent, the troopers and hunters would all be swept away.

Over in Montana most of the hunters who had outfitted the fall of 1883 as usual, spending many thousands of dollars, found nothing but bones and very hungry swarms of buffalo gnats. They came back bankrupt and finally drifted into mining, cowboying, or followed the roadagent and outlaw to Robbers Roost near the Black Hills or half a dozen other hideouts. Even the bone ricks along the last railroad to tap the hide country—the Northern Pacific—were shrinking until there were only a few loads brought in by settlers to trade for coffee and calico and shoes against the long hard winters. Bones had been going out ever since the railroad came. M. I. McCreight, former bone buyer, told of a pile at the west end of Devil's Lake, Dakota, that contained two hundred and fifty carloads, two thousand, one hundred twenty-five tons, with another hundred and fifty carloads at the southern shore, and a pile of three hundred at Mouse River. Fred Stoltz who bought buffalo bones, once had four, five hundred carloads on hand when the prices fell. In dry years the farmers lived off the bones they brought to Minot, at about twenty dollars a load, some accounts say; others put the price at seven or eight dollars a load. Not all loads were alike; perhaps the twenty dollars was paid for those hauled in the high, slatted bone racks of the time.

Indians too, began to pick up the last remains of the buffalo and instead of burning the prairie to crowd a herd closer together in a surround, they burned it now to show up the bones, although this sometimes cut the value. An advertisement by Bickett and Foote: 1000 TONS OF BONES WANTED ran in the Dickinson (Dakota) *Press* the spring of 1884. The June 27 issue said that twenty-seven yoke of oxen brought in bones yesterday and that thirty-four yoke arrived from Deadwood loaded with bones on the way in.

Dickinson, just east of the big herd, had been a main outfitting point for hunters, and now it was cleaning up on the
leavings.

One bone-buying firm estimated that over the seven
years, 1884-1891 they bought the bones of approximately
five million, nine hundred and fifty thousand buffalo skeletons, and there were many firms in the business. The Topeka
Mail and Breeze, speaking of "the extinct industry, bones,"
said that, allowing forty feet for a car, it would have made a
string of cars seven thousand, five hundred and seventy-five
miles long, enough to more than fill two tracks from New
York to San Francisco.

Suddenly now the alarmists who had long been predicting the extinction of the American bison found recep-
tive ears, when only two hundred and fifty buffaloes were left
on earth. A little investigation placed the figure higher: two
hundred and fifty-six in captivity, some of these in the crossbreeding herds, and about eight hundred and thirty-five wild
—all that was left of the fifty million, more or less, of 1867.
But most or all of the eight hundred thirty-five wild ones
might already be dead, for hunters no longer made their
killings public. Once there was word that the wild buffaloes had been reduced to fifty. Surely this was much, much
too close to complete extinction and at last some energetic
men went to work.

One of these was William Temple Hornaday, chief
taxidermist of the U. S. National Museum from 1882. He
was doubly alarmed. He had no good group for his museum,
and the noblest beast of the western world, only recently the
most numerous ruminant known, was in immediate danger
of extinction. He got his specimen in finest pelage in December of 1886, the hard winter that cleaned out the cattlemen
from the upper Missouri down into lower Colorado, and he
was largely responsible for both the preservation and the en-
largement of the buffalo herds.

Off on the Indian reservations there was another kind of activity for the buffalo, for his restoration. The ghost dancing started by the Indian prophet out in Nevada was to help bring back the great herds and to set the Indian back into his proper place. It was an old dream, one that fostered the earlier rebellions against the white man, such as the pueblo uprisings, the resistance of Tecumseh and his brother The Prophet, and inspired the Shakers of the northwest. The new prophet, called the Messiah, was Wovoka, son of the Prophet of Mason Valley, who died in 1870. By 1881 a young Kiowa had made medicine to bring the buffalo back and stirred up so much excitement that the year was called the Winter of the Buffalo Prophesies in the Kiowa calendar and caused the agent to report his uneasiness to Washington. In 1887 another Kiowa revived the prophesy and infected the whole tribe. They abandoned their camps and fled to their new prophet, but the day of delivery passed and the whites were still there, with not one buffalo in sight.

Now they had heard of this new Messiah and so great was their need that, in spite of the earlier disappointments, they sent a delegation to Nevada to see him. Other tribes also sent reliable men. They came back with news of great moment, particularly to the old buffalo country. They told of falling down on the ground in a dreaming in which they saw great herds of their brother, the buffalo, come running over the broken terrain, come from canyons and cuts and draws where not even a buffalo chip remained. As the headmen of the Sioux listened, they recalled the buffaloes that had appeared at the edge of the badlands only a few years ago, a whole herd to be killed for the hungry where none had been in a long time. And for those who doubted even now there was news. In September 1888, a hunter named John Whiteside had seen over sixty buffaloes while hunting off north from Bismarck. They were stampeding to water and he was almost caught in a ravine that led to the river while he stopped to shoot one. The buffaloes did not hesitate at the stream but swam across and when he saw them last they were going northwest, the first herd in the valley for many years.

"Ah, they were running, and they paid no attention to the white hunter," the old men said, and so they began to dance.

The agents everywhere were uneasy, and kept a close guard on the Indians but they knew little of the scouts that were kept out watching. Secretly these men slipped off to the rough country where the buffaloes would surely appear first, as those up at the badlands did in 1883; those first ones perhaps a sign from the dancing of the Kiowa prophet, and of Wovoka—a sign to get ready. It was true that no more came to answer all the buffalo medicine that the Sioux had made secretly, perhaps because the best, the sundance, was too big and a forbidden thing that the troops would surely break up. Now there was news of this little herd up north of Bismarck —once more buffaloes in a deserted region. Such things were not to be forgotten, no more than the memory of the meat they had tasted from the new-come herd they had helped butcher near the badlands, now that the hunger of the reservations had closed upon the dreamers once more.

They must think about this man out west, called the new Messiah, which was the name of the Christ that the missionaries followed. The Christ had come to save the white men and they hanged him from the crossed tree, as was clear in the pictures the priests brought, long, long ago. Now he had come to the Indians. But of this the Sioux who came back from him had very little to say. They admitted that the Messiah was not a stranger come from far off, only a man who had always lived around the reservations, yet he was the son of a prophet, and he became like dead before them and then returned and talked of what he had seen.

"What does he see?" the eager ones demanded, and those whose lips were still bitter from the treaty forced upon them in the stockade, the treaty that took their lands and the Black Hills with all their gold.

The Messiah told that he saw the Indians in a happy time again, free from the reservations, with the lodges full of meat and other good things, and with buffaloes all around. But for this happy time to be brought the Messiah said they must be peaceful and of good heart toward all people. They must make the dancing as he instructed, the ceremonials and the dancing, and soon it would all come.

Other men who had seen these dreams also spoke of the buffaloes on all sides, the white men gone as though they had never been, and all the dead ones of the Indians alive once more and right among them.

This last Sitting Bull and the others who had not accepted the Happy Hunting Ground of the whites into their religion could not suddenly believe in now. It had always been that the dead returned to the earth which fed them, as the flower returned, and the tree and the buffalo and all living things go back. They returned in gratitude to feed other growing things, all the grasses that fattened the buffaloes and the people. The spirit which is like the light in the coal goes out as the light does when the coal dies, returning once more to the light that is in the Great Powers, of whom all things are a part—the earth, the sky and all that lies between. To Sitting Bull and other old medicine and holy men this promise of the dead returning to life seemed thin as the morning fog along the creek bottoms, gone with one look from the sun.

But the Indians were hungry and very many of them sick with tuberculosis, trachoma, measles and other diseases. So they started the dancing again, men and women together everywhere, to last four days this time and then later again and perhaps once more. If they did everything in a certain way, with no hand or heart turned against any man, and persisted in this for some moons, not too many, the Messiah who had been hung to the crossed trees by the whites would bring all good things back to the Indians.

A tall tree trunk was set up out on the frozen winter

prairie. The head men stood beside it and the others in a circle around them and the tree, hands held together, moving, dancing, with the ghost shirts drawn over their clothing, the holy bullet-proof shirts that the Messiah showed them how to make. They danced from Friday afternoon until sundown on Sunday without food or water, each as he was led to do, alone or together with others, their moccasins whispering on the dead grass, murmuring on the frozen earth in shuffling, slow, steady supplication, the dancers perhaps becoming suddenly rigid, falling in trances. Revived, they told what they had seen. Many slipped into animal dances, bobbed on all fours like buffaloes, pawed the freezing ground, butted heads like the bulls, bawling, and then fell into the dreaming. Afterward they told of this place where the white men were truly rolled away, and all the dead relatives back among them, with buffalo herds coming dark over the horizon, and fast horses ready for the chase. So more joined hands and danced with the holy signs on them, danced on all the reservations of the buffalo country, singing the repeating songs of their dreams.

> They say there is to be a buffalo hunt over here!
> They say there is to be a buffalo hunt over here.
> Make the arrows! Make the arrows!
> Says the father, says the father,

an old warrior sang in his high thin voice, jumping on his gaunt legs, bare and painted below the flapping breechclout, numb in the December wind.

White men came to see them, many from everywhere. John Cook came too, the Johnny Cook of the buffalo hunting down around the Staked Plains where he had wondered once how he would feel if he were the son of an Indian and saw his buffaloes killed. He was still in the Indian service. He watched the dancing at one place a little while and then went sadly away.

At the Sioux agency at Pine Ridge, South Dakota, there was a new agent, with some newspapermen nearby who reported the ghost dancing as an uprising. With a little encouragement, particularly from one New York newspaper, they began to send out sensational stories of massacres, of white blood to flow and indeed already flowing, the bloodthirsty Sioux off the reservations and ravishing the settlements. Nobody said that not one Indian had left his reservation, except the few scouts out to herald the buffalo's coming. They watched out towards the Black Hills and on the path from the north, the way the buffaloes used to come hurrying to the shelter of Pine Ridge and the White River bluffs below it. The newspaper accounts alarmed both the settlers and the greenhorn agent, Royer, so he fled the agency and telegraphed for troops. They came, with four Hotchkiss guns and headed for Pine Ridge.

Up north, on Sitting Bull's reservation, the memory of the buffaloes that were suddenly there in 1883 was particularly poignant to those who had taken part in the hunt and eaten the flesh. Sitting Bull had been afraid that the troops would stop the dancing as they had the sundance, but he was reassured by the promise of the Messiah that there would be no violence, and no one could be hurt, because they would be wearing the sacred, bullet-proof ghost shirts.

So they danced, Sitting Bull too, for he had been a strong dreamer not many years ago. The agent there was an experienced man, and although no lover of old Bull, he knew that the dancing would soon wear itself out in the sub-zero weather of Dakota. He maneuvered to get the notoriety seeker, Buffalo Bill Cody and his newspapermen put off the reservation. But the army was less easily managed, and when orders came from Washington to arrest Sitting Bull, he held the army off a while, predicting general bloodshed if the troops came for the old medicine man. But the order was not rescinded and so he had to send out a force of his Indian police under Sergeant Bullhead to make the arrest.

Before the sleeting dawn of December fifteenth, 1890, the Sioux in the blue coats silently entered Sitting Bull's log cabin and dragged him naked from the sleeping robes. By the time they got him outside on his horse, the place was surrounded by the chief's old-time warriors, and even Sitting Bull's son taunted the old man for his quiet surrender. But the moment the police got rough with Bull, one of the warriors shot the leader of the Indian police. Bullhead fell, but he fired into the chief's body as he went down, and another policeman shot Sitting Bull too, through the head from behind, as though this had been prearranged.

So the most persistent exponent of the nomadic buffalo hunting life was dead. There was hand-to-hand fighting in that grey December morning light, but it was all gone for nothing, lost on the wind.

As the Indians heard that Sitting Bull was shot, they scattered, taking their women and children out of the way before the soldiers came and there was more killing. One group fled southward to Big Foot's band, and suddenly that chief's people were afraid too, and they forgot their dancing for the buffalo's return. Instead all ran together now, heading towards the badlands and then turning, struck south towards the Sioux on Pine Ridge Reservation. But people had been fleeing from there too, going north to the rough country, to Sheep Mountain in the badlands because there were troops riding up from the railroad just south in Nebraska.

Some of these troops overtook Chief Big Foot, with his one hundred six men and two hundred and fifty women and children, and ordered them to surrender. The Indians did this without protest. They couldn't fight; they didn't want to fight, even if they weren't practically without arms, and their old chief were not sick with pneumonia in one of the wagons. To show their good will some of Big Foot's warriors immediately enlisted as scouts to help bring in the Indians who had fled to the badlands camp, and started for them.

The troops were under Col. J. W. Forsyth, brother of the man the Indians surrounded with his scouts in the Beecher Island fight in 1868 on a branch of the Republican River. He had eight troops of the Seventh Cavalry here, among them a couple of grizzled old campaigners who were with the regiment since its organization twenty-four years ago, men who chased Indians with Custer back in 1867 around the Republican buffalo herd, men who had ridden upon the Cheyennes out of the blizzard down on the Washita, and who were surrounded by Indians up on Reno hill while Custer died on a ridge a few miles away.

But now it would be different than that last time. Even though the Indians had surrendered, the troops had the four Hotchkiss guns set up on a ridge that overlooked the tents as the grey winter morning dawned, and a company of Cheyenne Indian scouts to help them. With Big Foot's Sioux surrounded, the colonel ordered all the men out of the tents, leaving the women and children behind there unprotected, and motioned the Indians up close to the troops standing ready with their guns in their hands.

The men of the band came in a long slow file behind the sick chief, wrapped close in their blankets against the freezing wind. Slowly they squatted in a line on the winter ground facing the troops. It was only two weeks since Sitting Bull was disarmed and then shot down. The men who killed him were Indians, but the coats were the same, always the blue. Yet resistance now would mean death, immediate death, although perhaps that was all that lay ahead of them in any case, for it was well known that soldiers who come to an Indian camp bring the killing in their hands. They are not easily cheated by a pleasant surrender, like that of yesterday, or the waving of a white flag.

Almost at once the Indians were sent back to the tents to bring their guns, first one little group, then some others, and so on. Because only a few arms were brought, the troopers went to search the tents themselves, driving the frightened women and children out, to huddle together in terror, but with no place to run on the empty plain, the one ravine that was nearby too shallow for hiding. Their men watched helplessly, their dark faces hard and unmoving as the stone of the Black Hills. When no more weapons were found in the tents the troops prepared to search the warriors, but nobody knew quite how to do this dangerous thing. The Indian lets no one lay hands upon his body or the body of his people. There was a scuffle between two soldiers and a Sioux they were searching, and somehow a rifle was discharged. Then an excited young Indian shot into the sudden silence, and the troops fired a volley, so close to the Indians that their guns almost touched them. Nearly half of Big Foot's men went down before that one volley. Those left, mostly with no more than knives, clubs or perhaps a hidden revolver, charged into the carbines as though to smother their smoking mouths. On the ridge the Hotchkiss guns began their stuttering fire, but upon the tents and the women and children there, cutting them down, the tents jerking as if alive, with crying coming from the inside, and then going down in smoke, some of them blazing out in the strong grey wind.

A handful of Indians, mostly women and children, were left to run in panic, pursued by the blood-heated troopers and raked with the Hotchkisses swung upon their flight. The soldiers chased the Indians like rabbits fleeing over the prairie, some of the women left dead as far as two miles away where Indians had danced for the buffaloes' return only a few days ago.

The Pine Ridge Indians who had withdrawn to the badlands were surrendering when they heard the guns over at Wounded Knee Creek, and later they saw the handful of terrified and bleeding survivors. Some gave the desperate war cry of the Sioux warriors riding to their death and charged away from their trooper escort over to the battlefield, where, now, two hours after the fight, the soldiers were still hunting down the living. For a while the angry Sioux warriors drove the troops back, but it was only for a little while and with raw courage, for the Indians had no arms to fight off the cavalry. And in the afternoon snow began to fall, running in thin grey curls over the desolated ground at Wounded Knee, settling in little white drifts behind the bodies of the dead, the women and children, the chief and his men. As the snow deepened, they seemed more and more like great whitened carcasses scattered where they fell over the prairie.

Now the dream of the buffalo, too, was done.

BIBLIOGRAPHY
FOR THE GENERAL READER

THE GREAT PLAINS AS A WHOLE

Allen, Joel Asaph. "The American Bisons, Living and Extinct."
Memoirs of the Museum of Comparative Zoology, IV, No. 10. Cambridge, 1876.

Branch, E. Douglas. *The Hunting of the Buffalo*. New York, 1929.

Dodge, Col. Richard Irving. *The Hunting Grounds of the Great West*.
London, 1877.

Garretson, Martin S. *The American Bison*. New York, 1938.

Hornaday, William T. "The Extermination of the American Bison,
with a Sketch of Its Discovery and Life History," *U. S. National
Museum Report*, Part II, Washington, 1887.

McCreight, M. I. *Buffalo Bone Days*. Dubois, Pa. 1939.

Webb, Walter Prescott. *The Great Plains*. New York, 1931.

BOOK I

The literature of this period illustrates the extreme in the general postwar tendency to make heroes of the flamboyant and the violent. Perhaps the degree depends upon the bloodiness of the conflict.

Armes, Col. Geo. A. *Ups and Downs of an Army Officer*. Washington,
1900.

Blake, Herbert Cody. *Blake's Western Stories, the Truth about Buffalo
Bill*. Folder of Cody, Hickok and Doc Carver material with this
pamphlet in New York Public Library, including letters to and
from Wilstach about the killing of the Sioux chief, Whistler.

Brill, Charles J. *Conquest of the Southern Plains*. Oklahoma City, 1938.

Brininstool, E. A. *A Trooper with Custer*. Columbus, Ohio, 1925.

Butcher, S. D. *Pioneer History of Custer County*. Broken Bow, Nebr.,
1901.

Connelley, William E. *Wild Bill and His Era; the Life & Adventures
of James Butler Hickok*. New York, 1933.

Custer, Gen. George A. *My Life on the Plains*. New York, 1874.

Dawson, Charles. *Pioneer Tales of the Oregon Trail and Jefferson County*. Topeka, 1912.

Grinnell, George Bird. *The Fighting Cheyennes*. New York, 1915.

Helvey, Frank. "Experiences on the Frontier," *Nebraska Pioneer Reminiscences*. Cedar Rapids, 1916.

Inman, Henry. *The Old Santa Fe Trail*. New York, 1898.

Keim, De B. Randolph. *Sheridan's Troopers on the Border; A Winter Campaign on the Plains*. Philadelphia, 1870.

Logan, Herschel C. "Royal Buffalo Hunt." *American Rifleman*, Oct. 1952.

"Wild Bill-McCanles Tragedy," *Nebraska History Magazine*, Vol. X, No. 2.

Nichols, Col. Geo. Ward. "Wild Bill," *Harpers New Monthly Magazine*, February 1867.

Paine, Bayard H. *Pioneers, Indians and Buffaloes*. Curtis, Nebr., 1935.

Roenigk, Adolf, ed. *Pioneer History of Kansas*. Lincoln, Kans., 1933.

Sutley, Zack T. *The Last Frontier*. New York, 1930.

Van de Water, Frederic F. *Glory Hunter*. Indianapolis, 1934.

Walsh, Richard J. and Salsbury, N. S. *The Making of Buffalo Bill*. Indianapolis, 1928.

Wilstach, Frank J. *Wild Bill Hickok, the Prince of Pistoleers*. New York, 1926. Author's copy, with marginal notes by him, giving corrections and additional material sent him after publications, nailing all the more obvious tall tales he had included is in the New York Public Library, with an accompanying collection of letters, manuscripts and photographs.

Young, Harry (Sam). *Hard Knocks*. Chicago, 1915.

Youngblood, Charles L. *A Mighty Hunter*. Chicago, 1890.

BOOK II

Boswell, G. C. "Some Early Activities around Mobeetie," *West Texas Historical Association Year Book*, Vol. XII, 1936.

Cook, John R. *The Border and the Buffalo*. Topeka, 1907.

Crane, R. C. "Old Man Keeler," *West Texas Historical Association Year Book*, Vol. IV, 1928.

————. "Settlement of 1874–1875, Troubles in West Texas." *West Texas Historical Association Year Book*, Vol. I, 1925.

Dixon, Olive K. *The Life of "Billy" Dixon*. Dallas, 1927.

Dubbs, Emanuel, and others. *Pioneer Days in the Southwest*. Guthrie, 1909.

Jones, Charles Jesse. *Buffalo Jones' Forty Years of Adventure*. Ed. Col. Henry Inman, London, 1899.

Miles, Gen. Nelson A. *Personal Recollections of General Nelson A. Miles*. Chicago, 1897.

Mooar, J. Wright. "Frontier Experiences." *West Texas Historical Association Year Book,* Vol. IV, 1928.

Rister, Carl Coke. *No Man's Land*. Norman, Okla., 1948.

Vestal, Stanley. *Queen of the Cowtowns*. New York, 1952.

Wheeler, Col. Homer W. *Buffalo Days*. Indianapolis, 1925.

Wright, Robert M. *Dodge City, the Cowboy Capital and the Great Southwest*. Wichita, 1913.

BOOK III

Bitner, Grace. "Early History of the Concho Country and Tom Green County." *West Texas Historical Association Year Book,* Vol. IX, 1933.

Crimmins, Col. M. L. "Captain Nolan's Lost Troops on the Staked Plains." *West Texas Historical Association Year Book,* Vol. X, 1934.

Grant, Ben O. "Life in Old Fort Griffin." *West Texas Historical Association Year Book,* Vol. X, 1934.

Haley, J. Evetts. *Fort Concho and the Texas Frontier*. San Angelo, 1952.

Holden, W. C. "The Buffalo of the Plains Area." *West Texas Historical Association Year Book,* Vol. II, 1926.

Jacobs, John Cloud. "The Last of the Buffalo." *The World's Work,* Vol. XVII.

McCombs, Joe S. "On the Cattle Trail and the Buffalo Range." *West Texas Historical Association Year Book,* Vol. XI, 1935.

Nye, Capt. W. S. *Carbine & Lance, the Story of Old Ft. Sill*. Norman, Okla., 1937.

Roberts, Emmett. "Frontier Experiences." *West Texas Historical Association Year Book,* Vol. III, 1927.

Sandoz, Mari. *Cheyenne Autumn*. New York, 1953.

Wallace, Ernest and Hoebel, E. Adamson. *The Comanches, Lords of the Southern Plains*. Norman, Okla., 1952.

Webb, J. R. "Henry Herron, Pioneer and Peace Officer during Ft.

Griffin Days." *West Texas Historical Association Year Book,* Vols. XX to XXIV, 1944–1948.

BOOK IV

Burlingame, Merrill G.   "The Buffalo in Trade and Commerce." *North Dakota Historical Quarterly,* Vol. III, No. 4.

Johnson, W. Fletcher. *Life of Sitting Bull and the History of the Indian War of 1890–91.* Edgewood Publishing Company, 1891.

McLaughlin, James. *My Friend the Indian.* Boston, 1910.

Mooney, James.   "The Ghost Dance Religion and the Sioux Outbreak of 1890." *14th Annual Report,* Bureau of American Ethnology, Part II, 1895.

Roe, Frank Gilbert.   *The North American Buffalo.* Toronto, 1951.

Shields, Geo. O.   (Coquina) Articles in *American Field.*

Vestal, Stanley.   *Sitting Bull, Champion of the Sioux.* Boston, 1932.

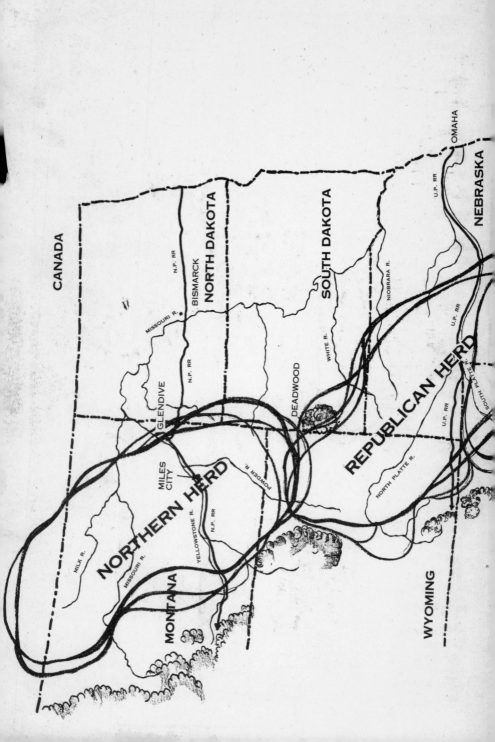